HANDBOOK OF HERALDRY

EFFIGY OF EDWARD THE BLACK PRINCE
FROM·HIS·TOMB·IN·CANTERBURY·CATHEDRAL.

HANDBOOK *of* HERALDRY

WITH INSTRUCTIONS FOR TRACING PEDIGREES

AND DECIPHERING ANCIENT MSS.

RULES FOR THE APPOINTMENT OF LIVERIES &c.

BY

JOHN E. CUSSANS

AUTHOR OF 'THE HISTORY OF HERTFORDSHIRE ETC.

FOURTH EDITION

WITH UPWARDS OF FOUR HUNDRED ILLUSTRATIONS

HERITAGE BOOKS
2009

HERITAGE BOOKS

AN IMPRINT OF HERITAGE BOOKS, INC.

Books, CDs, and more—Worldwide

For our listing of thousands of titles see our website
at
www.HeritageBooks.com

A Facsimile Reprint
Published 2009 by
HERITAGE BOOKS, INC.
Publishing Division
100 Railroad Ave. #104
Westminster, Maryland 21157

International Standard Book Numbers
Paperbound: 978-0-7884-1837-2
Clothbound: 978-0-7884-8223-6

TO

HENRY HUCKS GIBBS

OF ALDENHAM HOUSE, HERTFORDSHIRE, ESQUIRE

ETC. ETC. ETC.

This Book is Inscribed

BY HIS OBLIGED FRIEND

THE AUTHOR

'The songs with which the Northern Bards regaled the heroes at their "feasts of shells" were but versified chronicles of each ancestral line, symphonied by their stirring deeds. Through the oak-fire's uncertain flame the chieftain saw descend the shadowy forms of his fathers ; they came from the halls of Odin as the harper swept the strings, and deployed before their descendant, "rejoicing in the sound of their praise." No parchment told his lineage to the warrior of those days ; but the heroic names were branded each night upon his swelling heart by the burning numbers of the bard.

'Thus did the Northman chronicle his ancestry in those unlettered times. Afterwards, when the oak-fire was extinguished, the shell thrown by, and the night came no more with songs—when we reach the age of records—we find this love of lineage availing itself of the new method of commemoration. This strong ancestral spirit of the Norman may be traced partly to the profound sentiment of perpetuity which formed the principal and noblest element of his character, and partly to the nature of the property to which he was linked by the immemorial customs of the Teuton race.'

WARBURTON : Rollo and his Race.

PREFACE

SINCE 1869, two large editions of this book have been
issued, and for five or six years it has been out of
print.

The present edition may almost be said to be rewritten,
as will be seen by comparing it with the issues of 1869 and
1872, although no change has been made in the general plan.
The principal feature has been the substitution, in many
instances, of better-engraved examples than are to be found
in the former editions.

The heading of the second chapter of this book, *The
Accidence of Armory*, should really be its general title ; for
I profess to teach little but the names of heraldic charges
and the method of combining them. Without doubt, an
intimate knowledge of Armory is essential for a Herald,
but his duties are not so restricted. He has to assist at
Chapters where old Arms are confirmed and new ones
granted. His it is to marshal processions, to conduct the
ceremonies of Coronations, Royal Marriages, and Funerals ;
and at the Installation of Knights, and Creation of Peers,
the Herald is conspicuous. As, however, the College of
Arms consists but of one Earl Marshal, three Kings of

Arms, six Heralds, and four Pursuivants, an intimate knowledge of all their various duties can be of little use to the general public. Though myself protesting against the title of this book, I let it stand, inasmuch as the word Heraldry is at the present time popularly understood to be the same as Armory.

J. E. CUSSANS.

St. George's Day, 1882.

NOTE TO FOURTH EDITION

To the foregoing I have little to add. It will, however, be seen, by comparing this edition with the Third, that many modifications and, I trust, improvements, have been made.

J. E. C.

New Year's Day, 1893.

PREFACE

THE FIRST EDITION

I T is impossible for a modern work on Heraldry to be any other than a compilation ; and the only merit to which the author can lay claim is, that he has made a judicious selection from the materials before him. There is, of necessity, much in the following pages to be found in other text-books on the science ; on the other hand, there are several subjects which appear for the first time in such a work. Amongst these may be mentioned the directions for Emblazoning, tracing Pedigrees, deciphering ancient MSS., the appointment of modern Liveries, &c. ; and the chapters on French and American Heraldry.

In the treatise before the reader, the author has endeavoured to divest the noble science of Armory of those frivolous technicalities and conjectural interpretations to be found in the works of the early Heralds, which, by their abstruseness and uncertainty, tended to render the study so uninviting. Not only did the early teachers attach an allegorical signification to the various Colours and Charges —in which, by the way, there is as much diversity as in the books entitled ' The Language of Flowers '—but they even devised a separate nomenclature of the Tinctures, according to the rank of the person whose Bearings they blazoned. Thus, the Arms of Royalty were described by the names of celestial bodies ; of the nobility, by precious stones ; while the commonalty were obliged to be content with the simple Tinctures. *Or ; a Bend sable*, if borne by a king would be blazoned as *Sol ; a Bend Saturn ;* and if by a noble, *Topaz ; a Bend Diamond*. Others writers, again, have blazoned Arms by the Signs of the Zodiac, Months of the Year, Parts of the Body, the Elements, Flowers, Tempers, &c. According to the last method, *Or ; on a Mount vert, a Buck tripping sable, attired gules*, would be blazoned as *Blithe ; on a Mount bilious, a Buck tripping melancholy, attired choleric*. When Heralds indulged in such puerilities, it is no matter of surprise that the cause they espoused should be regarded by many persons as unworthy of serious attention.

The writer, remembering the difficulties he himself encountered in mastering the rudiments of the science, has endeavoured, in compiling this work, to place himself in the position of the student, and has, as much as possible, avoided throughout the use of terms which, though perfectly intelligible to a proficient, would not be so to an uninitiated reader. In some few instances he has not been able fully to carry out his intention ; whenever, therefore, a word occurs, the signification of which has not been previously explained, the student should refer to the Index.

J. E. C.

October 1, 1868.

CONTENTS

'Here shall shortlie be shewyd to blase all armys, if ye entende diligentli to youre rulys.'

BOKE OF SAINCT ALBANS

HANDBOOK OF HERALDRY

INTRODUCTION

' Il n'y a peut-être pas de science en apparence plus frivole, et sur laquelle on ait tant et si gravement écrit, que celle du Blazon.'— CHEVALIER DE COURÇELLES.

T has been asserted that 'he who careth not whence he came, careth little whither he goeth.' This is rather a bold statement to put forth, and, like many other trite aphorisms, one probably in which truth and strict propriety are sacrificed to epigrammatic force. Be this as it may, indifference as to the origin of their family is really felt by few ; for the pride of ancestry seems to be innate in nearly everyone ; those only affect to despise it who are ignorant of their descent, and can lay claim to no hereditary insignia of honour —practically expressing the sentiment of Montaigne : 'If we cannot attain to greatness ourselves, let us have our revenge by railing at it in others.'

Gibbon, in his Autobiography, very justly remarks : 'A lively desire of knowing and recording our ancestors so generally prevails, that it must depend on the influence of some common principle in the minds of men.

We seem to have lived in the persons of our forefathers ; it is the labour and reward of vanity to extend the term of this ideal longevity. The satirist may laugh, the philosopher may preach ; but Reason herself will respect the prejudices and habits which have been consecrated by the experience of mankind. Few there are who can seriously despise in others an advantage of which they are secretly ambitious to partake. The knowledge of our own family from a remote period will always be esteemed as an abstract pre-eminence, since it can never be promiscuously enjoyed. If we read of some illustrious line, so ancient that it has no beginning, so worthy that it ought to have no end, we sympathise in its various fortunes ; nor can we blame the generous enthusiasm, or the harmless vanity, of those who are allied to the honours of its name.'

Throughout the struggle with the Royalists, Oliver Cromwell and his adherents affected to ridicule that dignity which a long and unbroken line of ancestry undoubtedly confers ; but no sooner was the Protector firmly established in his position, than he assumed almost every kingly function. He was constantly addressed as 'Your Highness' ; his official proclamations commenced, 'WE, Oliver Cromwell ;' his Peers of Parliament were created by patent, in the margin of which was a representation of the Protector in regal robes, with his family escutcheon, containing all the quarterings to which he was entitled. He likewise assumed the imperial crown, as it appears on the second great seal of his predecessor, although he refused to be publicly invested therewith. From a manuscript in the Harleian Collection, preserved in the British Museum, it appears that an expense of nearly 1,600*l*. was incurred for the banners, standards, pennons, badges, &c., displayed at his funeral.[1]

[1] The following note is appended at the end of the list : 'The whole expense of the Protector's funeral amounted to 28,000*l*. The undertaker was mr. Rolt, who was payde but a small part, if any, of his bill.'

So, too, at the period of the great Revolution in France, all distinctions of rank and title were abrogated—even that of 'Monsieur;' but in a short time a new *noblesse* arose —not constructed out of the old aristocratic party, but, as Madame de Staël observes, of the partisans of equality. And this process of spontaneous creation of superior rank has always existed, and must continue to exist, amongst all people, and in all ages, as long as the power which wealth or ability naturally exercises, is acknowledged.

But, it may be urged, what actual service can the obsolete jargon and grotesque monstrosities of the old heralds possibly render now? Much, every way. If the study and practice of Heraldry served but to gratify the vanity of a few, and to excite the envy of many, then, indeed, would its teachings be useless—nay, worse than useless—absolutely pernicious. But, happily, this charming science has higher and nobler purposes to serve; its scope and influence are far more extended. Many are the incidents but faintly written in the pages of history, which would have remained for ever dark and illegible, but for the light flashed on them by the torch of Heraldry. A shield of Arms, a Badge, or a Rebus depicted on a glass window, painted on a wall, carved on a corbel or monument, will frequently indicate, with unerring precision, the date to which such relics are to be ascribed, and whose memory they are intended to perpetuate, when all verbal descriptions are wanting; and the identity of many an old portrait rests on no other authority than that of a coat of Arms painted at the side.[1] Mr. C. James, in his *Scotland in the Middle Ages*, writes: 'For the pursuit of

[1] The Trustees of the National Portrait Gallery in their thirty-first Annual Report (1888) state that a portrait formerly belonging to Mr. Fraser Tytler, and described as a portrait of Mary Queen of Scots, was found to be a portrait of her mother, Mary of Lorraine. The manner in which the Arms of France and Scotland are quartered, clearly indicates the date of the painting to have been 1560, when Francis II. and Mary ruled in France, and Mary of Lorraine was Regent of Scotland.

family history, of topographical and territorial learning, of ecclesiology, of architecture, it is altogether indispensable ; and its total and contemptuous neglect in this country (Scotland), is one of the causes why a Scotchman can rarely speak or write on any of these subjects without being exposed to the charge of using a language he does not understand.'

It is not to the antiquary and archæologist alone, however, that its teachings are valuable. Scarcely an hour passes but some branch of the science is presented to our notice ; and the education of no gentleman can be deemed complete which does not include, at least, an elementary knowledge of the subject. To one who is totally unacquainted with heraldic usances and phraseology, the writings of many of our best and most entertaining authors lose half their interest. The historical romances of Sir Walter Scott abound in armorial allusions. In *Marmion*, for example, we read—

> ' The ruddy lion, ramped in gold.'

Now, unless we were previously aware that a Red Lion rampant, on a gold field, within a tressure or border, was the device emblazoned on the standard of Scotland, this line would be unintelligible. How utterly devoid of meaning must be the opening speech of Shakespeare's *Richard the Third*,

> ' Now is the winter of our discontent
> Made glorious summer by this *sun* of York,'

to a person who is unacquainted with the fact that the *Rose-en-Soleil*, or White Rose placed within a Sun, was the Badge assumed by EDWARD IV. after the Battle of Mortimer's Cross ! In the last act of the same drama, Richmond, addressing his followers, says :

> ' The wretched, bloody, and usurping *boar*,
> That spoiled your summer fields and fruitful vines,
> *   *   *   this foul *swine*
> Lies now even in the centre of this isle,' &c,

RICHARD is here typified as the 'Boar,' that being his Cognisance or Badge. Unless, too, we know that 'Lucies' is the heraldic term for pike—which fish were borne as arms by SIR THOMAS LUCY, whom Shakespeare had good reason to dislike—we entirely miss the point of the somewhat coarse humour in the first scene of the *Merry Wives of Windsor*. Innumerable examples of a similar nature might be adduced, illustrative of the absolute necessity of possessing some knowledge of Heraldry.

Again, we see a Hatchment placed in front of a mansion ; to the uninitiated in armorial lore, this is but an unsightly diamond-shaped frame, covered with grotesque figures and scrawls ; but to one who possesses but an elementary know- ledge of the subject, a Hatchment is full of meaning. He sees at a glance that it is exhibited by a widow in memory of her deceased husband. The badge of Ulster—a red Hand on a silver inescutcheon—(see fig. 352) bespeaks him to have enjoyed the rank of a Baronet ; while the well-known motto, *Tria juncta in uno*, surrounding his shield, proclaims him to have been decorated with the Order of the Bath. It is seen, also, that his wife was an heiress.

In the hamlet of Whitwell, in Hertfordshire, is a public- house having for its sign *The Eagle and Child*. Immediately I saw it, I guessed that the Stanleys had at one time been possessors of the manor. Subsequent research proved the correctness of my supposition. In 1488 the manor was granted to Thomas Stanley, Earl of Derby, and it remained in that family for nearly a century. The date of the es- tablishment of a village ale-house is a matter of little moment, and I only adduce this instance to show how ex- tended are the historical lessons which may be learned by even a superficial knowledge of Armory.

Another purpose does Heraldry sometimes serve, which will, probably, be fully appreciated in this utilitarian age. In cases where lineal descendants have been wanting, armorial bearings have frequently been the means of indicating the consanguinity of collateral branches of the family, and thereby evincing their right of inheritance. A remarkable instance of the signal service thus rendered by Heraldry is given by Lord Eldon : ' While a barrister on the Northern circuit,' writes his Lordship, ' I was counsel in a cause, the fate of which depended on our being able to make out who was the founder of an ancient chapel in the neighbourhood. I went to view it. There was nothing to be observed which gave any indication of its date or history ; however, I observed that the Ten Commandments were written on some old plaster, which from its position I conjectured might cover an arch. Acting on this, I bribed the clerk with five shillings to allow me to chip away a part of the plaster ; and, after two or three attempts, I found the keystone of an arch, on which were engraved the arms of an ancestor of one of the parties in the law-case. This evidence decided the cause, and I ever afterwards had reason to remember with some satisfaction my having on that occasion broken the Ten Commandments.' Mr. Bigland bears further testimony to the practical value of Heraldry ; for, in his *Observations on Parochial Registers*, he writes : ' I know three families who have acquired estates by virtue of preserving the arms and escutcheons of their ancestors.' After these convincing proofs, who shall say that the study and practice of Heraldry is attended with no beneficial results ?

Heraldry has been described as one of the dead languages ; and so it is to some extent, for every branch of knowledge is a dead language when it has ceased to concern the majority of the people of the age. But there is a vitality remaining in true knowledge of every kind, which bids defiance to extinction.

CHAPTER I

THE RISE AND PROGRESS OF HERALDRY

'Coates of Armes were inuented, by our wise auncestors, to these 3 ends : The first was, to honour and adorne the family of him that had well deserued towardes his countrye. The seconde, to make him more worthy and famous aboue the rest, which had not done merit, and thereby they might be prouoked to doe the like. The third was, to differ out the seuerall lignes and issues, from the noble auncestor descending ; so that the eldest borne might be known from the second, and he from the thirde, &c.'—SIR JOHN FERNE.

HE science of Heraldry, or, rather, as has been pointed out in the Preface, of Armory (which is but one branch of Heraldry), is, without doubt, of very ancient origin. Enthusiasts there have been, such as Morgan, who assert that our first parents were the lawful bearers of 'cote-armure.' To Adam was assigned a shield *gules*, and to Eve another, *argent* ; which latter Adam bore over his as an inescutcheon, his wife being sole heiress. The same authority informs us that, after the Fall, Adam bore a garland of fig-leaves, which Abel quartered with *Argent ; an apple vert*, in right of his mother. In the *Boke of St. Alban's*, printed in 1486, we read, amongst other startling announcements, that, 'Of the offspringe of the gentilman Japeth came Habraham, Moyses, Aron, and the profettys, and also the Kyng of the right lyne of Mary, of whom that gentilman Jhesus, . . . by his modre Mary, prynce of cote-armure.' Ferne, in his *Blazon of Gentrie*, assigns distinctive armorial bearings to the ancient Egyptian kings, and to the gods of the Roman mythology. The arms of Alexander the Great were, according to Gerard Leigh, ' *Gules ; a golden lyon sitting on a chayer, and holding a battayle-axe of silver*'—which arms, together with those of eight other famous personages, constituting the Nine Worthies, were formerly, and I believe still are, to be seen sculptured in Gloucester Cathedral. The learned Bolton could find no more profitable employment for his time than by tracing or inventing Arms for almost all the heroes of antiquity ; amongst others, for Caspar and Balthazar, two of the kings who offered gifts to the Infant Jesus at Beth-lehem ; of the third king, strange to say, no mention is made.

From both sacred and profane history, we learn that it was the custom from the earliest ages for various communi-ties to adopt some peculiar device or symbolical sign, which, when depicted upon their standards afforded a ready means of distinguishing one army from another amidst the con-fusion of battle.[1] These insignia were originally confined solely to nations ; in process of time, military commanders adopted similar devices ; and, still later, they were used generally by individuals, as at the present time. History affords innumerable examples of national insignia, of which the Egyptian Ox, the Athenian Owl, and the Roman Eagle are familiar to everyone. Sophocles, Herodotus, Virgil, and other ancient writers, give minute descriptions of the devices represented on the shields of their heroes ;[2] but these can scarcely be considered as heraldic charges, although it was

[1] Numbers ii. 2 ; Psalms xx. 5 ; lx. 4 ; Isaiah xiii. 2.

[2] *Septem contra Thebas*, lines 380 to 646. *Æneid*, lib. ii. lines 386 to 392 ; lib. vii. line 657 ; lib. x. lines 180 to 188. Herodotus : *Clio*, § 171 ; *Calliope*, § 74.

from this source that Heraldry undoubtedly took its rise. The White Horse of the Saxons, and the Palm-tree and Crocodile of the City of Nismes, were borne long anterior to the period in which a system of Armory was established ; but these devices were never, as far as we can learn, emblazoned on shields. When, subsequently, Armory took a tangible form, and was brought within the compass of a science, these insignia were naturally retained.

'The Scriptures gave the standards or symbols of the Jewish tribes. By providing the chiefs of the Goths and Vandals with similar insignia, the art of Blazonry was traced to an origin almost equally primæval. Antiquity being the main object, antiquity was taken by storm ; while the violent invasion of truth was concealed by mysticism. In short, the herald's science, like many others, was guarded by its peculiar priesthood, who considered their interest as in a great degree consisting in mystery—whose traditional information afforded little light to themselves.'—*Gentleman's Magazine*, December 1829.

Leaving these questionable records of Armory, let us come at once to the period from which it can legitimately date as a Science. This is probably not earlier than the twelfth century ; for although, as I have already stated, standards bearing particular devices have served to distinguish communities during all ages, yet the earliest well-authenticated example of an heraldic charge, properly so called, adopted by an individual, is found on a seal of PHIL-LIP, COUNT OF FLANDERS, bearing date 1164, which device is a *Lion rampant*. Alexander Nisbet affirms that this same charge was borne by ROBERT le FRISON ninety years previously, but of this there exists no positive proof. STEPHEN, EARL of RICHMOND, anno 1137, is represented on his seal as bearing on his right arm a shield charged with figures resembling *Fleurs-de-lys ;* but it is very probable that this device was simply used as diapering, and was not intended as an armorial bearing. Diapering as a method of relieving the

monotony of a plain surface, was very early practised ; and
to this custom must be ascribed the curious fact that a
chessman, preserved in the Bibliothèque
Nationale at Paris, and supposed to have
belonged to Charlemagne (temp. 827), is
represented supporting a shield, apparently
fretty. The pattern, however, on this shield
so much resembles the general features of
the diapering displayed on the tablet to
GEOFFREY PLANTAGENET (fig. 131), that there
seems little room to doubt but that the design in both was
the same.

Fig. 1.

There certainly are manuscripts extant of the thirteenth
and fourteenth centuries in which the Saxon kings appear
with their shields duly charged ; but it must be borne in
mind that chroniclers have ever been given to anachronisms,
when no authentic record has been before them, which the
following instance—one out of many that might be adduced
—sufficiently proves. In 1087, William I. directed a
number of knights to take possession of the monastery at
Ely. Their portraits and arms were subsequently painted
and exhibited in the great hall ; but it is curious to observe
that the knights were represented as wearing round helmets
—which fashion was not adopted until the fourteenth century
—while the form of their shields, on which their arms are
depicted, was still more modern. When, therefore, we find
a warrior encased in armour of a description which we know
was not in vogue during the period in which he lived, the
accuracy of the other portions of the drawing must be regarded with suspicion.

Seals are, of all records, those on which the greatest reliance can be placed ; for being contemporary witnesses, no
doubt can exist of their historical value. It is much to be
regretted that so few matrices, or their impressions, remain to
us. Several circumstances have tended to their destruction.
In the first place, seals were frequently effaced during the

lifetime of their possessors, or by their immediate successors, to prevent any fraudulent use being made of them ; [1] for when but few persons could write their names, a seal attached to a document answered the purpose of a signature ; and until the reign of Richard II., they constituted the only marks of attestation affixed to royal deeds and charters.[2] Again, being sometimes fashioned in gold or silver, or engraved on precious stones, such as were not destroyed by the owners were frequently purloined for their intrinsic value.   Wax impressions being so fragile, it is not surprising that so few should have survived.   Until comparatively of late years, they were seldom preserved out of mere curiosity, or it is possible that some of an earlier date than 1164 might be discovered charged with arms.

The arms assigned to EDWARD the CONFESSOR (A.D. 1065) are a *Cross patonce*, surrounded by five *Martlets*.   This is a legitimate heraldic charge ; but the earliest and chief authority on which the assumption is based, that the Confessor bore a shield so emblazoned, is found on the tomb of Henry III. in Westminster Abbey, on which it was sculptured during the reign of Edward II.—nearly three centuries after the Confessor's death.   Cotemporaneous

Fig. 2.

authority is usually the strongest, and on coins of Edward the Confessor we find a cross between *four* birds, which birds are certainly not Martlets.[3]

---

[1] A relic of the ancient custom of destroying disused seals survives unto the present time, with regard to the Great Seal of England. On the accession of a monarch to the throne, he strikes the seal of his predecessor with a hammer ; it is then declared to be broken, and becomes the perquisite of the Lord Chancellor.

[2] The Latin word *signum* was used indifferently to express either an impression on wax, or a sign manual.

[3] The purpose of a cross on the reverse side of a coin was simply to indicate where it might be cut so as to provide small change.   Half-

The floor of the guard chamber in the *Abbaye aux Hommes*, at Caén—founded in the year 1064—is partly paved with tiles bearing armorial devices, which fact several writers have adduced as a proof that Heraldry was understood and practised at that early period ; but, unfortunately for this theory, one of the tiles is *semé of Fleurs-de-lys*, probably intended for the Arms of France, but they were not adopted as such for nearly a hundred years later ; on another of the tiles, Arms are represented as *quartered*, which system was not devised until the close of the thirteenth century. The shield of MAGNAVILLE, EARL of ESSEX, who died in the year 1144, and whose monumental effigy is in the TEMPLE Church, appears charged with an heraldic device—an *Escarbuncle*—which Arms, if really borne by him, constitute the oldest example extant in England ; but in the Roll of Arms compiled in the reign of Edward II., the arms of MAGNAVILLE are given as *Quarterly, or and gules*, without any Escarbuncle ; and on the seal of HUMPHREY de BOHUN, EARL of HEREFORD and ESSEX (A.D. 1297–1321), the same arms are repeated. This monument in the Temple has been attributed to Earl Magnaville on the authority of a Chronicle of Walden Abbey, which bears internal evidence of having been written as late as 1409, at which time the identity of the monument was probably as much a matter of speculation as at the present day.

If armorial distinctions had been in vogue at the time of the Conquest, the tapestry at Bayeux would certainly afford corroborative proof. In this marvellous work, in which minute details are scrupulously noticed, there is nothing which can be legitimately considered as a representation of Arms ; perhaps the nearest approach thereto is a plain cross charged upon the flag of a Norman vessel. In another por-

pennies and four-things were halves and fourths of real pennies. At the present time in Greece, halves of Bank-notes—divorced from their other halves—pass current for just one-half of the integral value of the note itself.

tion of the tapestry, William appears holding a small banner similarly charged ; but the two Lions or Leopards ascribed to him, and sculptured on his monument at Caen in the year 1642, are nowhere to be seen. Many of the shields of the Normans appear as charged with Bordures, Crosses, Fesses, and Roundles ; but from the irregular manner in which they are disposed, as well as from their frequent repetition, I am inclined to think that these figures are but bands and bosses for the purpose of strengthening the shields ; especially as in one place a Bordure appears on the *inside* of a shield. The Roundles, strange to say, are only depicted on the shields in battle-scenes, from which I infer that it is possible they were intended to represent marks and indentations caused by the weapons of the enemy. The prominent leaders, moreover, who appear as bearing these shields, are not in other scenes distinguished by the same devices. On the cornice of the tomb of ELIZABETH in KING HENRY the SEVENTH's Chapel, the arms ascribed to the CONQUEROR are

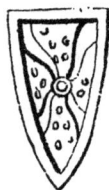

Fig. 3.

actually *impaled* with those of his wife MATILDA, daughter of BALDWIN, fifth EARL of FLANDERS. This flagrant example of anachronism in representing two coats of arms as impaled in the eleventh century, which system was unknown until many years later, shows how little dependence is to be placed on records compiled at a period long subsequent to that in which the occurrences they celebrate were enacted.

In an account written by John, a monk of Marmoustier in Touraine, about the year 1130, of the knighthood of GEOFFREY PLANTAGENET, subsequent to his marriage with MAUDE, daughter of HENRY I., it is stated that he was invested with a hauberk, chaussés, and gilt spurs ; and a shield charged with little Lions of gold was hung upon his neck ; and on an enamelled plate preserved in the Museum at Mans, he is represented as bearing a long, kite-shaped shield, *azure*, charged with *six Lions rampant, or ; three, two, and one ;* and his grandson, WILLIAM LONGESPÉE, EARL of SALISBURY, appears with the same arms in SALISBURY Cathedral.

STEPHEN, on his Great Seal, appears on horseback, holding on his arm a long Norman shield, *uncharged*.   This is a very significant fact, and plainly proves that, even if his predecessors did exhibit two Lions on their shields, they were only personal Arms, and not considered as hereditary.   It has been commonly asserted that HENRY II. added a third Lion, in right of his wife, ELEANOR of AQUITAINE, to the two he already emblazoned ; and from that time (A.D. 1154),

Three Lions passant guardant in pale, have been the national Arms of England ; but on the seal of his son John, before he became King, appear but *two Lions passant*, and on the first seal of RICHARD I. in 1190 are *two Lions combattant* (fig. 4), of which, however, but one is seen, by reason of the convexity of the shield.   Four years later, on his return from Palestine, he devised

Fig. 4.   another seal, on which the *three Lions passant guardant* were represented as they still remain in the Royal Arms (fig. 5).

It therefore appears from the instances adduced, that

armorial devices were first probably borne by kings and nobles, as personal decorations, during the twelfth century ; but it was not until the reign of HENRY III. that Heraldry was reduced to anything like a definite system, and was worthy the title of a science.

To the Tournaments originating in Germany, and passing successively to France and England, must be

Fig. 5.   attributed, in a great measure, the introduction of individual Armorial bearings.   These exercises were regarded with great favour by the early English monarchs, as they served to familiarise the nobles with the use of arms, and to foster a spirit of chivalrous daring amongst them. It was the custom, in these encounters, for the combatants to assume some conspicuous device or figure —at first arbitrarily, but which in many instances was retained as an hereditary mark of distinction—by which they could be easily recognised, when their features were concealed by their helmets. Single figures would naturally constitute the earliest charges ; and such Arms are generally considered the most honourable, as they imply that they are the most ancient. Towards the close of the twelfth and commencement of the thirteenth centuries, however, so many fresh claimants had established their right to armorial bearings, that several distinct charges were displayed on one shield, in order to produce a composition differing from any then in existence.

When the Hermit Peter, animated by religious enthusiasm, induced the flower of European chivalry to take up arms against the infidel Saracens, it became necessary for the immense army which assembled, composed of so many different nationalities, to adopt certain distinctive insignia whilst engaged in the expedition. Thus, the English had a white Cross sewn or embroidered on the right shoulder of their surcoats ; the French were distinguished in a similar manner by a red Cross ; the Flemings adopted a green Cross ; and the Crusaders from the Roman States, bore two keys in saltire.[1] These, however, were but general distinctions ; individuals, with but few exceptions, had not yet assumed personal Arms. As a further means of inducing alike the devout and the daring to embark in the glorious enterprise,

---

[1] Lithgow, a Scotchman, who, in the reign of James I., published an account of his travels in the East, states that all the pilgrims with whom he journeyed towards Jerusalem were marked on the arm with a device (as in the margin), resembling that borne by the ancient Crusader-kings of Jerusalem,—which was *Argent ; a Cross pommé*, and subsequently, *potent, between four others humetté, or.*

Fig. 6.

not only was plenary absolution granted by the Church for all past and future sins, but the soldier, of whatever rank, who, fighting under the Banner of the Cross, slew an infidel was declared Noble,[1] and, as such, was permitted to assume whatever device his fancy might dictate, as a memento of the gallant exploit.   Hence arose a multitude of charges hitherto unknown in Armory ; such as *Palmers' staves ; Escallop-shells ; Bezants*—gold coins of Byzantium ; *Water-bougets*—leathern vessels for containing water ; *Passion nails ; Crescents ; Saracens' heads ; Paschal lambs ; Scimitars ;* &c.   But the Cross being the object of the greatest veneration, it is natural to suppose that it was more in favour as a device than any other ; and numberless modifications of its form were devised for this purpose, as will be seen hereafter. To the Crusaders, too, are we probably indebted for the introduction of such grotesque figures as the *Wyvern, Dragon, Harpy*, and similar monstrosities, which appear to have an Eastern origin.

Before coats of Arms were considered as hereditary possessions, a knight of noble birth bore his shield plain, until by some martial exploit he had *achieved* for himself the right of wearing a device.   In allusion to this, the Welsh bard, Hywel al Owain Gwynedd, in a poem supposed to be written about the year 1176, thus laments his failure in obtaining the prize at a national contest : ' Another has been the successful competitor ; he carries the apple-spray, the emblem of victory ; whilst my shield remains white upon my shoulder, not blazoned with the desired achievement.'   On becoming entitled to bear a charge upon his escutcheon, a knight was permitted to assume whatever Arms he pleased, provided they had not been previously appropriated by another ; but at that period, when travelling was expensive, and communication necessarily restricted—before the College of Heralds was in existence, and authentic records of Armorial

[1] This deed is specially mentioned in the *Boke of St. Alban's* as qualifying a person to bear ' cote-armure.'

Bearings could be readily obtained,—many mistakes and dis-
putes as to the rightful ownership of certain Arms naturally
arose.   If arbitration failed to induce either claimant to
resign Arms which both had adopted, the dispute was settled
by single combat, in which strength was deemed innocence,
and weakness, guilt.   One of the most remarkable instances
in which recourse was had to arms to settle a difficulty of
this kind was in the year 1389, when no less than three
families, SCROPE, CARMINOW, and GROSVENOR, bore similar
arms—*Azure ; a bend or.*   The contest between Scrope and
Carminow was not conclusive, and ultimately both families
were permitted to bear the same Arms, as they do at the
present day.   In the trial which ensued between Lord
Scrope and Sir Robert Grosvenor, the latter was forbidden
to carry such Arms unless he surmounted them with a silver
Bordure.   This he refused to do ; and assumed in its stead,
Azure ; a Garb (wheatsheaf) *or*, part of the arms of the
Earldom of CHESTER, to which he was entitled by descent
from RANDOLF de MESCHINES.

A knight was also permitted to adopt for his Arms those
of a vanquished enemy.   Bossewel writes on this subject :
'If an English man in field doo put to flight any gentleman, enemy to his Prince, . . . he may honor his own
cote in the sinister quarter with the proper cote of the
gentleman so fled away.'   In Isaacke's *Remains of Exeter*,
it is stated that Robert Carey, in the reign of Henry V.,
engaged in a trial of arms, at Smithfield,
with a Spanish knight, whom he defeated ;
'and whereas, by the law of Heraldry,
whosoever fairly in the field conquered his
adversary might justify the wearing and
bearing of his arms whom he overcame,
he accordingly took on him the coat-
armour of the Arragonese, being, *Argent;*

Fig. 7.

on a Bend sable, three Roses of the first, which is ever since
borne by the name of CAREY, whose ancient coat of Arms

was, *Gules ; a Chevron argent, between three Swans proper,* one whereof they still retain in their crest.'

So thoroughly were nobles identified with the arms they bore, that in the old ballad, entitled 'The Battle of Towton,' written in the Fifteenth Century, the various knights who took part in the engagement are enumerated, not by name, but by the Badges which they wore, as the following brief extract will show :

' The way unto the North contre, the *Rose*[1] ful fast he sought ;
W[t] hym wente y[e] *Ragged Staf,*[2] y[t] many men dere bought ;
The *Fisshe Hoke*[3] came into the felde w[t] ful egre mode,
So did the *Cornysshe Chowghe,*[4] and brought forth all hir brode,' &c.

As early as the reign of King John, we find, by the seal of that monarch, that it was the custom for nobles to wear

Fig. 8.   Great Seal of King John.

a Surcoat, or long loose robe, over their armour ; originally intended, as stated in the thirty-ninth stanza of the *Avow-*

[1] Earl of March.
[2] Earl of Warwick.
[3] Lord Fauconberg.
[4] Lord Scrope of Bolton.

vnge of King Arthur, a romance of the Fourteenth Century, for the purpose of protecting the hauberk from the rain and from the heat of the sun, which would render the armour uncomfortable to the wearer.[1] In an illumination of the time of Richard II., archers are represented as wearing sur-coats of leather, called *jacques* (from whence our modern 'jacket'), of edge-ringed mail over their hauberks ; and in the *Chronicles* of Bertrand de Guesclin, written about the same period, we read, 'S'avoit chascun un jacque par dessus son haubert.' On the Surcoats of nobles were subsequently embroidered their Armorial Bearings, in coloured silk and metal ; and on the jacques of common soldiers, their lord's Badge, worked in worsted or other inexpensive material. The custom of thus depicting Arms seems to have been adopted about the close of the Thirteenth Century : the earliest examples being the seal of Edward I., and a brass to Sir Robert de Stetvans, at Chartram, in Kent. It is probable that Armorial Bearings were formerly depicted on many of the plain surcoats which we see on monumental effigies, now become obliterated by time.

In the *Canterbury Tales*, the knight relates how

> ' thei founde,
> Thurgh girt with mony a grevous blody wounde,
> Two yonge knightes liggyng by and by (*side by side*),
> Both in oon armes clad ful richely ;
> Not fully quyk, ne fully deed thei were,
> But by here coote-armure, and by here gere,
> Heraudes knew them well.'

So universally was the practice of embroidering arms upon the Surcoat adopted, that (according to Sir Thomas de la More) Gilbert de Clare, Earl of Gloucester, lost his life at Bannockburn by neglecting, in his haste, to put on his Surcoat : being taken prisoner, his captors, judging

---

[1] ' Gay gownes of grene,
    To hould thayre armur clene,
        And were hitte fro the wete.'

from the absence of his insignia of nobility that he was not worth a ransom, put him to death.

The long Surcoat, proving inconvenient to the wearer when on foot, the front part was, towards the end of the

Fig. 9. Prince John of Eltham, A.D. 1334, Westminster Abbey.

Fig. 10. Sir John de Creke, circa 1325, Westley Waterless, Co. Cambridge.

reign of Edward II., cut off at the waist, still leaving the garment flowing behind : thus modified, it was termed a *Cyclas*, or *Ciclaton*. It is open to doubt, however, whether the Cyclas should be regarded as a heraldic garment, notwithstanding that it was worn by nobles, and frequently emblazoned with their Arms, inasmuch as it was also worn by ladies and citizens. The term Cyclas, or Ciclaton, however, meaning the shortened surcoat in vogue during the reign of Edward III., is so usefully expressive, that though it may not be quite legitimate, it may be suffered to remain.

Prince JOHN Plantagenet, 'of ELTHAM,' is represented on his monumental effigy in WESTMINSTER ABBEY, Anno 1334, as wearing a Cyclas, which reaches below the knees behind, and to the lower part of the thighs in front, being open at the sides as far as the hips (fig. 9) ; and on the west front of Exeter Cathedral are the figures of two knights similarly habited. Although it was not adopted as a knightly garment until the early part of the Fourteenth Century, the Cyclas was in use many years before, as appears from Matthew Paris, who, in describing the pageants attending the marriage of HENRY III. with ELEANOR of PROVENCE, in 1236, writes, that the citizens of London 'were adorned with silk garments. and enveloped in cyclases woven with gold.'

The Cyclas then gave way to the *Jupon*, which was a surcoat without sleeves, reaching only to the waist. At the period when the Jupon was in fashion, the custom of making elaborate and costly display of Armorial Bearings on garments reached its zenith. Of all the follies indulged in by that weak-minded and luxurious sovereign, RICHARD II., extravagance of dress was perhaps the chief. Hitherto, the surcoat, under its various forms, was worn only by warriors when actually engaged in the field ; but now, everyone attending the sumptuous court of that effeminate monarch appeared in a jupon of the most costly description, on which, as well as on other articles of dress, were depicted, in silk, tissue, and beaten gold, the Arms of the wearer.

The Jupon did not long remain in vogue ; for, in the early part of the succeeding reign, we find it superseded by the *Tabard*. The Tabard was originally a loose garment commonly worn by labourers, somewhat resembling the modern smock-frock.[1]　In the *Plowman's Prologue,* attributed to Chaucer, we read,

> ' He tooke hys tabarde, and hys staffe eke,
> And on hys heade he set hys hatte ; '

and, again :

> ' In a tabarde he rood upon a mere.'

The Tabard, as formerly worn by Nobles—and which still constitutes a conspicuous part of the Herald's official

Fig. 11.　From a brass to John Shelley, in Clapham Church, Sussex.

Fig. 12.　Tabard of King Henry VI., formerly in St. George's Chapel, Windsor.

costume—descended to a little below the waist, and was furnished with square or rounded sleeves, extending nearly to the elbows.　It was open at the sides ; and the Armorial Bearings of the wearer were emblazoned both on the front and back as well as on the sleeves.

The monument of Sir JOHN PECHÉ, in LILLINGSTONE

---

[1] In some parts of Devonshire, the word is still used : a long apron suspended by a string from the neck, and fastened around the waist, in the manner adopted by brewers' draymen, is called a *tabby.*　It is possible, however, that this word is but a corruption of the French *tablier* ; the Devonshire dialect, especially that of the southern part of the County, has many words derived from that source : for example, ' *goshy,*' *left-handed;* '*foche* ' (forche), *the fork of a road.*　The spot where the lane from Blackawton joins the highroad between Totnes and Dartmouth is called Blackawton Foches.

Church, Kent, affords a magnificent example of this knightly garment.

Heralds formerly bore the Royal Arms upon their Tabards, so that they might be recognised at a distance, and

Fig. 13.   Richard III.   From the Warwick Roll,
College of Arms, A.D. 1484.

allowed to pass unmolested, when bearing a message to a hostile party ; and Gerard Leigh mentions that he once saw a Herald, 'for lack of the queen's coat of arms, take two trumpet-banners, and, by fastening them together, formed a tabard ' From the custom of thus depicting Armorial Bearings on the Surcoat, arose the term 'COAT OF ARMS;' which has since become more extended in its signification, and is frequently used to express a Shield of Arms.

Not only were Arms emblazoned on the Shield, Banner, or Pennon, and Surcoat of a Knight, but they were profusely scattered over the Caparisons of his Charger. The earliest example of this practice occurs on the Great Seal of EDWARD I. Ladies were also permitted to charge upon their garments their Paternal Arms, as well as those to which they became entitled by marriage. On this subject I shall have more to say hereafter, when treating on *Monumental Heraldry*.

The custom of engraving Arms on plate, and articles of domestic use, seems to have obtained at a very early date, as appears from an inventory of the Crown Jewels taken in 1334, at which time many of the articles therein enumerated bore the Royal Badges. EDMUND MORTIMER, EARL of MARCH, by his will bearing date 1380, bequeathed a silver spice-box, engraved with his Arms, to Gilbert, Bishop of Hereford; and twelve years later, RICHARD, EARL of ARUNDEL, devised to his son 'a silk bed, with a half tester, or canopy, embroidered with the quartered arms of Arundel and Warren.' Amongst the legacies bequeathed by ELEANOR BOHUN, Dowager DUCHESS of GLOUCESTER, who died in 1399, was 'a Psalter, richly illuminated, with clasps of enamelled gold, with white swans, and the arms of my lord and father enamelled on the clasps.'

It is almost needless to remind the reader how largely Heraldry was employed as an ornamental accessory to Architecture. During the reigns of the first three Edwards, comprising what is commonly known as the Decorated Period, Armorial devices were introduced in the principal edifices to a considerable extent, of which the Cathedrals of Canterbury and York afford noble examples; but when the Decorated gave place to the Perpendicular style of architecture, Heraldic devices and shields of Arms were employed to a still greater extent, and formed an integral part of the design. Placed alone, held in the hands of saints, or supported by grotesque figures, they form corbeilles and brackets ; and are frequently to be found over doorways and windows, on the spandrils of subsillia, or stone benches ; enriching gables and dripstones ; on the altar ; and in compartments of monuments and fonts. That Armorial Bearings were not thus displayed merely for the purpose of gratifying personal vanity, but rather as forming an important element in the architectural plan, is evident from the fact that very many shields still remain uncharged. In like manner were niches contrived, which, though at the time of building they contained no statues, were evidently intended for their subsequent reception. It may readily be imagined that when Heraldry was a living science, and the possession of Arms an indubitable mark of honour, not to be acquired by wealth alone, such evidences of hereditary dignity should be conspicuously displayed in the castles and mansions of the Nobility. Within and without, on the windows, walls, gates, battlements, and vanes, were exhibited the devices of their illustrious owners. Shakespeare, in allusion to the practice of emblazoning arms on stained windows, makes Henry Bolingbroke, on his return from banishment, exclaim :

> ' You have fed upon my signories,
> Disparked my parks, and felled my forest woods ;
> From my own windows torn my household coat ;
> Razed out my impress, leaving me no sign,
> Save men's opinions and my living blood,
> To show the world I am a gentleman.' ·

Notwithstanding that our churches and baronial mansions were at one time so profusely decorated with shields of Arms and Badges, it is little matter of surprise that comparatively so few objects of Heraldic or general Archæological interest have survived to the present day. Besides the natural influence of time, there were two epochs in the history of this country which proved especially destructive to such records. Henry VIII., stung by the refusal of the Roman Church to assist him in his infamous designs, revenged himself by destroying the greater part of those invaluable mementoes which could in any way be considered as connected with Papal institutions, as well as the records of those families who had rendered themselves obnoxious to him. Thus we find the Royal Commissioners, who were appointed for this service, writing to the King, regarding the Priory of Christchurch, Hants, as follows : ' In the church we found a chapel and monument made of Caen stone, prepared by the late mother of Reginald Pole for her burial, which we have caused to be defaced, and all the arms and badges clearly to be delete' (erased). The fanatical zeal of Cromwell and his followers well-nigh completed the work of spoliation instituted by Henry. The cathedrals were converted into barracks for soldiers and their horses ; stained windows were ruthlessly broken ; altars and screens were destroyed ; effigies were mutilated ; monumental brasses were stripped for their metal ; and even the vaults of the dead were rifled for the valuables they might contain.

But Henry VIII. and Cromwell are not solely responsible for the destruction of ancient monuments. Our grandfathers were very Vandals, and their grandsons are frequently but little better. I do not like to gibbet certain respectable parsons now living, but of my own knowledge the following desecrations have taken place quite recently in churches in one small county :—Two east windows, with Fourteenth-Century arms, entirely destroyed to make room for modern abominations : a dozen old brasses in the chancel covered with a foot of material, topping up with encaustic tiles, so as to raise the floor-line : (in this case no great harm is done, as the brasses are intact beneath) : a magnificent old altar-tomb cleared away to make room for a stove : old incised slabs taken from the church ; some now used as the floor of a baker's oven, others to pave the rector's pig-sty. This last-named appropriation was made in a village near Hertford, in the year 1879.

During the brilliant wars of Edward III., Heraldry attained the perfection which it continued to hold for upwards of a century. Several causes combined to bring about its decadence ; the general decline of the arts did much towards it ; the too prodigal concession of Arms did more. From the time of Edward IV., *Augmentations* were frequently granted ; and by the Tudors this custom was increased to an extent only paralleled by the Stuarts. It needed but the heralds of the Seventeenth and Eighteenth Centuries to complete, what their immediate predecessors had commenced. The Augmentations granted to Sir EDWARD PELLEW, Lords NELSON, EXMOUTH, and HARRIS, Sir CHARLES HARDINGE, Bart., and Sir EDWARD KERRISON, for example, are ridiculous in the extreme, and it is totally impossible to emblazon them correctly from any verbal description. Landscapes, Marine views, and legitimate Charges are huddled together in one composition, in the most picturesque confusion, utterly in defiance of all heraldic usance. How would it be possible for any two persons to delineate the following Augmentation, granted to Lord NELSON, alike ? *On a chief undulated argent, waves of the sea ; from which a palm-tree issuant, between a disabled ship on the dexter, and a battery in ruins on the sinister, all proper.*

Then for crest : *On a wreath of the colours, upon waves of the sea, the stern of a Spanish man-of-war, all proper ; thereon inscribed, ' San Joseff.'* The Armorial Bearings granted to the TETLOWS of LANCASTER in 1760, are perhaps even still more preposterous ; they are as follows : *Azure ; on a Fess argent, five musical lines sable, thereon a Rose gules between two Escallops of the third ; in chief a Nag's head erased of the second, between two Crosses crosslet or ; and in base a*

Fig. 14.

Harp of the last. Crest : *On a Book erect gules, clasped and ornamented or, a silver Penny on which is written the Lord's Prayer ; on the top of the book, a Dove proper, holding in the beak a crowquill Pen sable.* Motto : *Præmium virtutis honor.* This heraldic curiosity is said to have been granted in commemoration of the grantee's brother having written the Lord's Prayer on a silver penny.

Even Turner, who delighted so much in strange aërial effects, would have been puzzled to paint the crest of the TONGUE family : *On an Oaktree, a nest with three young Ravens, fed with the dew of heaven, all proper.*

It is with no intention of casting ridicule on the science of Heraldry that I adduce these instances, but only to show how the most noble institutions may become degraded, and be rendered contemptible, when perverted from their legitimate purposes. Happily, a reawakening is taking place to the practical importance of Heraldry as an exponent of History. Stripped of the absurdities with which a few zealous enthusiasts have loaded it, it once more vindicates its title as a science ; and if its lessons be learned aright, the student will discover a mine of valuable knowledge, which will richly repay him for exploring. With regard to modern Heraldry, a recent writer justly observes: ' It is not a blind following, and much less is it a mere inanimate reproduction, of mediæval Heraldry, and a reiteration of its forms and usages, that will enable us to possess a true historical Heraldry of our own. What we have to do is, to study the old Heraldry ; to familiarise ourselves with its working ; to read its records with ease and fluency ; and to investigate the principles upon which it was carried out into action. And, having thus become heralds, through having attained to a mastery over mediæval Heraldry, we shall be qualified to devote ourselves to the development of a fresh application of the science, that may become consistently, as well as truthfully, historical of ourselves. The mediæval authorities will have taught us both what Heraldry is able to accomplish, and the right system for its operation ; and with ourselves will rest the obligation to produce a true historical Heraldry, that we may transmit to succeeding generations.'

In the *Art Journal* of the year 1854, will be found five excellent papers by W. Partridge, entitled 'What is Heraldry ?' These I recommend to the careful perusal of the heraldic student.

Fig. 15. Jupon of Edward the Black Prince in Canterbury Cathedral.

Fig. 16.

CHAPTER II

THE ACCIDENCE OF ARMORY

The Shield

NOBLES, as we have already seen, formerly bore their Arms charged upon their shields, and in the same manner Heraldic Devices have continued to be represented. There is no definite rule to determine the form of the Escutcheon ; much is left to the taste of the draughtsman, to adopt that which is most agreeable to the eye, and best adapted to receive the various charges. The arms of widows and unmarried ladies (the Queen excepted) must always, however, be represented on a diamond-shaped shield, heraldically termed a *Lozenge.*[1]

It is much to be regretted that, although ancient seals and monuments furnish us with so many examples of shields which might be advantageously adopted, modern heralds have so frequently neglected to avail themselves of them. The earliest form of shields is that known as the *Norman*,

[1] The custom of emblazoning the arms of ladies upon lozenges did not generally obtain in England until the sixteenth century ; though Mackenzie notices that Muriel, Countess of Strathern, who died in the year 1284, bore hers in this manner.

or *kite-shaped* (p. 25), which is very graceful, but is not
sufficiently wide at the base for general heraldic display ; it
is, however, admirably adapted for a single charge—such as
a *Lion rampant.* At the commencement of the Fourteenth
Century, shields were considerably shortened, and, from
their triangular form, are commonly called *Heater-shaped*
(fig. 17).

The shields represented on the tomb of Edward III., in
WESTMINSTER ABBEY (fig. 18), are both effective and convenient ; but perhaps the best adapted to the requirements

Fig. 17. Fig. 18. Fig. 19.

of the modern herald are those in the compartments of the
monument to EDWARD the BLACK PRINCE, at CANTERBURY,
which are more tapering towards the base than the last, and
particularly graceful in their contour (fig. 19).

When a coat of Arms comprises several Charges, or *Quar-*
terings, the *Écusson à bouche* (so called
from its being notched in the dexter chief
to support the spear) may be employed
with advantage, on account of the ample
space afforded at the base. The example
here given is from the tomb of Abbot
RAMRYGE, in ST. ALBAN'S Cathedral. Somewhat similar to this, but with a plain
instead of a fluted surface, is the shield of

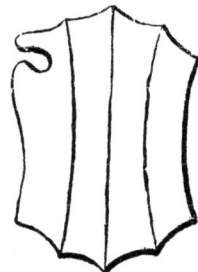

Fig. 20.

the arms of HENRY PLANTAGENET, PRINCE of WALES, afterwards HENRY V., from his stall-plate in ST. GEORGE'S Chapel,
Windsor (fig. 21). Another form of the *Écusson à bouche* is
shown at the heading of this chapter. It is taken from a

beautifully illuminated MS. in the British Museum (*Harl.
MS.* 12,228), executed about the year 1350.

Fig. 21.

Fig. 22.

The shields of arms which decorate the
friezes of the tombs of MARY QUEEN of SCOTS
and of Queen ELIZABETH, in WESTMINSTER
Abbey, are very unsightly, and should only
be used when many Charges, or Quarterings,
have to be introduced.

The form of the shield seems in a great
measure to have followed that of the arch with which it was
contemporary ; for as the Lancet arch was superseded by the
Equilateral of the Decorated Period, and this in turn by the
Obtuse-angled of the Perpendicular, so, in like manner,
Escutcheons expanded until they assumed the almost square
form represented above, which was so much in favour
amongst the Tudors.

It does not necessarily follow, that because shields of any
particular form may have anciently been in actual use, that
they are, therefore, adapted for the service of the armorists
of the present day.   On a monument of HENRY V., for example, are, amongst others, two shields, both unsuited for

Heraldic display. One is a square shield *à bouche*, extremely formal and ungraceful ; and the other is an oblong shield, of which the top and bottom are bent outwards at an angle of about forty degrees, designed to prevent a spear or arrow glancing off and wounding the horse or rider. I would particularly warn the student against adopting the grotesque forms of escutcheons, so much in vogue amongst the armorists of the Seventeenth and Eighteenth Centuries, than which nothing can be conceived more unsuitable, or in worse taste.

Parts of the Shield

It must be remembered that the shield, when in actual use, was held by the knight in front of him ; the right-hand side, therefore, would be towards the left of a spectator ; and in a representation of a coat of arms, that part of the shield which appears on the *left* side is called the DEXTER, and that on the *right*, the SINISTER. In Blazoning, the words right and left must never be used.

For the purpose of accurately determining the position a charge is intended to occupy upon the escutcheon, its various parts are thus distinguished :

A Dexter Chief.
B Chief.
C Sinister Chief.
D Honour Point.
E Fess Point.
F Nombril Point.
G Dexter Base.
H Base.
I Sinister Base.

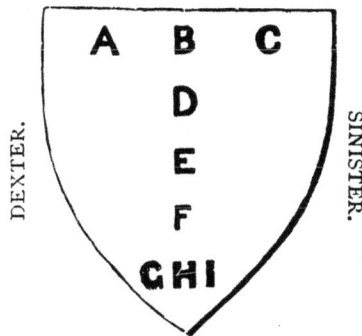

Fig. 23.

The Chief and Base are not restricted to the precise points indicated by B and H.   If, for example, a shield were

D

blazoned as bearing *three Escallop-shells in chief*, they would be severally placed at A, B, and C, and descend as low as D. In English Heraldry, mention is seldom made of the Honour and Nombril Points. I know of no blazon of arms in which these terms are employed.

Dividing Lines

The *Field*, or surface of a shield, is not always of one uniform colour ; it is frequently divided by various lines drawn through it, which take their name from the *Ordinaries*. When thus divided, they are described as follows, and are said to be *Party per* such Ordinary :

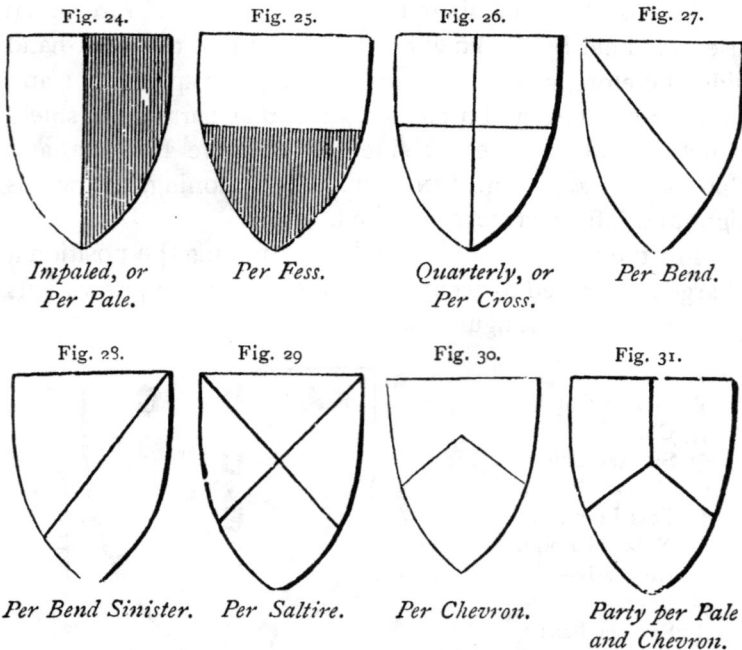

Fig. 24.   Fig. 25.   Fig. 26.   Fig. 27.

Impaled, or Per Pale.   *Per Fess.*   *Quarterly, or Per Cross.*   *Per Bend.*

Fig. 28.   Fig. 29   Fig. 30.   Fig. 31.

Per Bend Sinister.   *Per Saltire.*   *Per Chevron.*   *Party per Pale and Chevron.*

To these may also be added what is sometimes called *Grafted*, but would be better expressed by *Party per Pale and Chevron* (fig. 31). On such a shield, George I. and his successors bore the triple Arms of Hanover, which were omitted from the Arms of England on the Accession of our present Queen, on acconnt of the Salic law which obtains in Hanover.

Shields are subject to other divisions, such as *Gyronny, Barry*, &c., as will be seen hereafter.

A shield divided into any number of parts, by lines drawn through it at right angles to each other, is said to be *Quarterly* of the number, whether it be of four parts or more ; thus, fig. 32 would be described as *Quarterly of eight*. If one or more of these quarters should be subdivided into other like divisions, it is said to be *Quarterly-quartered ;* and the quarter thus quartered is called a *Grand quarter*. The accompanying diagram

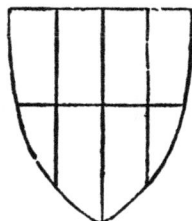

Fig. 32.

would be described as *Quarterly ; the First and Fourth Grand quarters, quarterly-quartered*. When a shield is divided into four quarters, it is sufficient to describe it as *Quarterly ;* that number being always implied, unless another be specified.

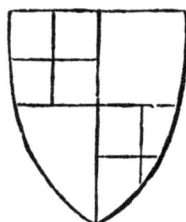

Fig. 33.

The lines by which a shield is divided are not always straight ; they may assume any of the following forms :

Fig.

34. *Engrailed.*

35. *Invected.*

36. *Undé, or Wavy.*

37. *Nebulé.*

38. *Indented.*

39. *Dancetté (but 3 indentations).*

40.   *Embattled.*

41.   *Potent.*

42.   *Ragulé.*

43.   *Dovetailed.*

44.   *Rayonné.*

45.   *Nowy.*

46.   *Escartelé.*

47.   *Angled.*

48.   *Bevilled.*

Examples of the last four partition-lines are seldom, if ever, to be met with in English Armory.

In French Heraldry, wherein all the terms employed are in that language, the terminations of the adjectives and participles are modified according to the gender and number of the substantives to which they refer,—as *un lion affronté,* and *deux têtes affrontées* ; but in English Blazonry, it is not advisable to attempt this distinction ; for to describe two hands as *appaumées,* because the word MAIN is feminine in French, savours somewhat of pedantry. A person may be a good Armorist, and a tolerable French scholar, and still be uncertain whether an Escallop-shell, covered with *bezants,* should be blazoned as *bezanté* or *bezantée.* I have therefore taken the liberty of systematically ignoring grammatical correctness in this respect, and have placed all descriptive terms in the masculine singular, without regard to the gender and number of the nouns they qualify. At any rate, the plan I have adopted cannot be more incorrect than that of blazoning a *Chief* or *Saltire* as *Undée—Chef* and *Sautoir* being masculine ; yet it is commonly so written by English Armorists.

Fig. 49.

Écusson à bouche, from the seats in the choir of Worcester Cathedral, temp. Henry IV.

CHAPTER III

TINCTURES

THE TINCTURES employed in Heraldry are of three kinds : METALS, COLOURS, and FURS ; which are as follows : [1]

Metals

	Heraldic Term.	Abbreviation.
Gold	OR	*Or*
Silver	ARGENT	*Arg.*

Although Heralds make a distinction between Metals and Colours, both are really *colours* in the ordinary acceptation of the term. Thus we find lions *or*, which means of a golden colour ; but in blazoning a Charge, or part of a Charge, supposed to be actually composed of metal—such as a chain, or the clasps of a book—the terms *gold* and *silver* should be employed. This rule, however, is not persistently carried out, for Crowns, Gem-rings, Collars around the necks of beasts, and other metallic objects, are commonly, though incorrectly, described as *or* or *argent*, instead of *gold* or *silver*.

Colours

	Heraldic Term.	Abbreviation.
Red	GULES	*Gu.*
Blue	AZURE	*Az.*
Black	SABLE	*Sa.*
Green	VERT	*Vert*
Purple	PURPURE	*Purp.*

[1] For the colours to be used in emblazoning Arms, see Chapter xxiii.

To the above colours are sometimes added, TENNÉ (bright chestnut), and SANGUINE, or MURREY ; but they are seldom, if ever, employed in Armory ; PURPURE is also rarely to be found in English Coats of Arms.

In the celebrated *Roll of Caerlaverock* (A.D. 1300), the Arms of DE LACI are given—*Or; a Lion rampant, purpure;* and the official Arms of the Regius Professor of Civil Law at Cambridge University appear on a field of this tincture.

TENNÉ and SANGUINE should be considered rather as *Livery Colours (q.v.).* Some writers have declared them to be *stainant,* or disgraceful ; but this can scarcely be the case, or they would not have been voluntarily adopted by noble families as the distinctive colour of their retainers' uniforms. TENNÉ was the livery colour of the BISHOP of WINCHESTER, and Blue of the DUKE of GLOUCESTER. This explains the passage in the *First part of King Henry VI.,* where, in the quarrel between them, the Duke says :

> ' Draw, men, for all this privileged place ;
> *Blue coats to tawny coats.*
> * * * * * *
> Now beat them hence. Why do you let them stay ?
> Thee I'll chase hence, thou wolf in sheep's array !
> *Out, tawny coats!* '

When a charge is to be emblazoned in its natural colour and form (as distinguished from the conventional), it is described as PROPER (*ppr.*). Thus a *Red Rose, leaved and stalked proper*—the emblem of England—would be very unlike a *Rose gules, leaved and stalked vert.* The form of the Heraldic Rose will be found under the head of *Common Charges.*

Furs

ERMINE.	VAIR.
ERMINES.	COUNTERVAIR.
ERMINOIS.	POTENT.
PEAN.	COUNTERPOTENT.

In Blazoning, the names of the Furs are usually written in full. The introduction of Furs into Heraldry probably originated from the ancient custom of covering bucklers with the skins of beasts ; which formed a sufficient protection against arrows and other missiles then in use.

The various Tinctures are represented in engravings and on seals in the following manner :

OR.—Plain, powdered with dots.

Fig. 50.

ARGENT.—Plain.

Fig. 51.

GULES.—Parallel lines drawn in Pale.

Fig. 52.

AZURE.—Parallel lines drawn in Fess.

Fig. 53.

SABLE.—Lines crossing each other at right angles.

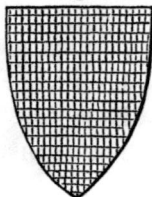

Fig. 54.

VERT.—Diagonal lines drawn
   from dexter to sinister.

Fig. 55.

PURPURE.—Diagonal   lines
   drawn from sinister to
   dexter.

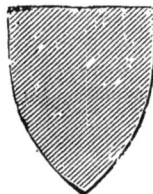

Fig. 56.

TENNÉ is represented by diagonal lines drawn from the
sinister to the dexter, crossed by perpendicular lines ; and
SANGUINE by diagonal lines, intersecting each other.

The method of indicating the various tinctures by lines
is ascribed both to De la Columbière and Silvester Petra-
sancta.   The earliest example in England occurs in some of
the seals attached to the death-warrant of King Charles I.,
though it was probably in vogue some years earlier. Another
mode of indicating the Tincture of Charges upon a shield of
arms is by ' *Tricking,*' a description of which will be found
in Chapter xxiii.

ERMINE is represented by an Argent field, powdered with Sable ' *spots.*'

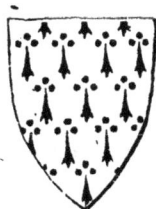

Fig. 57.

ERMINES is the reverse of Ermine,
being Sable powdered with Argent
' *spots.*'

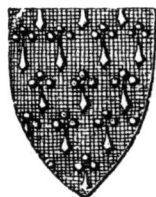

Fig. 58.

ERMINOIS is Or with Sable '*spots.*'

Fig. 59.

PEAN is Sable powdered with Or '*spots.*'

Fig. 60.

VAIR is formed by a number of small bells, or shields, of one tincture, arranged in horizontal lines, in such a manner that the bases of those in the upper line are opposite to the bases of others, of another tincture, below.

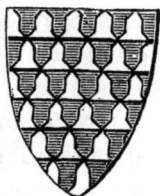

Fig. 61.

COUNTERVAIR, the same as Vair, except that the bells, placed base to base, are of the same tincture.

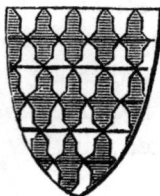

Fig. 62.

POTENT is formed by a number of figures, bearing some resemblance to crutch-heads, arranged in horizontal lines, in the same manner as Vair.[1]

Fig. 63.

---

[1] 'Potent' is an old name for crutch, and is still used in that signification in Norfolk, where it is pronounced 'pottent.' Chaucer, in the *Romaunt of the Rose*, writes:

'When luste of youth wasted be and spente,
    Then in hys honde he takyth a potent.'

COUNTERPOTENT. In this the Po-

Fig. 64.

tents are arranged as in Countervair.

ERMINITES and VAIR-EN-POINT are sometimes included amongst the Furs. The former is similar to ermine, with the addition of a red hair on each side of the '*spots ;*' and in the latter, the bells are so arranged that the bases of those in the upper line rest upon the points of those beneath.

The Furs VAIR, COUNTERVAIR, POTENT, and COUNTER-POTENT are always to be blazoned *Argent* and *Azure*, unless otherwise specified. If the field were *Or*, and the bells *Gules*, it would be blazoned as *Vairy*, *Or* and *Gules*. They are usually represented as of four rows, heraldically termed TRACKS.

Furs are known by the name of DOUBLINGS, when used in the linings of mantles ; but when coming under the denomination of Tinctures, they are called each by their respective name.

Although *Ermine* is usually re-presented as in fig. 57, the oldest and undoubtedly the best form is as here shown.

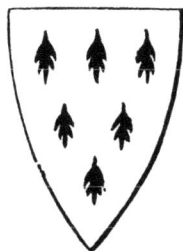

Fig. 65.

CHAPTER IV

CHARGES

Ordinaries, Roundles, and Guttæ, or Gouttes

BY a Charge is implied any figure placed upon a shield, which is then said to be *charged* with such device. Thus in the Royal Arms of England, the shield is *charged* with three Lions.

English Armory affords a few examples of families who bear no charge upon their escutcheon: the WALDEGRAVES, for instance, bear for Arms a shield *Party per pale arg. and gu.* (fig. 24); the ASTONS, *Per chevron arg. and sa.*; the SERLES, *Per pale or and sa.*; and the FAIRLEYS, the same tinctures reversed.

Charges may be divided into two classes—ORDINARIES, and COMMON CHARGES.

Armorists usually divide the Ordinaries into HONOURABLE ORDINARIES and SUB-ORDINARIES; but I have ventured to deviate from this plan, and include them all under one head. I am induced to do this from the fact that out of twenty-five writers on Heraldry whose works I have consulted, but five are agreed as to which devices should be severally included in the two classes. In the *Grammar of Heraldry* I have followed the majority, and placed under the head of Honourable Ordinaries, the CHIEF, PALE, BEND, BEND-SINISTER, FESS, BAR, CHEVRON, CROSS, and SALTIRE.

ORDINARIES

The CHIEF is an Ordinary which occupies the upper third portion of the shield.

'The diminutive of the Chief is the *Fillet*, which is one-fourth its depth, and is placed in the lowest portion thereof.' I cannot recall to my memory any instance of a Fillet being employed in English Armory.

Fig. 66.

The PALE is a perpendicular band, placed in the centre of the shield; of which, like the Chief, it occupies one-third.

Its diminutives are the *Pallet* and *Endorse*, which occupy one-half and one-fourth of the Pale respectively. When the Endorse is used, two of them are placed one on either side of a Pale, which is then said to be *Endorsed*.

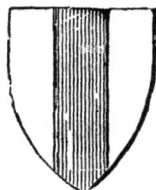

Fig. 67.

The BEND is an Ordinary which crosses the shield diagonally from dexter to sinister. When charged, it occupies one-third of the shield; but when uncharged, only one-fifth.

Fig. 68.

The diminutives of the Bend are the *Bendlet*, or *Garter*, which is half the width of the Bend; the *Cost*, or *Cotice*, which is half the Bendlet; and the *Riband*, half of the Cost. Costs never appear alone in a shield; they are generally borne in couples, with a Bend, Fess, or other charge between them; which charge is then said to be *cotised* (fig. 69). The *Riband* does not extend to the extremities of the shield; its ends being *couped*, or cut off.

Fig. 69.

Fig. 70.

The BEND-SINISTER differs from the Bend, in being drawn in the opposite direction, viz., from the sinister chief to the dexter base.

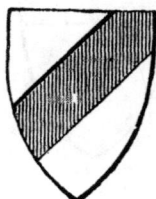

The diminutives of the Bend-sinister are the *Scarpe*, which is one-half its width, and the *Bâton*, which is one-fourth. The latter, like the Riband, is *couped* at the extremities, and both are generally considered as marks of Illegitimacy.

Fig. 71.

The FESS is an Ordinary crossing the shield horizontally, of the same width as the Pale.

Fig. 72.

The BAR, although generally reckoned as a separate Ordinary, may be more justly considered but as a diminutive of the Fess, as the only difference between them is in their width, the Bar occupying but one-fifth of the field.

The *Closet* and the *Barrulet* are severally one-half and one-fourth the width of the Bar.

Fig. 73.

Barrulets are frequently placed together in couples ; when so borne, they are called *Bars-gemelle*.

Two, three, or four Bars may constitute a charge, but a single Bar is never borne alone. The Fess differs from the Bar and its diminutives in this respect—that the former always occupies the middle of the field, whilst the latter may be placed in any portion thereof.

The CHEVRON is formed by two Bars, one-fifth the width of the Shield, issuing respec-

Fig. 74.

tively from the dexter and sinister bases of the Shield, and *conjoined* at its centre (fig. 74).

The *Chevronel* contains one-half, and the *Couple-close* one-fourth, of the Chevron. The latter is borne—as its name implies — in couples, and usually appears *cotising* a Chevron.

The term *Cotising* is applied indifferently to Costs, Barrulets, and Couples-close, when respectively placed on both sides of a Bend, Bar, or Chevron.

Cotises may be of any of the dividing lines given on pp. 47 and 48, as in the Arms of Kendal (fig. 75). *Argent; a Bend vert, between Cotises dancetté gules.*

The Bend, Fess, and Chevron—particularly in Foreign Heraldry—are sometimes represented as *arched*, or *bowed*.

Fig. 75.

The SALTIRE is but a variation of the Cross, and is formed by the combination of a Bend and a Bend-sinister. It has no diminutive. *Azure ; a Saltire argent*, forms what is commonly known as the CROSS OF ST. ANDREW.

Fig. 76.

The CROSS is an Ordinary, produced by a perpendicular band one-fifth the width of the shield (or if charged, one-third), meeting a horizontal band near the Fess point ; the four limbs thus formed being of the same width.

No Ordinary is subject to so many modifications of form as the Cross. Being considered as the emblem of Christianity, it was eagerly adopted by the Pilgrims and Crusaders, and subsequently retained by them to perpetuate their exploits. To prevent the confusion which would necessarily arise from so many individuals bearing the same

Fig. 77.

charge, an almost endless variety of forms was devised ; some, indeed, retaining but a slight resemblance to the original figure. It would be impossible to enumerate all the varieties of this favourite device.　Gwillim mentions thirty-nine different Crosses ; Gerard Leigh, forty-six ; Edmondson, one hundred and nine ; and Robson no less than two-hundred and twenty-two.　Those which are most commonly employed in English Heraldry are the following :

The GREEK CROSS (fig. 77), which is the simplest form of this Bearing, and the only one which can be justly regarded as an Ordinary ; the others being, strictly, but *Common Charges*.

Such a Cross *Gules*, upon a field *Argent*, constitutes the CROSS OF ST. GEORGE of England.

When '*a Cross*' only is specified in a Blazon, it is always to be represented as a GREEK CROSS.

The LATIN CROSS has its horizontal limbs *couped* and

Fig. 78.

enhanced (or set higher than their usual position), so that each is of the same length as the upper limb.　A charge but seldom used.

The Latin Cross is sometimes called a *Passion Cross ;* but in the latter, all the limbs should be couped, that is the top and bottom of the Cross should not touch the extremities of the shield, while still retaining the distinctive features of the Latin Cross.

The PATRIARCHAL CROSS is a Greek Cross, the upper limb of which is traversed by a shorter (fig. 79).

The CROSS OF ST. ANTHONY, or TAU CROSS, resembles the Greek letter of that name (fig. 80).

Fig. 79.

Fig. 80.

The CROSS HUMETTÉ, or COUPED, as its name implies, has its extremities cut off (fig. 81).

The CROSS POTENT has its four limbs terminated by others placed transversely, bearing a resemblance to the Fur of that name (fig. 82).

The CROSS PATÉ, or FORMÉ. In this Cross the limbs are very narrow where they are conjoined, and gradually expand ; the whole forming nearly a square (fig. 83).

Fig. 81.   Fig. 82.   Fig. 83.

The MALTESE CROSS, or CROSS OF EIGHT POINTS, differs from the Cross Paté in having the extremities of each of its limbs indented or notched (fig. 84). This Cross was the Cognisance of the Knights Templars and Hospitallers.

The CROSS FLEURIE (fig. 85) and CROSS FLEURETTÉ (fig. 86) are very similar : in the latter, the *Fleurs-de-lys* are generally represented as issuing from the limbs, and not forming a part of the Cross itself.

Fig. 84.   Fig. 85.   Fig. 86.

The CROSS BOTONNÉ, or TREFLÉ, differs from the Cross Fleurie in having *Trefoils* or triple buds in the place of the *Fleurs-de-lys* (fig. 87).

E

A Cross, the limbs of which are terminated by a single ball, is termed a CROSS POMMÉ, or POMMELLÉ.

The CROSS PATONCE resembles a Cross Fleurie with its extremities expanded (fig. 88).

The CROSS MOLINE (fig. 89) has its extremities formed like *Fers-de-moline*, or *Mill-rinds* (*see* COMMON CHARGES).

Fig. 87.   Fig. 88.   Fig. 89.

A Cross Moline with its eight points *rebated*, or cut off, is termed a CROSS FOURCHÉ.

The CROSS RECERCELÉ resembles a Cross Moline with its floriations more expanded (fig. 90).

The CROSS NOWY has the angles formed by the conjunction of its limbs rounded outwards (fig. 91).

The CROSS QUADRATE, or NOWY-QUADRATE, has its centre square, instead of round, as the last (fig. 92).

Fig. 90.   Fig. 91.   Fig. 92.

All the varieties of the Cross may be *Nowy* or *Quadrate*.

The POINTED CROSS, CROSS URDÉ, or CHAMPAIN, is pointed at the extremities (fig. 93).

The CROSS RAYONNANT has rays of light behind it, issuing from the centre (fig. 94).

The CROSS-CROSSLET—a very frequent charge—has each of its limbs crossed (fig. 95).

Fig. 93.

Fig. 94.

Fig. 95.

A Greek Cross, having its limbs traversed in the manner of a Cross-crosslet, would be described as a CROSS CROSSED, or a CROSS-CROSSLET FIXED. The term *fixed*, applied to Crosses, signifies that their limbs extend to the extremities of the Escutcheon.

When the central part of the four limbs of a Cross is cut out, it is said to be VOIDED, as shown at fig. 96 ; when the *voiding* is continued to the extremities of the shield, it is VOIDED THROUGHOUT. If only that part where the limbs are conjoined be removed, it is termed QUARTERLY-PIERCED (fig. 97). A Cross with a square aperture in its centre, smaller than the last example, is QUARTER-PIERCED.

The Base of a Cross is sometimes represented as pointed : it is then said to be FITCHÉ. Fig. 98 is a CROSS CLECHÉ, *fitché*. Crosses of this description are said to have been carried by the early Christians in their pilgrimages, so that they might be readily fixed in the ground whilst performing their devotions.

Fig. 96.

Fig. 97.

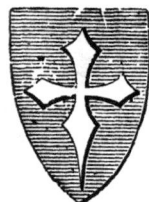

Fig. 98.

A Cross set on Steps (usually three) is DEGRADED, or ON DEGREES. By a CROSS FIMBRIATED is implied a Cross having around it a narrow Border, which forms an integral part of the Charge itself ; and, in emblazoning, the Fimbriation, and not the Cross, must be shaded. The CROSS OF ST. GEORGE, and the SALTIRE OF ST. PATRICK, as they appear on the British Ensign (Chap. xx.), afford examples of Fimbriation. Any other Charge besides a Cross may be thus represented.

Sometimes a Cross is charged upon another, as in the accompanying example, which would be blazoned, *Vert ; on a Cross argent, another humetté of the field.*

Particular attention must be paid to the shading of a Cross when imposed upon another. At a casual glance, figs. 96 and 99 seem identical ; on examining them, however, it will be seen that the shading of the inner cross is differently disposed.

Fig. 99.

The shield in the margin, containing the Arms of Heydon, would be blazoned :— *Argent and azure ; a Cross engrailed counterchanged.* The meaning of *Counterchanging* will be found a few pages later.

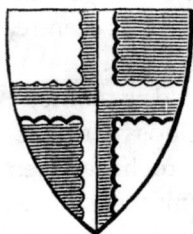

The foregoing Ordinaries are not always represented by straight lines ; they may be formed by any of the Partition lines shown at pages 47 and 48. Thus we find Chiefs, Chevrons, Crosses, &c., *engrailed, ragulé, wavy, indented,* &c. Fig. 101 is an example of a *Chief wavy.*

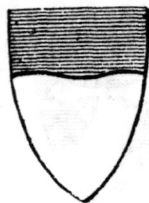

Fig. 100.

When a Fess, Bend, or Chevron, is bounded on *each* side by the lines embattled, potent, or ragulé, it must be blazoned as *Embattled-counter-embattled,* or *Potent-counter-*

Fig. 101.

potent, as the case may be (fig. 102). This
rule does not apply to Pales, Crosses, and
Saltires, which are always bounded on *both*
sides alike, although *counter* be not expressed. A Fess, described simply as *embattled*, is supposed to be plain on the lower
edge.

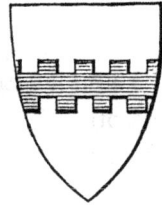

Fig. 102.

It will be observed that, in fig. 102, the projections on the
upper side of the Fess are opposite to the indentations below. When the projections are
opposite to each other, as in the accompanying
example, it is not to be blazoned *Embattled-
counter-embattled*, but *Bretissé*.

Fig. 103.

Crosses and other Ordinaries may also be
formed by arranging small charges in the form
of such figures, as will be hereafter explained.

The following charges are generally termed SUBORDI-
NARIES :

The PILE is a figure in the form of a wedge, and, unless
otherwise specified in the Blazon, occupies
the central portion of the escutcheon, and
issues from the middle chief. It may, however,
issue from any other extremity of the shield,
and there may be more than one. Piles, like
other Ordinaries, may also be charged, and may
be of any of the *Dividing lines*, as in the
Arms of BYDE :—*Or ; on a Pile engrailed
azure, three Anchors of the field* (fig. 105). Fig. 106 is an

Fig. 104.

Fig. 105.

Fig. 106.

example of a charged cross :—*Azure ; on a Cross or, five Mullets gules*, for VERNEY.

The length of the Pile depends, in a great measure, on the other figures which may occupy the shield.   If no other charge intervene, it may extend to the Nombril-point, or even lower.

Fig. 107.

The QUARTER, as its name implies, occupies one-fourth part of the shield. It is formed by two straight lines, drawn in the direction of the Fess and the Pale, and meeting at the Fess-point. Examples of this charge are very rarely to be met with.

The CANTON may be regarded as a diminutive of the Quarter, as it occupies but one-third portion of the Chief (fig. 108).   It is usually placed in the Dexter chief ; if on the other side, it is termed a CANTON SINISTER.

Fig. 108.

The GYRON is formed by a diagonal line, bisecting a Quarter *bendwise* (fig. 109).   It is usually repeated so as to cover the entire surface of the shield ; in which case it is blazoned as GYRONNY, and the number of Gyrons specified. Thus, fig. 110 would be blazoned, *Gyronny of eight, arg. and az.*

The GYRON, CANTON, and QUARTER are always contained within straight lines, and never within the irregular Dividing lines given on pages 47 and 48.

Fig. 109.

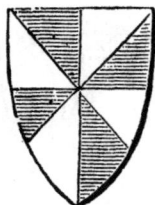

Fig. 110.

The BORDURE is a band one-fifth the width of the Shield, which it entirely surrounds. This Ordinary may be formed of any of the Dividing lines; it is always, however, to be represented plain, unless the contrary be specified.

When a Bordure is charged upon a shield, it surmounts any other Ordinary, except a Chief. Bordures are themselves commonly charged, as, for example, in the Arms of WIL-

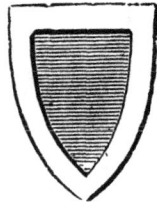

Fig. 111.

LIAMS :—*Argent; within a Bordure engrailed gules charged with eight Crosses paté or, alternating with as many Bezants; a Greyhound courant in Fess sable, between three Cornish Choughs proper* (fig. 112).

Fig. 112.

Fig. 113.

For further modifications, to which the Bordure and its diminutives are subject, see IMPALING and QUARTERING.

A Bordure or other Ordinary composed of Metal and Colour alternately, is termed COM-PONY or GOBONY (fig. 114). The example, fig. 113, would be blazoned, *Argent; a Bend compony gules and azure, cotised sable*, for LEVENTHORP.

Fig. 114.

If there be two *Tracks*, it is then said to be COUNTER-COMPONY (fig. 115); if more than two, Chequé.

Fig. 116 is an example of a Bordure quarterly : First and Fourth, *argent*; Second and Third, *azure*.

Fig. 115.

Fig. 116.

A Bordure of Metal should not be placed upon a Field of the same. Sometimes, though very rarely, instances of Colour imposed on Colour are to be met with. As a general rule, the Bordure is of the same Tincture as the principal Charge of the Coat, as in the Arms of Scotland (fig. 120).

Bordures, when charged with Bends, Bars, Chevrons, &c., show merely the extremities of such ordinaries as would appear upon the Bordure, were they produced entirely across the Escutcheon. The accompanying example would be blazoned, *Ermine ; within a Bordure argent, charged with two Chevronels gules.*

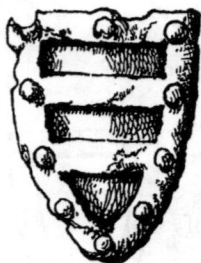

Fig. 117.

Small charges, such as *Escallop-shells* and *Bezants* (small circular gold plates), are frequently emblazoned on Bordures. Unless otherwise specified, the number of these charges is restricted to eight. An early example of thus charging a Bordure is to be found on the monumental Effigy of a Knight in Whitworth Churchyard, Durham, in which, however, the Bordure is charged with ten Roundles. The Arms of RICHARD, EARL of CORNWALL, son of KING JOHN, were *a Lion rampant, within a Bordure bezanté.*

Fig. 118.

Armorists formerly used several distinctive terms in blazoning a charged Bordure, to signify the nature of such Charge : as *Enaluron*, if charged with Birds ; *Entoyre*, with inanimate Charges ; *Enurny*, with Lions ; *Verdoy*, with Plants or Flowers ; and *Purflewed*, if composed of a Fur. This method is now obsolete ; but, in the *Visitations of the Heralds*, and other ancient documents, these terms are frequently employed.

The ORLE is half the width of the Bordure, and does not extend to the extremities of the Shield (fig. 119).

The TRESSURE is one-fourth of the Bordure, and is usually borne double, and *Fleury counter-fleury*,—that is, with eight *Fleurs-de-lys* issuing from each Tressure, as in the Arms of Scotland, which are : *Or ; a Lion rampant within a Tressure fleury counter-fleury gules* (fig. 120).

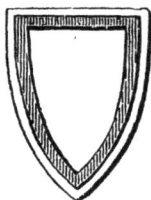

Fig. 119.   Fig. 120.

The Tressure is frequent in the Arms of Scottish families, and is generally considered as indicative of Royal descent by the female side.

The INESCUTCHEON, or SHIELD OF PRETENCE, is a small shield, borne on the centre of the Field (of which it occupies one-fifth), on which a husband emblazons the Arms of his wife, when an Heiress. (See MARSHALLING.) An Inescutcheon is sometimes added to a Coat, and charged with some special *Augmentation*, or Mark of Honour, by the Sovereign, as in the Arms of DIMSDALE :—*Argent ; on a Fess dancetté azure, between three Mullets sable as many Bezants ; over all on an Inescutcheon or, a sinister Wing erect Sable.*

Fig. 121.

When borne on any part of the shield other than the Fess-point, or when more than one occurs, as in the Family Arms of the HAYS, EARLS of KINNOUL, and CECILS, MARQUESSES of SALISBURY (fig. 123), it is called an *Escutcheon*. As an

Fig. 122.

Inescutcheon is always supposed to be a real object laid upon
the shield, its outline must be drawn and shaded accordingly.

The LOZENGE is a diamond-shaped figure set perpendicu-

Fig. 123.

larly on the shield (fig. 124). It may be of any tincture, as
in the Arms of Sir JOHN DE CREKE (fig. 10), which were
Or ; on a Fess gules, three Lozenges vair. It may also be
charged.

The FUSIL is an elongated Lozenge (fig. 125). I am inclined to think that the Fusil was originally the head of a

Fig. 124.

Fig. 125.

Pick. As this is no place for discussion, I will content myself with observing, as one argument in favour of my supposition, that the various branches of the family of PICOT or
PIGOT bear indifferently Fusils and Pick-heads.

The Fusil was formerly represented of an oval form,
pointed at the top and bottom, like a spindle covered with
thread. In this form it was commonly called a *wharrow-
spindle*, and is so borne by the Family of TREFUSIS.

The MASCLE is a Lozenge *voided*, so that the Field appears through the opening (fig. 126).

The RUSTRE differs from the Mascle in being perforated with a round instead of a Lozenge-shaped opening (fig. 127). Some Armorists blazon a Rustre as *a Mascle pierced round.*

The FRET is a figure formed by two narrow bands in saltire, interlaced with a Mascle (fig. 128).

Fig. 126.   Fig. 127.   Fig. 128.

The BILLET is a small oblong figure, frequently to be met with in Armory, supposed to represent a *billet*, or letter, as shown in the first Quarter of fig. 311. When a Shield or Charge is *Semé*, or strewn, with Billets, without regard to position or number, it is termed *Billeté.*

FLANCHES, which are always borne in pairs, are formed by circular lines, proceeding from the upper angle of the Shield, on either side, towards the respective Base-points

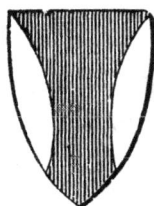 

Fig. 129.   Fig. 130.

(fig. 129). Flanches are not of common occurrence in English Armory, but we have an example in the Arms of that good man and soldier, the late Sir BARTLE FRERE :—
Gules ; between Flanches or, two Leopards' faces in pale of

the last (fig. 130).   Although in the two examples here given the Flanches are not represented quite in the same manner both forms are correct, or at least admissible. Should there be, say, three Lions passant in Chief, the draughtsman would commence his Flanches at the angles, so as to afford more space for the charges ; but if there is nothing of importance to occupy the chief, he would be justified in representing his Flanches as in the arms of FRERE.

FLASQUES and VOIDERS are Flanches which encroach less on the Shield.   They arc even of rarer occurrence than Flanches.

Charges are frequently blazoned as *In Fess, In Pale, In Cross, In Orle,* &c., which means that they are to be disposed in the forms of such Ordinaries.   Fig. 136 would be blazoned as *Azure ; a Chevron argent, in chief three*

Fig. 136.

Fig. 137.

Crosses paté of the last, for BARCLAY.   The next example shows charges *on* a Chief :—*Or ; on a Chief indented sable, three Crescents argent,* for HARVEY.

The shield on page 13 shows three Fusils conjoined in fess.

Unless any other number be particularly expressed, Charges, either *On an Orle,* or *In an Orle,* always consist of eight.   For further directions as to the disposition of small Charges, see Chap. vii.

When a Shield contains a Cross, and in each of the four

Quarters there is a Charge, the Cross is said to be *Cantoned* by such Charges.

All the Ordinaries (but not their diminutives, or the Fusil, Mascle, Rustre, or Fret) may be charged.

The *Pallet* is an exception to this rule, and may receive a Charge.

A Shield consisting of more than one Tincture, and the division formed by a line drawn in the direction of any of the Ordinaries, is said to be *Party per* that Ordinary. Fig. 24 would be blazoned as *Party per Pale, argent and gules ;* and fig. 25, *Party per Fess, argent and gules.* A Shield is never *party* of any of the Diminutives, or of the Chief or Bar : thus it would be incorrect to blazon fig. 66 as *Party per Chief, azure and argent*—it should be, *Argent ; a Chief azure.*

In blazoning, the word *Party* is commonly omitted ; *Per Fess,* or *Per Chevron,* is sufficiently explicit.

Roundles and Guttæ

Roundles are small circular figures—of frequent occurrence in Heraldry— forming a distinct group of Charges. These are generally reckoned to be seven, which are distinguished from each other by their several Tinctures,— they are :

				Fig.
The Bezant	. . . .	*or*	. .	138
The Plate .	. . . .	*arg.*	. .	139
The Torteau (pl. *Torteaux*)	.	*gu.*	. .	140
The Heurte	. . . .	*az.*	. .	141

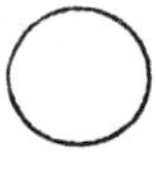

Fig.

THE PELLET, or OGRESS   .   .   *sa.*   .   .   ⚫   142

THE POMME   .   .   .   .   *vert.*   .   .   ◐   143

THE FOUNTAIN . *barry wavy of six, arg. and az.*   ◉   144

In an Illuminated Manuscript of the early part of the Fourteenth Century (*Add. MSS. No.* 10,293, *Brit. Mus.*) is a drawing of a river which is represented as rising from a fountain depicted as above.

'A Bend between six Fountains forms the Coat of the Stourton Family, borne in signification of the six springs whereof the River of Stoure, in Wiltshire, hath its beginning, and passeth along to Stourton, the seat of that Barony.'

To these may be added—GOLPES (*Purpure*), GUZES (*Sanguine*), and Oranges (*Tenné*), of which examples are occasionally to be met with in Foreign Heraldry.

Bezants are said to have been derived from the gold coin of Byzantium, and to have been introduced into Armory by the Crusaders on their return from the East.

The Bezant, Plate, and Fountain, are always to be repre-

Fig. 145.

Fig. 146.

sented flat ; but the others in relief, and they must be shaded accordingly.

A Roundle may also be blazoned *of a Fur*, and is sometimes charged, as in the Arms of DACRES :—*Argent ; a Chevron sable between three Torteaux, each charged with an Escallop of the first ;* and as in those of DOCWRA :— *Sable ; a Chevron engrailed argent, between three Plates, each charged with a Pallet gules* (figs. 145 and 146).

In the *Boke of St. Albans* all the Roundles, with the exception of the Bezant or Talent, are described as Tortels, or *little cakes.* The learned authoress thus describes in Latin, French, and English, the Arms which modern Heralds would blazon as *Or ; three Torteaux,* for COURTENAY :— 'Portat tres tortellas rubias in campo aureo.' 'Il porte d'or et trois torteaulx de gowles.' 'He beareth golde and three cakes of gowles.' The late Mr. Planché points out that the Bordure bezanté of Richard, King of the Romans, had nothing to do with Bezants, as coins, but that the charge was simply Peas (*Poix*), being the Arms of *Poi*tiers or *Poi*ctou. These Peas were gold, and as he was also Earl of Cornwall, fifteen golden peas or Bezants became the Arms of the County of Cornwall, and were adopted by many families who were settled in it, as shown on the cover of this book.

GUTTÆ, or GOUTTES, as their name implies, are drops, and, like the Roundles, are distinguished by their Tinctures :

GOUTTES D'OR	.	.	.	.	*or.*
,,	D'EAU .	.	.	.	*arg.*
,,	DE SANG	.	.	.	*gu.*
,,	DE LARMES .	.	.	.	*az.*
,,	DE POIX	.	.	.	*sa.*
,,	D'OLIVE	.	.	.	*vert.*

The terms *d'eau, de sang,* &c., are not always employed when blazoning Gouttes ; it is equally correct, and, at the same time, more simple, to blazon Gouttes by their Tinctures. Thus the accompanying example might be blazoned as *Argent ; gutté de larmes,* or *Argent ; gutté azure.* I am strongly in favour of the latter method.

Fig. 147.

CHAPTER V

VARIED TINCTURES OF FIELDS AND CHARGES

W E have already seen that a Field or Charge may be divided by Partition-lines, as well as by others drawn in the direction of the Ordinaries. Besides these, Fields, and Charges themselves, are sometimes covered with a repetition or combination of the Ordinaries, so as to form a sort of pattern.

PALY signifies that the Shield is to be divided into an even number of partitions *palewise*, specifying the number of such divisions. The example in the margin would be blazoned thus : *Paly of six ; argent and gules.*

It is to be particularly observed that, in emblazoning a Field or Charge composed of more than one Tincture, that which is first

Fig. 148.

mentioned must be placed in the most honourable position. Thus, if a Shield be divided *per Bend, or and azure*, the *or*, being first specified, must occupy the upper portion, and the *azure* the lower. . So, in fig. 148 the gules yields precedence to the argent, which latter is placed towards the dexter.

BENDY. A Shield, or its charge, is said to be *Bendy* when it is divided into an even number of Bends.

BARRY means that the Field is to be divided into a number of Bars, in the same manner as the foregoing. Fig. 149 would be blazoned as, *Barry of six, argent and izure.* When a shield is traversed by more than eight Bars, it is said to be *Barruly.*

Paly, Bendy, and Barry, must always be composed of an even number of Pales, Bends, and Bars ; for if, in fig. 149, there were another division, it would become, *Argent ; three Barrulets gules.*

Fig. 149.

PALY-BENDY is when the Field is divided by lines drawn in the directions of the Pale and Bend. Fig. 150 is *Paly-bendy, argent and gules.* A field is PALY-BENDY-SINISTER, when the lines are drawn in Pale and Bend-sinister (fig. 151).

BARRY-BENDY is formed by the intersection of lines drawn *Barwise* and *Bendwise*, as in the subjoined diagram : (fig. 152).

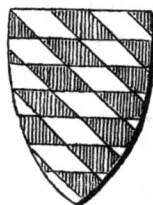

Fig. 150.   Fig. 151.   Fig. 152.

Besides these may be mentioned PALY-BENDY-SINISTER, BARRY-BENDY-SINISTER, and CHEVRONY ; the meaning of which terms is obvious.

GYRONNY has already been described at p. 66.

LOZENGY is produced by lines drawn in the direction of the Bend and Bend-sinister ; thus forming a number of Lozenges (fig. 153).

FUSILLY is similar to Lozengy, except that the lines are more vertical, and form Fusils, instead of Lozenges.

COMPONY, and COUNTER-COMPONY. These arrangements, which have been previously

Fig. 153.

described are only applicable to small Charges ; for it is

F

evident that a Field *Compony or and vert* would be *Paly* of the same (see figs. 114 and 115).

CHEQUÉ signifies that a Field or Charge is divided into a number of squares, formed by lines drawn in the directions of the Pale and Fess.

Bossewell, in the *Armorie of Honor*, published in 1597, says, that Chequé is intended to represent a chess-board. 'In the olde time, it was the play of Noble men ; and therefore the Table thereof is not unworthy to be borne in Armes.'

Fig. 154.

It is to be observed, that the foregoing divisions of a surface are not Charges, but are supposed to represent Tinctures in themselves : they must not therefore be shaded, but be indicated by a fine line on both sides alike.

FRETTY. A surface is thus described when it is covered with a number of narrow bars or sticks— usually eight—lying in the directions of the Bend and Bend-sinister, interlacing each other. When more than eight pieces occur, the number should be specified. Although Fretty does not constitute a Charge, the bars of which it is composed must be duly shaded. See also *Trellis*.

Fig. 155.

DIAPERING

DIAPERING was a device much practised by the Mediæval armorists, to relieve the monotony of any considerable uniform surface, particularly in Coats of Arms painted on glass, and monumental tablets. This was usually effected by covering the shield with a number of small squares, or Lozenges, and filling them with a variety of simple figures ; or sometimes a running ornament was employed for the same purpose. Monuments, Seals and Illuminated MSS., of the

Thirteenth and Fourteenth Centuries, abound in this kind of ornament,—some of them extremely beautiful. The enamelled Tablet to GEOFFREY PLANTAGENET (A.D. 1150), preserved in the Museum of MANS, affords one of the earliest examples of Diapering (fig. 131).

The quartered shield of ROBERT DE VERE, on his monumental effigy in the Church of HATFIELD BROADOAK, in ESSEX, furnishes a magnificent specimen of this style of ornamentation, executed in low relief (fig. 133). The shield contains but one Charge, a Mullet, in the First Quarter ; and, were it not for the Diaper by which the plain surface is relieved, it would appear flat and uninteresting.

On the shield of RALPH, Earl of STAFFORD (A.D. 1370), in ST. STEPHEN's Chapel, WESTMINSTER, both the Field and Charge—a Saltire—are most delicately diapered. Several other shields of Arms are to be seen in the same Building, similarly ornamented.

Nor was Diapering restricted to Fields and Charges, for in the effigy of EDWARD III. in WESTMINSTER ABBEY, the boots are covered with a delicate diapering composed of trellis-work with a Lion passant in every lozenge.

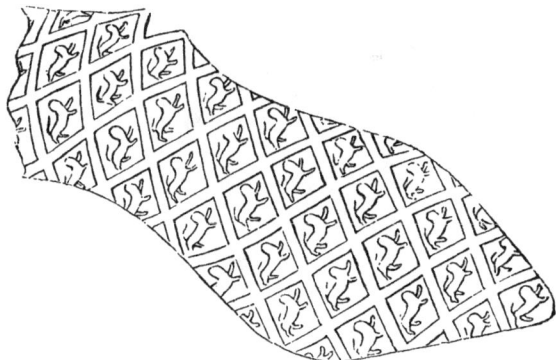

Fig. 156.

The examples, 132 and 134, are taken from Illuminated Manuscripts of the Fourteenth Century, and may be advantageously introduced on Shields or principal Charges.

F 2

The enamelled shield on the Monument of WILLIAM DE
VALENCE, Earl of PEMBROKE, also in WESTMINSTER ABBEY,
affords a fine example of Diapering of another description,
but equally adapted to the use of modern armorists as the
former (fig. 135). In Diapering, everything is left to the
taste of the emblazoner, to adopt such figures as may be agreeable to the eye, without approaching too closely to the form
of any Charge, so as to cause it to appear as though it were
an integral part of the Coat.   Sir John Ferne says, ' a Coat-
armour Diapre may be charged with any thing, either quick
or dead ; but plants, fruits, leaves, or flowers, be aptest to
occupy such Coates.'

Fig. 157.   Diapered surcoat—*Gules ; three Clarions argent*—from a window
in Tewkesbury.

When Diapering is employed as a means of ornamentation, particular care should be exercised not to render the
colours too vivid.   The Charge. it must be remembered, is

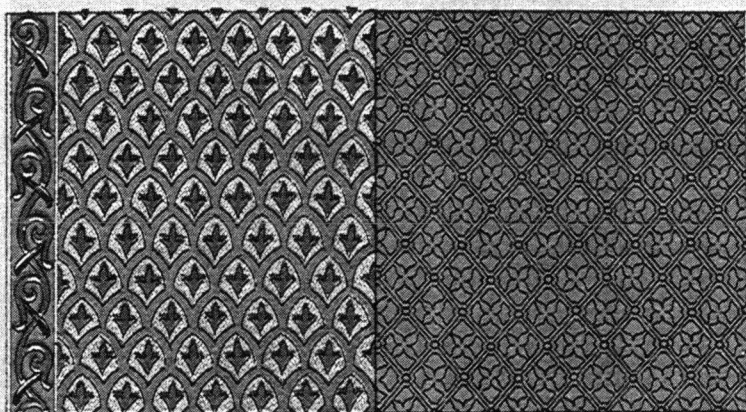

131   132

135

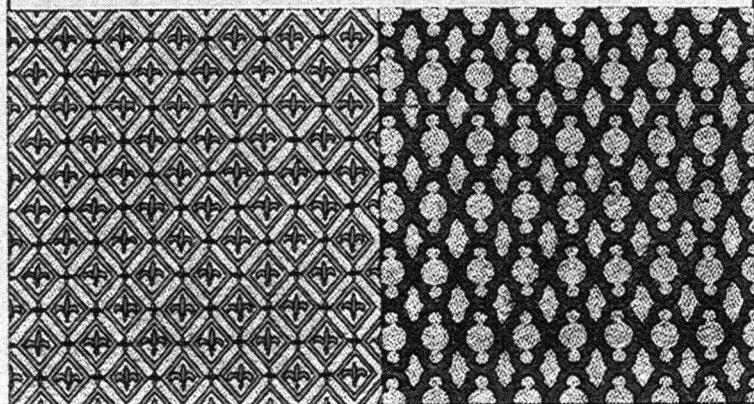

133   134

the principal object, to which the Diapering must be subservient. A good method to adopt is to represent the Diaper by a slightly darker tint of the same tincture as that on which it is laid. Gamboge and Roman ochre, pale red, or fine black lines, may be advantageously used on a gold surface ; another simple but effective mode of Diapering upon gold is to trace out the desired pattern with an agate point. Further directions on this subject will be found in the Chapter on Emblazoning.

Diapering being merely a fanciful embellishment, does not, of course, enter into the Blazon of a Coat of Arms.

When a Field consists of two Tinctures—Metal or Fur and Colour—a Charge placed thereon is sometimes COUNTER-CHANGED ; which implies that both the Field and Charge are of the same Tinctures, but reversed. Thus, in fig. 158 —the Arms of BAKER, of BEYFORDBURY—which would be blazoned, *Per pale ermine and gules ; a Greyhound courant between two Bars invected ; in chief two Quartrefoils, and a third in base, all counterchanged*, it will be seen that ermine is placed upon gules, and gules upon ermine.

  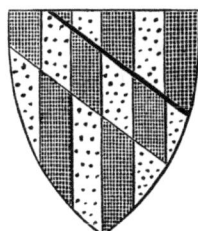

Fig. 158.   Fig. 159.   Fig. 160

The Arms of OLIVE afford another illustration :—*Per pale sable and argent ; a Chevron between three Greyhounds' heads erased, all counterchanged* (fig. 159).

Another form of counterchanging is sometimes to be met with, as in the Arms of CALVERT :—*Paly of six, or and sable ; a Bend counterchanged* (fig. 160). It will be noticed that in this example the perpendicular lines which form the six Pales are continued throughout the shield, but that the Pales themselves are *rompu*, or broken by a Bend, and that the tinctures of that Bend are exactly opposite the tinctures of the Pales.

Fig. 161.

When a Roundle is counterchanged, it loses its distinctive name. In the following blazon, for instance, *Per pale, or and vert; three Roundles, two in chief, and one in base, counterchanged,*—those in chief are, severally, a *Pomme* and a *Bezant ;* and the one in base is partly of one Tincture, and partly of another (fig. 161).

CHAPTER VÍ

COMMON CHARGES

EVERY device depicted upon a Shield, other than the Ordinaries already mentioned, is styled by Armorists a *Common Charge.* It would be impossible to give a complete list of Common Charges : for anything animate or inanimate, and even creatures which exist but in the imagination of Heralds, may be employed as Armorial Bearings.

Of all Charges, the LION is that which is most commonly to be met with. Possessing, in an eminent degree, strength, courage, and generosity,—as the early Heralds were taught to believe, and believed and taught,—it is not surprising that, in the days of a semi-barbaric chivalry, when Armorial Devices were intended to be emblematical of their Bearers, the Lion should be esteemed the most fitting wherewith to emblaze the shield. So generally was this Charge adopted, that, prior to the Thirteenth Century, it constituted, with but few exceptions, the sole Armorial Device.

The Lion may be represented as of a Metal, Fur, or Colour, and in a variety of positions, the principal of which are the following :

STATANT : Standing in profile, looking before him.

** Charges are always to be represented as moving to-wards the Dexter side of the Escutcheon, unless otherwise specified.

When a Lion or other Charge is moving towards the Sinister, it is described as *Contourné.*

It is usual to pronounce such words as *Statant, Rampant, Courant*, &c., as they are written ; and not to give them their French pronunciation.

PASSANT : As if walking, with the Dexter paw raised from the ground (fig. 163) ; and, like Statant (fig. 162), looking towards the Dexter.

PASSANT-GUARDANT : Walking in the same manner as Passant ; but with the head *affronté*, or full-faced (fig. 164). *Three Lions passant-guardant in pale or, on a field gules*, constitute the Arms of England.

Fig. 162.   Fig. 163.   Fig. 164.

Old Armorists—and even Porny, who wrote in 1766—assert, that a Lion should never be blazoned as passant-guardant : when in that position, they say, it should be described as a *Leopard*. Whether the Shield of England originally contained three Lions or Leopards has been the subject of many learned dissertations. In the year 1235, Ferdinand II., Emperor of the West, presented Henry III. with three Leopards, in allusion to his Arms ; and that there was a recognised distinction between the animals, is evident from an inventory of the Royal menagerie in the Tower, compiled in the reign of Edward III., where, amongst other items, are mentioned, 'one lyon, one lyonesse, and one leparde.' In the *Roll of Caerlaverock*, which contains a list of the Arms of all the Nobles who laid siege to the castle of that name, in the year 1300, the Banner of Edward I. is described as being emblazoned with *three Leopards courant*.

That they were regarded as Lions in the Sixteenth Century, if not earlier, appears from a line which occurs in Shakespeare :

> ' Either renew the fight,
> Or tear the Lions out of England's coat.'
>
> *First Part of King Henry V.*, act i. sc. 5.

PASSANT-REGUARDANT differs from passant-guardant only in having the head *contourné*, or turned towards the Sinister (fig. 165).

RAMPANT : Standing on the Sinister hind-leg, with both fore-legs elevated, the Dexter above the Sinister, and the head in profile (fig. 166). Such a Lion gules, on a Field or,

Fig. 165.   Fig. 166.

within a Bordure fleury-counterfleury, constitutes the national Arms of SCOTLAND (fig. 120).

Fig. 167.   Fig. 168.   Fig. 169.

RAMPANT-GUARDANT, and RAMPANT-REGUARDANT, differ from Rampant in having the head *affronté* and *contourné* respectively.

SALIENT : With both hind-legs on the ground, and the fore-paws elevated equally, as if in the act of springing on his prey (fig. 167).

SEJANT : Sitting down, with the fore-limbs erect (fig. 168).

COUCHANT : Reclining at full length on the ground ; but holding the head erect (fig. 169).

DORMANT : Lying down in the same manner as Couchant, with the head resting between the paws as though asleep.

A Lion, with its tail between its legs, is said to be *Coward ;* when furnished with two tails, *Queue fourché*, or *Double queued ;* and, if it be destitute of that appendage, *Defamed.* Two rampant Lions, face to face, are said to be *Combattant ;* and, when placed back to back, *Addorsed.*

When an Ordinary *surmounts*, or is placed *over*, a Lion, or other animal, it is said to be *Debruised*, or *Oppressed*, by that Ordinary. The Arms of *Holland* (fig. 170) are blazoned,

   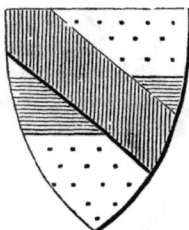   

Fig. 170.   Fig. 171.   Fig. 172.

Azure ; semé-de-lys, a Lion rampant argent, debruised by a Bend gules.[1]   The words *Over all* or *Surmounted by* might be used instead of *Debruised by ;* but in the case of one Ordinary lying on another, *Surmounted by* or *Over all* is always used, and never *Debruised by.*   Thus the Arms of ELWES are *Or ; a Fess azure, surmounted by*, or, *over all, a Bend gules* (fig. 171).   In some cases, where it is self-evident that one charge lies over another, it is not necessary to say *over all ;* as in the Arms recently granted to the SEE OF ST. ALBANS :—*Azure ; a Saltire or ; a Sword proper, hilted of the second in pale, pointing to a Celestial Crown in chief gold* (fig. 172).

[1] The HOLLAND Arms are contained in the first and fourth Quarters. The engraver has made the Bend argent, instead of gules. The second and third Quarters belong to HIBBERT.

Particular attention must be paid to the Heraldic signification of the word *over*. It must never be taken to mean *above*, but *upon*.

A portion only of an Animal may constitute a Charge, as :

A DEMI-LION RAMPANT, which is the upper portion of a Lion rampant *couped*, or cut off straight, beneath the shoulder, including that part of the tail which is above the line (fig. 173).

Fig. 173.

Fig. 174.

A LEG, styled heraldically a JAMBE, or GAMBE, which is usually represented as *erased*, or torn from the body, as in the diagram (fig. 174).

If the Jambe extend only to the first joint, it is called a PAW.

A HEAD, which may be turned in any of the directions before-mentioned.

Fig. 175.

Fig. 176.

A TAIL, or QUEUE : the Family of CORK bears for Arms, *Three Lions' tails erect, erased gules*, on an Argent Field.

When any portion of an Animal is ragged, as though torn violently from the body, it is said to be *Erased*, as in the Arms of HALSEY :—*Argent ; on a Pile sable, three*

Griffins' heads erased of the first (fig. 175) ; but if it be cut clean off, as the Boars' heads appear in the Arms of Bowles (fig. 176), it is said to *Couped.*

It is highly important, in blazoning the head or a limb of an Animal, to specify whether it be Couped or Erased ; for, unless this be done, it would be impossible to represent the Charge with accuracy.

A Boar's Head is sometimes couped close to the shoulders, exhibiting the neck (as in the Arms of the Sloanes) ; and, sometimes, close behind the ears. In the former case, the term *Couped at the neck* is employed ; and, in the latter, *Couped close,* or *Couped* (fig. 176).

Sometimes Charges, particularly Demi-lions, are blazoned as *Issuant,* or *Naissant.* Both words have nearly a similar import, and mean *Rising from;* but there is a great difference in their application. When the former term is employed, the Charge is represented as issuing from the bottom of a Chief (as at fig. 177) ; but, in the latter case, the Charge

Fig 177.   Fig. 178.

appears to rise from the centre of an Ordinary (usually a Fess) ; or, sometimes, from a Common Charge. Fig. 178 would be blazoned, *Ermine ; naissant from a fess azure, a Demi-lion rampant argent.* Lions charged on an Ordinary, or when three or more appear on a Shield, are by some Heralds called *Lioncels,* or young Lions; but, as Robson very justly remarks, this title is absurd ; for, if there be a number borne on one Coat, they must be reduced in size accordingly, which cannot imply age. It is, therefore, more correct to call them *Lions,* irrespective of size and number. In the

Arms of DE BOHUN, for example (fig. 179), the animals are always described as Lions.

In blazoning a Lion, it is necessary to state the Tincture of its *arms*, which are its teeth and claws ; and of its tongue, or *langue*. Lions are usually represented as *armed* and *langued gules*, unless the Field, or they themselves, are of that Tincture, when *azure* is substituted.

Fig. 179.

BEARS, TIGERS, BULLS, BOARS, WOLVES, ANTELOPES, STAGS, GOATS, FOXES, BADGERS (called by Heralds GRAYS), TALBOTS, or hounds, ALANTS (mastiffs with short ears [1]), HORSES, BEAVERS, SQUIRRELS, and many other animals, are to be found blazoned as Charges, of which it is unnecessary to give illustrations. The HERALDIC TIGER, HERALDIC ANTELOPE, &c., are described amongst '*Imaginary Beings.*'

In blazoning the Tails of certain animals, particular terms are commonly employed. The tail of a Fox is called the BRUSH ; of a Deer, the SINGLE ; of a Boar, the WREATH ; of a Wolf, the STERN ; of a Hare or Rabbit (heraldically termed *Coney*), the SCUT, &c. Heralds should not be accused of pedantry in making these distinctions, seeing that others, who are not Heralds, are equally open to censure. Thus two Ducks are a Couple, but two Pheasants, which in October are a Brace, are in April a Pair.

In addition to those already mentioned, the following descriptive terms are applied to Animals :

ADDORSED : Two Charges placed back to back.

BAILLONNÉ : A Lion rampant, holding in its mouth a Staff or Bâton, is thus described.

BRISTLED : This term is used in blazoning the Tincture of the Bristles on the neck and back of a Wild Boar.

---

[1] ' About his chare wente alaunz,
     Twenty and mo, as grete as eny stere,
     To hunte at the lyon, or at the bere.'—*Chaucer.*

CAPARISONED : A War-Horse covered with Trappings or Housings is said to be *caparisoned.*

When Animals are charged upon the Caparisons of a Horse, they must be represented on both sides of it, as though moving towards its head.

CLYMANT : A term applied to Goats when in a rampant position.

COLLARED : Having a Collar about the neck. When an Ape is thus described, the collar is affixed around its loins.

COUNTER-PASSANT : Two Animals walking in opposite directions on the same plane ; if one were above the other, they would be blazoned as *Counter-passant in Pale.*

COUNTER-SALIENT : Two Animals leaping— one in Bend, the other in Bend-sinister, as in the Arms of WILLIAMS.

COURANT : Running.

CRINED : Used to express the tincture of the mane of a Horse, Unicorn, &c., or the hair of a Human Figure, or Mermaid : the Charge is then said to be *Crined* of such tincture.

DISMEMBERED, or TRONONNÉ : A Charge cut into small pieces, which, though separate from each other, are placed sufficiently close to preserve the original form of such Charge. A *Lion rampant dismembered* is borne by the MAITLAND Family.

DISTILLING : Dropping.

EMBRUED : A weapon stained with blood is thus described. The same term is applied to the mouths of Lions, &c., when dropping blood whilst, or after, devouring their prey.

GORGED : Having a Coronet or Ring around the throat or neck.

HORNED : Used in the same manner as *crined,* when an Animal has horns of a different tincture from its body.

INCENSED : An Animal is thus described when fire is issuing from its mouth and ears.

PASCUANT : Applied to Deer, Oxen, &c., when grazing.

REGARDING, or RESPECTANT : Said of two Animals face to face, and not *combattant* (see fig. 196).

TRONONNÉ : See *Dismembered*.

TUSKED : Having tusks, as a Boar or Elephant.

UNGULED : Horses, Unicorns, Boars, Oxen, Deer, &c are said to be *unguled* of their hoofs.

VORANT : Devouring.

VULNED : Wounded.

Other descriptive terms will be found by reference to the Index.

In blazoning Stags, certain terms are used which are not applicable to other Animals. If *statant affronté*, they are said to be AT GAZE ; if *passant*, TRIPPING ; if *running*, AT SPEED ; if *salient*, SPRINGING ; and, if *sejant*, LODGED. They are ATTIRED, not *armed*, of their *Tynes*, or horns. The REINDEER is distinguished by having double attires.

BIRDS

The EAGLE, on account of its strength, swiftness, and courage, was considered by the early Heralds to hold the same position amongst Birds as the Lion amongst Animals ; hence it is a Charge of frequent occurrence, and is to be found emblazoned on the Escutcheons of some of the most ancient families. The most common attitude in which the Eagle appears in Heraldry, is *Displayed*. This term is peculiar

Fig. 180.

to Birds of Prey ; when other Birds (such as the Dove) are represented with their wings expanded, as in the accompanying example, they are said to be *Disclosed*.

The Heraldic student must bear in mind the difference between *An Eagle displayed* and *An Eagle with wings displayed;* when the latter term is employed, the Bird is supposed to be perched. The Eagles of ancient Rome, France, and the United States, would be blazoned as *with wings displayed;* those of Russia, Austria, and Prussia, as *displayed*.

According to some authorities, a double-headed Eagle— as that of Russia—is blazoned as an *Imperial Eagle*. This, however, is manifestly incorrect; for the German Eagle is no less *Imperial*, although it has but one head.

A Bird of Prey is said to be *Armed* of its beak and claws ; but other Birds are *Beaked* and *Membered*. The same law which regulates the Tinctures of the Arms and Tongues of Lions (mentioned at p. 89) is observed with regard to the claws, beaks and tongues of Birds of Prey.

When FALCONS or HAWKS are represented with Bells on their legs, they are blazoned as *Belled* ; and when the *Jesses*, or straps with which the Bells were attached, are *Flotant*, or hanging loose, they are *Belled and Jessed ;* if to the end of the Jesses are affixed VERVELS, or small rings by which the Falcon was fastened to its perch, it is described as *Belled, jessed, and vervelled* (fig. 181). Falcons may also be *Hooded.* They are always to be represented with wings *close*, unless otherwise specified.

Fig. 181.

After the EAGLE and the FALCON, the Birds of most frequent occurrence in Armory are the SWAN, GAME-COCK, CORNISH CHOUGH, PELICAN, HERON, POPINJAY (or Parrot), CROW, GOOSE, SHELDRAKE (a kind of Duck), OSTRICH, RAVEN, OWL, DOVE, PEACOCK, and BAT. The ALLERION and MARTLET will be found under the head of '*Imaginary Beings.*'

An OSTRICH is generally represented as holding a horse-shoe in its mouth.

A PEACOCK *affronté*, with its tail expanded, is blazoned as *In its pride* ; it is also *Eyed* of the variegated spots on its tail.

When a PELICAN is represented in her nest, and feeding her young in the conventional manner in which we usually see it, it is described as a *Pelican in her piety*, or *Vulning herself.*

The Pelican in her piety—as an emblem of benevolence and parental affection—is frequently to be found in places of worship. Beautiful specimens of this device are preserved at UFFORD, in SUFFOLK, and NORTH WALSHAM, in NORFOLK, surmounting the Fonts. The brass Lectern in NORWICH Cathedral is a Pelican ; and, previous to the Reformation, there was another in the Cathedral of DURHAM. It was also frequently represented on Monuments : the Brass of WILLIAM PRESTWYCH, Dean of HASTINGS, in WARBLETON Church, SURREY,—bearing for motto, ' *Sic Christus dilexit nos,'*—and the mural Monument of one of the EARLS of COVENTRY, in the Church of CROOME-D'ABITOT, in WORCESTERSHIRE, afford fine examples. A *Pelican in her piety* is carved under the east window outside ST. PAUL'S Cathedral.

Some writers make a distinction between a *Pelican vulning herself,* and *in her piety.* By the former term they mean that the bird is alone, wounding her breast ; and by the latter, that she is surrounded by, and feeding, her young.

A GAME-COCK, besides being *Armed* of his beak, claws, and spurs, is *Crested* of his comb, and *Jowlopped* of his wattles.

A CORNISH CHOUGH, which forms part of the Coat of WILLIAMS, of HERRINGSTON, Co. DORSET (fig. 112), is always represented *Sable, beaked and membered gules.*

When in a blazon a *Swan's neck* occurs, it comprises the head and neck as far as the body. It is frequently *Gorged,* or encircled with a coronet.

Parts of Birds, especially the wings, are often used as Charges. When a pair of wings appears as in the diagram, they are said to be *Inverted,* or *Conjoined in lure.*

A pair of wings thus fastened together was used by Falconers, wherewith to train their Hawks, and was called a *Lure.* To this was affixed a long line, one end of which the

Fig. 182.

G

Falconer held in his hand, when the wings were thrown in the air to imitate a bird flying.[1]

A single wing is sometimes called a *Demi-vol*. It must be mentioned in the blazon whether it be the dexter or the sinister wing, and whether the tip be *inverted*. Unless otherwise directed, wings are always supposed to be erect, as in the Arms of DIMSDALE (fig. 122).

FEATHERS are also included amongst Heraldic Charges. They are always borne straight, except those of the Ostrich, the tips of which are drooping. A PLUME OF FEATHERS consists of three, as in the Badge of the PRINCE OF WALES, unless some other number be mentioned. If there be two or three rows above each other, they are termed *Double* or *Triple plumes*. In such a case, the upper row has one feather less than that immediately beneath it. When more than three rows occur, they are termed a *Pyramid of feathers*, or *Panache*. Sir Samuel Meyrick says, that 'the distinction between the Panache and Plume is, that the former was fixed on the top of the Helmet, while the latter was placed behind, in front, or on the side.' A Feather borne with the quill transfixed through a scroll of parchment is styled an *Escroll*, though this term is more applicable to the narrow band at the base of an Achievement on which the Motto is inscribed.

Fig. 183.

The following descriptive terms are employed in blazoning birds.

ADDORSED: This term, when applied to the wings of birds, means that they are to be represented partially open, and inclining backwards. When in that position, however, they are more usually and better described as *Elevated*, as in the Arms of WOLRICH

---

[1] 'My Falcon now is sharp, and passing empty ;
  And, till she stoop, she must not be full gorged ;
  For then she never looks upon her lure.'
        Taming of the Shrew, Act iv. sc. 1.

or WOOLRYCH :—*Azure ; a Chevron between three Swans with wings elevated argent.*

CLOSE : With wings closed. This term is only applicable to those birds which are addicted to flight—as Eagles, Swans, Doves, &c. It is unnecessary thus to describe an Ostrich, or Game-cock, as their wings, in Armory, never appear expanded, unless they are so directed in the blazon.

ERECT, when used in blazoning wings, signifies that the principal wing feathers make nearly a right angle with the back of the bird.

MEMBERED : The *Members* of a bird are those portions of its legs which are destitute of feathers.

RISING, or ROUSANT : About to rise, or take wing. This term is usually employed in blazoning Swans. The wings may appear as *Addorsed.*

SOARING, or VOLANT : Flying.

TRUSSING has the same signification when applied to birds, as *Vorant* has to animals (fig. 184). PREYING ON is, however, a better expression, as *Trussed* is frequently used by old Armorists to mean *Close.*

It sometimes occurs that the term ' *a Bird,*' or ' *Birds,*' only is given in the blazon, without any particular variety being specified. In this case they should be drawn in the form of Blackbirds.

Fig. 184.

FISH

Amongst Fish, the DOLPHIN is that which is most commonly represented in Heraldry. Its usual position is *Embowed*, as shown in the example. When moving towards the sinister side, it is said to be *Counter-embowed* ; and when straight, which is an infrequent position, *Extended.*

In France, the bearing of this Charge was exclusively restricted to the DAUPHIN, or heir to the Throne.

Fig. 185.

The other Fish which have been most in favour amongst Heralds are the LUCIE, or PIKE; ROACH, SALMON, STURGEON, EEL, TROUT, and HERRING.

When in a blazon '*a Fish*' is mentioned, and no kind specified, it should be drawn as a Herring.

The position of Fish in the escutcheon is signified by the following Terms.

NAIANT : Swimming in fess towards the dexter (fig. 186).

HAURIANT : In pale, with the head in chief (fig. 187).

URINANT : Also in pale, but with the head in base (fig. 188).

Fig. 186.   Fig. 187.   Fig. 188.

Fish are described as being *Scaled* and *Finned*, of whatever Tincture they may happen to be.

SHELL-FISH afford a few Charges, but they are of comparatively rare occurrence in Armory. The Families of DYKES, CRABB, ATSEY, and PRAUN, bear respectively a LOBSTER, CRAB, CRAY-FISH, and PRAWN.

Fig. 189.—Arms of SCALES :—Gules ; six Escallops or, three, two and one.

Fig. 190.—Arms of KIDSTONE :—Sable ; three Salmon hauriant proper ; on a Chief or, three Goats' heads erased of the first, within a Bordure argent.

The ESCALLOP and WHELK are the only SHELLS employed by Heralds. The former is borne by the RUSSELLS, TRACEYS, and many other Families, and the latter by the SHELLEYS (see page 34). The Escallop is a very old and honourable Bearing, having been assumed by the Pilgrims on their return from the Holy Land. It is represented as at fig. 189.

REPTILES AND INSECTS

Of Reptiles introduced into Heraldry, the SERPENT, SCORPION, and TORTOISE are the most common ; and of Insects, the BEE, BUTTERFLY, and GRASSHOPPER.

Serpents may be *Nowed*, twisted or knotted (fig. 191) ; *Erect*, placed in pale ; *Erect wavy* ; or *Involved*, which last means, curved in a circle. In blazoning, the names SERPENT, SNAKE, ADDER, and VIPER are frequently used indiscriminately.

BUTTERFLIES and BEES are usually depicted *Volant* ; the latter, *Volant en arrière*, that is, with the back presented to the spectator, as in the well-known cognisance of the BOURBONS. The Arms of the ROWE family are, *A Bee-hive, beset with Bees, promiscuously volant.*

Fig. 191.

THE HUMAN FIGURE

Human Figures are of frequent occurrence in Armory, principally as Supporters to Shields.

As Charges, portions only are commonly employed.

The SAVAGE, or WILD MAN, is represented naked, and usually *Wreathed* about the temples and waist with leaves, and holding a club. Two of such figures constitute the supporters of the Arms of DENMARK.

A DEMI-SAVAGE (couped at the waist) is frequently seen both as a Crest and a Charge. The Crest of WIGHTMAN, and the Arms of BASIL-WOODD, furnish examples. The Heads of a MOOR, or BLACKAMOOR, and a SARACEN, are *wreathed* about the temples with a fillet of twisted silk, the Tincture or Tinctures of which must be mentioned.

The same rules are to be observed in blazoning a portion

of a Human Figure as have been already given for Animals. In blazoning a Hand, besides stating what position it occupies, and whether it be the Dexter or Sinister, and erased or couped, it must be mentioned whether it be *clenched* or *appaumé* (open).

The LEG, HEART, ARM, HAND, and HEAD are the parts of the Body usually blazoned as Charges. An Arm encased in armour is *Vambraced* : thus, fig. 192 would be blazoned as, *Argent ; a sinister Arm, erased at the shoulder, embowed, vambraced, hand gauntleted, all proper.* If the Hand had been turned towards the sinister side, it would have been *counter-embowed.* A Hand is never supposed to be *gauntleted,* unless so specified. A clothed figure is said to be *Vested* or *Habited* ; and when the clothes are bound tightly round about the waist, *Close-girt.*

Fig. 192.

IMAGINARY BEINGS

To the fertile imagination of the ancient Oriental warriors, we are in a great measure indebted for the fabulous creatures which appear as Heraldic Charges. These devices were freely adopted by the victorious Crusaders as mementoes of their expedition, and thus they became introduced into Western Europe. Some few, however, such as the PHŒNIX and the SAGITTARIUS, seem to deduce their origin from the Heathen Mythology.

Fig. 193.

Fig. 194.

The DRAGON (fig. 193) is a winged monster, covered

with scales, and having four legs : its tail and tongue are armed with a conventional sting. Both the head and wings frequently appear as separate Charges.

The GRIFFIN (fig. 194) is an Animal the head, shoulders, wings, and fore-feet of which resemble an Eagle ; the body, hind-legs, and tail being formed like a Lion. When in its usual attitude, Rampant, with wings expanded, as in fig. 194, it is described as *Segreant.* It may also be *Passant,*

Fig. 195.

Fig. 196.

as in the Arms of CHESTER (fig. 195). Demi-Griffins also appear as Charges, as in the Arms of SMITH, of WATTON, Co. HERTS (fig. 196).

A MALE GRIFFIN is destitute of wings, and is further distinguished by two straight horns rising from the forehead, and rays of gold which issue from various parts of the body. This is an unusual charge.

The COCKATRICE has the head, body, wings, and feet of a Cock (scales being substituted for feathers), and the tail of a Dragon (fig. 197). It is *Armed, Crested* and *Jow-lopped* in the same manner as the Game-cock. The head alone is a frequent Charge.

Fig. 197.

As modern Natural Histories are deficient in details connected with Cockatrices, I have translated and condensed the best account I have found, which is from a MS. (No. 10,074) in the Royal Library in Brussels :—'When the Cock is past seven years old an egg grows within him, whereat he greatly wonders. He seeks privately a warm place, on a dunghill, or in a stable, and scratches a hole for a nest, to which he goes ten times daily. A toad privily watches him, and examines the nest every time the cock leaves it, to see if the egg yet be laid. When the toad finds the egg, he rejoices much, and at length hatches it, producing an animal with the head, neck, and breast of a cock, and from thence downwards the body of a serpent. And that is a Cockatrice.'

Fig. 198.

The WYVERN differs from the Cockatrice in having the head of a Dragon, and is usually without spurs (fig. 198). The wings of the Dragon, Griffin, Cockatrice, and Wyvern are always represented as addorsed.

The HERALDIC TIGER and ANTELOPE differ essentially from their zoological prototypes. The former is represented with the head of a Dragon, except that the tongue is not *armed*, and with three or four tufts of hair along the neck, and one on the breast : in other respects, it resembles a natural Tiger. The HERALDIC ANTELOPE has the body of a Stag, two straight horns, a short tusk on the nose, and tufts of hair on the neck, chest, and tail, which latter is like that of a Lion.

Fig. 199.

The PASCHAL or HOLY LAMB is a Lamb *passant* supporting with its dexter fore-leg a staff, usually in bend-

Fig. 200.

Fig. 201.

sinister, from which depends a Banner, charged with a Cross of ST. GEORGE. See FLAGS.

The TRITON and MERMAID (figs. 200 and 201) are more commonly employed as Supporters than as Charges, and thus appear flanking the shield of the *Fishmongers' Company*. The upper part of the Triton's body is, however, in that example armed like a knight. A Triton is sometimes called a MERMAN or NEPTUNE.

In addition to these may be enumerated the CHIMERA, possessing the head of a Lion, the body of a Goat, and the tail of a Dragon ; the PEGASUS, or WINGED HORSE ; the SAGITTARIUS, or CENTAUR, an Animal produced by the combination of the head and bust of a Man with the body of a Horse, and holding in its hands a bent bow ; the LION-POISSON, or SEA-LION, which has the head and shoulders of a Lion, with fins for paws, and the *nowed* tail of a Fish for a body ; the SEA-HORSE, which is a combination of a Horse and a Fish, similar to the last ; the UNICORN ; the SALA-MANDER, which is always *passant* amidst flames of fire ; the WINGED BULL, LION, and DEER, &c. The dexter supporter of the arms of LORD HUNSDON, in WESTMINSTER ABBEY, is a BAGWYN, which is a beast like an Heraldic Antelope, with the tail of a Horse and the horns of a Goat.

To this list may be added a few imaginary Birds ; which are ; the PHŒNIX, a demi-eagle displayed issuing from flames of fire ; the HARPY, a Vulture with a woman's head and breast, borne as Arms by the City of NUREMBERG : the MARTLET, which is a Swallow without feet, as in the Arms of DEEDES (fig. 202), and the ALLERION, which is an Eagle destitute of feet and wings. The *Martlet* is a very common Bearing, and constitutes the Mark of Distinction of the fourth son. See DIFFERENCING.

Fig. 202.

CAMDEN says that GODFREY DE BOULOGNE, 'at one draught of his bow, shooting against David's Tower at Jerusalem, broached three feetless birds called Allerions upon his arrow, and therefore assumed in his shield, *Or* ; *on a Bend gules, three Allerions argent*.' It has been conjectured, however, that the House of LORAINE did not bear this charge on their Escutcheon on account of the exploit of their ancestor narrated by Camden, but simply because the letters contained in the words *Loraine* and *Alerion* form a perfect anagram.

THE CELESTIAL BODIES

The SUN is always supposed to be *Proper*, or *In his Glory*, or *Splendour*, and is blazoned *Or*, unless otherwise specified. It is represented by a Disc, on which is sometimes depicted a human face, and is surrounded by a number of rays, alternately straight and wavy, which issue from its circumference. A single Ray may constitute a Charge, as in the Arms borne by the family of ALDHAM, which are : *Azure ; issuant from the dexter corner of the escutcheon, a Ray of the Sun, in bend proper*. When blazoned as *Eclipsed*, it is tinctured sable.

The proper Tincture of the MOON is Argent ; and when full-faced and shining, it is described as *In her complement* or *Plenitude*. It is usually environed with a number of short, straight rays. The Moon, when Eclipsed, is said to be *In her Detriment*, and is emblazoned sable.

A Half-Moon, with the horns directed upwards, is a

Fig. 203.　　　　　　　　Fig. 204.

CRESCENT (fig. 203, in base). This Charge is also used as the *Difference* by which the second son is distinguished. A

Crescent with the horns directed towards the Dexter, is said to be INCRESCENT ; and if towards the Sinister, DECRESCENT.

The STAR, or ÉTOILE, is represented with six *wavy* points (fig. 204). See MULLET (fig. 250).

The SIGNS OF THE ZODIAC, PLANETS (fig. 203, in Chiet, JUPITER), RAINBOWS, and CLOUDS, are sometimes, though very rarely, employed as Charges.

TREES, PLANTS, AND FLOWERS

Of Trees, the OAK, PINE, OLIVE, PALM, and LAUREL are the most commonly blazoned in Armory ; but others are sometimes to be met with. Branches of Trees more frequently appear as Crests, than as Charges. They are generally blazoned *proper*, or in their natural colours, although they may be of any Tincture.

The following Terms are employed in describing Charges of this class :

ACCRUED : Full-grown.

BARBED : Leaved. This term is usually applied to Roses, in describing the tincture of the little leaves, or Involucra, which encircle the flower, and does not refer to the ordinary leaves growing on the stem.

BLASTED, or STARVED : A Branch destitute of Leaves.

BLOSSOMED : Bearing Flowers or Blossoms.

COUPED : Cut off evenly.

ERADICATED : Torn up by the Roots.

FRUCTED : Bearing Fruit. An Oak-tree is *fructed* of its Acorns ; and a Pine, of its Cones.

JESSANT: Shooting, or springing out of.

JESSANT-DE-LYS : The accompanying cut (fig. 205) represents the Arms of CAN-TELUPE, or CANTELOW :—*Azure ; three*

Fig. 205.

Lions' faces, jessant-de-lys or. In the Arms of the SEE of HEREFORD the Lions' faces are *Reversed*, that is, turned upside down.

NERVED : Leaves are thus described when the Nerves or Fibres are of a different tincture to the Leaf itself.

PENDENT : Drooping or hanging.

SEEDED : Applied chiefly to roses, in blazoning the Seeds in the centre.

SLIPPED : Torn or broken off. The term *Erased* is never applied to Trees or Plants. See ERADICATED.

The Stump of a Tree is sometimes called a STOCK ; and amongst Scotch Heralds a Branch is termed a SCROG.

The FLEUR-DE-LYS is one of the most ancient and fre-quent of Heraldic Charges. The origin of the Fleur-de-lys

Fig. 206.

has been variously accounted for : by some it is supposed to represent a Lily, by others a Lance-head ; others, again, assert that it is a *Rebus*, founded on the name of LEWIS the SEVENTH of FRANCE, who adopted it on his seal in the year 1137 ; to this last supposition most authorities incline. They were quartered with the Arms of ENGLAND from the year 1299, when EDWARD the FIRST married MARGARET of France, until the Union of ENGLAND and IRELAND in 1801, when they were relinquished.

It is very evident that Fleurs-de-lys were not intended to represent Lilies, for in the Arms of ETON COLLEGE, granted in 1449, we find both Charges mentioned : *Sable ; three* LILIES *slipped argent : a Chief party per pale, azure, and gules ; on the dexter side a* FLEUR-DE-LYS *or :*

Fig. 207.

on the sinister a Lion passant guardant of the last. The Lily, moreover, consists of five leaves or petals, and is represented with a stalk, as in the margin. WILLIAM WAYNFLETE, Bishop of WINCHESTER, the founder of MAGDALEN COLLEGE, OXFORD, bore *three Lilies slipped argent* ; which device still appears in the Arms of that College.

' There are extant some volumes written under King Edgar, and by his command, touching the reformation of monastic life in England, wherein he is pictured with a crown fleuri. So, also, the crowns that are put on the heads of most ancient kings in pictures of the holy story of Genesis (*MSS. in Bib. Cott.*), translated into Saxon in those times, are ensigned with Fleurs-de-lys. This flower, being considered as an emblem of the Trinity, is, perhaps, the reason why it was afterwards used, and is still continued, as an ornament in the crowns of almost all Christian nations.' (Condensed from a MS. of Stephen Leake, Garter King-at-Arms.)

The ROSE is sometimes blazoned *proper*, exhibiting the stem and leaves ; the Rose of ENGLAND is thus represented. When, however, *a Rose* only is mentioned in a Blazon, it is always understood to mean the *Heraldic Rose*. The five small points around the flower represent the leaves of which it is said to be *Barbed*.

Fig. 208.

A *Rose barbed and seeded ppr.* does not imply *a Rose ppr.*, but *an Heraldic Rose, barbed vert and seeded or.*

Fig. 209. Fig. 210. Fig. 211. Fig. 212.

The four examples of Heraldic Roses here given are taken from good authorities, but the second is the best form to employ in Armory.

It will be remembered that a Rose *gules* was assumed by the Lancastrian party as a Badge, and a Rose *argent* by the Yorkists. In the year 1461, EDWARD the FOURTH surrounded his white Rose with rays of the Sun, thus forming the ROSE-EN-SOLEIL, which was subsequently adopted by his adherents ; and still appears on the *Union Jack*, or '*Regimental Colour*,' of the Guards, and other Regiments.

The COLUMBINE ; CLOVE-PINK, or GILLY-FLOWER ; CYANUS, or BLUE-BOTTLE ; and THISTLE, are almost the only other flowers used as Charges, and these but rarely : the first three are severally borne by the families of HALL, JORNEY, and CHERLEY ; and the Thistle, which is the emblem of SCOTLAND, appears in the arms of PEMBROKE COLLEGE, OXFORD.

Fig. 213.

The TREFOIL, QUATREFOIL, and CIN-QUEFOIL, are leaves which bear three, four, and five cusps respectively. The Trefoil is usually blazoned as *Stalked* and *Slipped* ; that is, with a stalk, and that stalk broken off, not cut. *Slipped*, applied to a plant, is the same as *Erased* to the limb of an animal. The DOUBLE QUATREFOIL, as the name implies, is a leaf with eight cusps, but there are few examples of this Charge in English Armory.

Fig. 214.—*Argent; three Cinquefoils sable*, for SEBRIGHT.

When LEAVES are borne on a shield they are always supposed to be *erect* ; if they are intended to be placed horizontally or diagonally, their position must be expressed as *Bar-wise, Bend-wise*, &c.

WHEAT-EARS are occasionally to be met with in Armory ; but a more frequent Charge is a Sheaf of Wheat, called a GARB. The *Band* around the Garb is supposed to be of the same Tincture, unless the contrary be specified in the Blazon. When a Garb is of any grain other than wheat, it must be mentioned ; as, a *Garb of Oats*, &c. Sometimes the straw is of a different tincture from the ears ; as, *a Garb vert, eared or*. Garbs are usually *or*, and when of this tincture are frequently blazoned *Proper*.

Fig. 215.

But few FRUITS are used as Heraldic Charges ; the principal are, the FIR-CONE, commonly called PINE-APPLE ; the ACORN ; and the PEAR.

The Student must not confound the Pine-apple with the West-Indian fruit of that name. The latter is Heraldically known as the ANANAS.

The base of a shield, for about one-fifth of its entire depth, is sometimes occupied by a rising piece of ground, tinctured *Vert*, as though covered with grass : such a Charge is termed a MOUNT ; as in the arms of BOSANQUET :—*Or ; on a Mount vert, a Tree proper ; on a Chief gules, a Crescent between two Mullets argent* (fig. 216).

Fig. 216.

CHAPTER VII

COMMON CHARGES (CONTINUED)

Miscellaneous Inanimate Objects

IN the following list of Charges, I do not profess to include all those which have been at various times adopted by Heralds ; for, as I have before stated, *anything* may constitute a Charge. I shall also omit such common objects as a Book, Key, Horse-shoe, &c., the form of which is too familiar to require an explanation.

ALPHABET, LETTERS OF THE : Capital letters are sometimes used as Charges ; as in the Arms of KEKITMORE, *Gules ; three S's or* ; of TOFTE, *Argent ; two Chevronels between three T's sable* ; of BRIDLINGTON PRIORY, *Per pale sable and argent, three B's counterchanged* ; and in the Arms of RASHLEIGH, of MENABILLY, appears a T argent. The family of LANG bears on a Fess between other charges in chief and in base, the letters ABCDEF.

ANCHOR : Unless otherwise expressed in the Blazon, this charge should be represented in pale, with the flukes in base, and without a cable, as in fig. 105.

ANNULET : A plain ring, frequently used as a Charge ; it is also the *Mark of Difference* of the fifth son (see fig. 275).

ARBALESTE : A Cross-bow (fig. 217).

ARCH, or BRIDGE : Usually drawn as in fig. 218.

ARROW : A bundle of Arrows bound together in the centre is termed a SHEAF, and consists of three : one in pale, and two in saltire. It is said to be *Armed* or *Barbed* of its head, and *Flighted* of its feathers. Unless otherwise directed, the heads are to be in base, as in the Arms of MAUSERGH MAUSERGH.

Fig. 217.

Fig. 218.

ATTIRES : The Horns of a Stag.

BAND : A Fillet with which a Garb or Sheaf of Arrows is bound.

BANDEROLL : A narrow Streamer affixed to the head of a Crosier, and usually depicted as enveloping the Staff.

BARNACLES, or BREYS (fig. 219) : An instrument used to compress the nose of an unbroken or restive Horse. Barnacles are sometimes represented as open, as in the arms of DE GENEVILLE or DE JOINVILLE, Seigneurs DE BROYES, where they appear as at fig. 220, taken from an old Roll of the Thirteenth Century, now in the College of Heralds. To bray is to break, bruise, or pound, and is used in that sense in the *Pro·verbs*, 'Though a fool be brayed in a mortar.' A HEMP-BREY (fig. 242) is really the same instrument as a HORSE-BREY, except that they were used for different purposes, and that the former is in Armory always represented as being upon a wooden stand (fig. 242).

Fig. 219.

Fig. 220.

H

Barnacles, as shown above, are always described as a *pair of Barnacles*, and must not be confounded with the BARNACLE, which is a Bird somewhat resembling a Goose.

BAR-SHOT : A missile formerly employed in warfare, consisting of a short bar of iron, with a ball at each end, resembling a Dumb-bell.

BATTERING-RAM : An engine used to effect a breach in the wall of a besieged Town or Castle. It is blazoned as *Armed* (or *Headed*), *Ringed*, and *Banded*, and sometimes as *Garnished*, which term includes the three foregoing. Fig. 221 would be blazoned, *Argent ; a Battering-ram in fess gules, garnished azure.*

BATTLE-AXE (fig. 222) : It is described as being *Helved*

Fig. 221.   Fig. 222

of its handle. The LOCHABER AXE (shown on the Dexter) has a broader blade, and is usually shaped like an *Increscent*. The helve, also, is slightly curved. The BROAD AXE is represented as on the Sinister.

BEACON, or FIRE-BEACON : An iron vessel—containing some combustible substance in flames—placed on a pole, against which is placed a ladder (fig. 223).

Fig. 223.   Fig. 224.   Fig. 225.

BELLS : In blazoning, it is necessary to state whether CHURCH BELLS or HAWK BELLS are intended. They are represented as in fig. 224—the former in Base, and the latter in Chief.

BIRD-BOLT : A blunt arrow, sometimes borne with two or three heads. When furnished with more than one head, the number must be specified (fig. 225).

BOTTEROLL, CHAPE, or CRAMPETTE : The piece of iron with which the bottom of a scabbard is shod. The Crampette is an infrequent Charge : it was the ancient Badge of the Lords DELAWARR ; and it also occurs in the Arms of the late Queen ADELAIDE. It is shown on a Canton in the third Quarter of fig. 311.

BRASSETTS : Armour to protect the Arms.

BROAD ARROW : See PHEON.

BRUSH : The tail of a Fox,—which animal was styled by the old Heralds a TOD, the head of which is borne as Arms by several branches of the TODD family.

BUCKLES, sometimes called ARMOUR-BUCKLES : In blazoning, the form, whether round, oval, square, or lozenge, must be specified. The tongue is always to be represented as *erect*, unless described as *pendent*. See the Buckle attached to the Helmet of Sir JOHN SAY on the Frontispiece

Fig. 226.

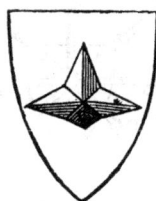

Fig. 227

BUGLE : See HUNTING-HORN.

CALTRAP, or CHEVAL-TRAP : An instrument used to retard the progress of an enemy's cavalry, by laming the horses. It was formed of four short but strong spikes, or *Gads*, conjoined in such a manner that, when thrown on the

ground, one would always be erect (fig. 227). *Argent;
three Caltraps sable*, is borne by the family of TRAPPS. Caltraps also occur in the Arms of Sir EDWARD WALKER, of
BUSHEY, Bart : *Erminois ; on a Pile embattled azure, a
Mural Crown, between two Caltraps in pale or* (fig. 228).

Fig. 228.

Fig. 229.

CARBUNCLE, or ESCARBUNCLE : A very ancient conventional Device, usually represented as at fig. 229. The extremities of the *Staves* are sometimes connected by a band.

On the seal of THIERRY, eighth EARL of CLEVES (A.D.
1311), the Carbuncle is represented as in fig. 230, but in the
Arms of NAVARRE the ends of the staves are connected by
a chain (*una varra-Navarre*) as shown in fig. 231.

Fig. 230.

Fig. 231.

CASTLE : An embattled Fortress, on which are commonly
placed three towers (fig. 232). When the tincture of the
Field is to be seen through the windows or ports, they are
said to be *Voided of the Field*.

CATHARINE WHEEL : Supposed to represent the wheel upon which ST. CATHARINE suffered martyrdom (fig. 233).

CHAMFRAINE, or CHAMFRON : Armour to protect the head of a war-horse (fig. 234).

Fig. 232.   Fig. 233.   Fig. 234.

CHAPLET, or GARLAND : These terms are frequently, but erroneously, used to signify the same object. A Chaplet should be composed of four Roses, arranged at equal distances in a circle, the intervening spaces being filled up with leaves ; and a Garland should be formed of laurel or oak leaves, interspersed with acorns. It should always be stated of what the Chaplet or Garland is composed. They are usually tied in base with ribbon, the ends *flotant*, and always *erect*, so as to appear as circles. See WREATH.

CHESS-ROOK : This Charge is represented in Heraldry very dissimilar in form to that of the modern Rook : it bears a greater resemblance to the Bishop. The family of WALCOT, amongst others, emblazon this ancient Charge upon their Escutcheon.

Fig. 235.   Fig. 236.

CLARION : See REST.

CORONET : See Chap. xiv. When a Coronet is blazoned

as a Charge, it is represented as a Ducal Coronet, but without the velvet cap. The Arms of TOULMIN, of ST. ALBANS, afford an example of Coronets being employed as Charges :— *Argent ; a Chevron ermines between three Coronets sable* (fig. 236). For the various forms of CROWNS which are used as Charges, see the Chapter on *Coronets and Helmets.*

CRAMPETTE or CHAPE : See BOTTEROLL.

CRONEL : The head of a tilting spear, borne in the Arms of WISEMAN.

CROSIER : A staff bearing a Cross at the top, belonging to an Archbishop, as an emblem of his dignity (fig. 237 ; Archbishop Chichely, Canterbury, A.D. 1443). Bishops and Abbots are commonly, though erroneously, supposed to bear a Crosier with a rounded head, somewhat resembling a Shepherd's Crook. This should properly be called a PASTORAL STAFF (fig. 238). From both a narrow streamer—called a *Banderoll, Vexillum,* or *Orarium*—frequently depends, fastened near the head of the Staff.

Fig. 237.

In Illuminations and Monumental Effigies, the Pastoral Staves of Bishops and Abbots are identical in form. There is, however, one invariable distinction observed, by which those dignitaries can be readily distinguished from each other on monumental effigies : an Abbot holds his Staff in his right hand ; whilst a Bishop holds it in his left, his other hand being elevated, as though he were pronouncing a Benediction.

Abbesses on their seals and monuments, are frequently represented as bearing a Pastoral Staff, as in the Brass to ISABEL HERVEY, ABBESS of ELSTOW, in Bedfordshire.

The accompanying Illustration of a Pastoral Staff is taken from an example of the Fourteenth Century, about which period they were usually ornamented with Crockets, the Staff itself being hexagonal or octagonal. In the Fourth volume of the *Transactions of the London and Middlesex Archæological Society*, page 231, will be found a copy of the Initial Letter to the Charter granted by King Richard II. to the Minor Canons of St. Paul's. The King is between the Archbishop of York and the Bishop of London. The Crown of the King and the costume, Mitres, and Staves of the Bishops, are worthy of careful attention. See, also, Initial Letter of Chap. x.

Fig. 238.

CROSS-BOW : See ARBALESTE.

CUBIT ARM : An arm couped at the elbow. It is necessary to state in the Blazon whether the Arm be the dexter or sinister ; and its position, such as *Erect, In fess*, &c. ; also, whether the Hand be *Appaumé* or *Clenched*. The Hand is always supposed to be bare, unless in the blazon it is stated to be *gauntleted*.

ESCARBUNCLE : See CARBUNCLE.

FALCHION : A Sword, the blade of which is broad, and slightly curved.

FAN, FRUTTLE, SHRUTTLE, or WINNOWING-BASKET (fig. 239), as in the Arms of SEPTVANS.

FETTER-LOCK, or SHACK-BOLT : A somewhat rare Charge. *A falcon on a Fetter-lock* was one of the Badges assumed by EDWARD the FOURTH. Admirable examples of this Badge are to be seen on the bronze gate leading to Henry the Seventh's Chapel, in Westminster Abbey.

Fig. 239.

GAD : A rectangular plate of steel, borne in the Arms of the IRONMONGERS' COMPANY. Gads are also the spikes affixed to the knuckles of a gauntlet, to inflict a more dangerous wound, when the wearer was engaged in the *mêlée*. (See Frontispiece.)

GALLEY : See LYMPHAD.

GARLAND : See CHAPLET.

GAUNTLET : An iron glove, usually depicted without fingers, which is its most ancient form (see fig. 386). It must be stated in the Blazon whether it be the dexter or sinister gauntlet, and if *Appaumé* or *Addorsed.*

In emblazoning a Gauntlet *appaumé*, the Student must bear in mind that it should not be mailed on the palm, as it would have been impossible, in that case, for the wearer to have grasped a weapon firmly. The palm of the hand was either covered with a leathern glove, or the gauntlet was affixed by straps to the fingers.

GIMMAL, or JUMELLE RINGS : When two or more Annulets are interlaced, they are sometimes termed Gimmal Rings.

A Gimmal or Jumelle Ring was formed of two flat hoops of gold, which fitted accurately within each other, and constituted but one ring. They were sometimes made triple ; and it was customary at a Betrothal for each of the contracting parties to retain one portion, and to give the other to the witness. At the marriage, the three pieces were reunited, and formed the wedding-ring. *Emilia* says, in OTHELLO :

‘ I would not do such a thing for a joint-ring.’

GORGE, or GURGE (fig. 240) : A whirlpool ; borne on the Shields of the GORGES and CHELLERYS. This Charge covers the entire Field, and is always blazoned *Argent and Azure.*

GRIECES : Steps or Degrees.

HABICK : An instrument used in dressing cloth. An unusual Charge. Two Habicks appear in the Arms of the *Clothworkers' Company* (fig. 241).

Fig. 240.   Fig. 241.

HARP : When represented as in the Third Quarter of the Royal Arms, it is usually termed a WELSH HARP.

HAWK-BELL : See BELL.

HELMET : When blazoned as a Charge, is represented as that of an Esquire. See Chap. xiv.

HEMP-BREAK or HACKLE : An instrument used for bruising hemp or flax (fig. 242). A Hackle was the device of Sir REGINALD BRAY, who, during the reign of Henry VII., in a great measure restored the Chapel of St. George, at Windsor, where it repeatedly occurs in various parts of the building.

HUNTING-HORN, or BUGLE : A very ancient and common Bearing. It is usually blazoned as *Stringed*, which signifies that it depends from two strings, or ribbons, tied in a knot above ; and *Garnished*, which refers to the mouthpiece, and the rings which encircle it (fig. 243).

Fig. 242.

Fig. 243.

JAVELIN : See TILTING-SPEAR.

KNOTS : See Chapter ix.

LETTERS OF THE ALPHABET : See ALPHABET, LETTERS OF THE.

LURE : Two wings conjoined (as in fig. 182), to which is attached a line and ring.

LYMPHAD, or GALLEY : A vessel, usually with two masts ; one at the stem, and the other at the stern. It is represented with the sail furled, and propelled by oars. Many Scotch families bear this Charge, among others that of Sir ANDREW LUSK, Bart., as in fig. 244, which would be blazoned as

Azure ; a Lymphad with three masts argent ; on a Chief of the last, a Woolpack between two Mullets gules.

Fig. 244.

Fig. 245.

MANCHE, or MAUNCHE : A hanging sleeve.　Fig. 245 is taken from *Harl. MSS.* No. 6079, and is the form in which it is usually depicted.　A fine example of this Charge occurs on the Brass of JOHN DE HASTINGS, EARL OF PEMBROKE, in ELSYNG Church, NORFOLK (A.D. 1347).

The oldest form of the Manche is as shown in fig. 246 (temp. Hen. III.), but later on, that is, during the Fourteenth Century, we find it as represented by fig. 245 and fig. 247.

Fig. 246.

Fig. 247.

MILLSTONE (fig. 248) : An old but not a very frequent Charge.　The iron clamps which support it on either side, called the MILL-RINDS, or FERS-DE-MOLINE, are more commonly borne separately as Charges than the stone itself. The Arms of MILLS (fig. 249) would be blazoned as *Ermine ; a Mill-rind sable.*　There are twelve families of MILLER who bear Crosses-Moline in their Arms, and none who bear Millstones or Mill-rinds.　It is tolerably evident, therefore, that the Charges which are now Crosses-Moline, were originally devised as Mill-rinds.

Fig. 248.

Fig. 249.

MORION : A Helmet. In illustrations, it appears under a variety of forms. It is sometimes shaped after the fashion of the helmet of the well-known bust of Ajax found in Adrian's Villa ; and at other times it assumes the form of the Casques worn by the soldiers of the Commonwealth, which was a steel cap fitting close to the head, having a wide and slightly arched brim.

MOUND must not be confounded with MOUNT. The latter is a green hillock in the base of a shield (see fig. 216) : the former is a jewelled ball, the emblem of sovereignty.

MULLET : A Figure resembling a spur-rowel of five points (fig. 250). When of more than five points, the number must be specified. It is generally *pierced*, as in the diagram. Compare the *Mullet* with the *Étoile* (fig. 204).

PALL : An archiepiscopal vestment made of lamb's-wool, and worn over the shoulders. Only one-half is apparent in

Fig. 250.

Fig. 251.

Fig. 252.

Armorial illustrations ; it is always fimbriated, and charged with Crosses *paté fitché*. It appears in the Arms of the Sees of CANTERBURY and ARMAGH (fig. 251).

PALMER'S, or PILGRIM'S, STAFF : A Charge, the origin of which is obvious. The PILGRIM'S SCRIP is sometimes represented with the Staff, as in fig. 252.

PHEON : The barbed head of a dart (fig. 253). A Pheon engrailed on the outer edge is blazoned as a BROAD ARROW.

PLAYING-TABLES : This Charge, which is but seldom employed, is drawn with twenty-four points, like a Backgammon-board.

PORTCULLIS : An iron gate formed of bars armed at the base, and bolted *in trellis ;* at both sides is a chain pendent from rings at the top (fig. 254). A Portcullis is the principal Charge in the Arms of the CITY of WESTMINSTER ; and, as a Badge of HENRY the SEVENTH, it is conspicuous as an ornament in his Chapel added to the Abbey.

 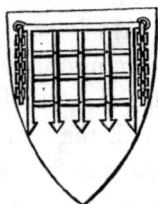 

Fig. 253.   Fig. 254.   Fig. 255.

PRESTER- or PRESBYTER-JOHN : Borne in the Arms of the See of CHICHESTER. *An Ecclesiastic sitting on a tombstone, in his sinister hand a Mound, his dexter hand extended, or : on his head a linen mitre, and in his mouth a Sword in fess, proper.*

REST, CLARION, CLARICORD, or SUFFLUE : Various opinions have been given by Armorists as to the origin of this Charge. Some incline to the supposition that it was intended as a rest to receive the lance when a Knight was on horseback, and others that it was a musical instrument. They probably constituted, at one time, two distinct devices, but they are now considered as identical. It is commonly represented as at fig. 255, but the six illustrations given below, taken from competent authorities, show the various methods in which it was delineated. My own opinion is, that the Rest or Clarion was a rude type of a musical instrument, analogous to the Pandean pipe.

CLARIONS or RESTS.—Figs. 256-261.

SCALING-LADDER : A very ancient Charge, though somewhat uncommon. It is generally represented *bendwise*, resting against a wall, and furnished at the top with two grappling-claws.

SCIMETAR : This weapon differs little from the Falchion. The blade is, however, rather more curved, and somewhat narrower.

SCRIP : See PALMER'S STAFF.

SEAX : A Falchion with a semicircular notch at the back of the blade, seen in the Arms of the County of MIDDLESEX ; which are : *Gules ; three Seaxes fesswise in pale argent* (fig. 262).

Fig. 262.

Fig. 263.

SHAKEFORK : Resembles a Pall, humetté and pointed (fig. 263).

SPEAR : See TILTING-SPEAR.

SPUR : This Charge may either be represented in its modern form, with a revolving rowel, or with a single point. The latter is the most ancient, and is known as the PRYCK-SPUR. The example in the margin is taken from a Brass to Sir ROBERT DE

Fig. 264.

BURES, in ACTON Church, SUFFOLK (A.D. 1362). The monumental effigy of JOHN PLANTAGENET, of ELTHAM, in WESTMINSTER ABBEY (A.D. 1336), affords a fine example of an octagonal-shaped pryck-spur. RICHARD the FIRST, on his great seal, is the first king who appears wearing a ROUELLE-SPUR. Spurs are sometimes represented with a circular guard around the points.

SWORD : The Sword differs from the Falchion, Seax, and Scimetar in being represented straight, instead of curved. See the third Quarter of fig. 311. In all of these weapons, the hilt, pommel, and sometimes the *Gripe*, or that part by which they were held, differ in tincture from the blade, which difference must be noted in the Blazon. When no position is assigned, the hilt is to be placed in base.

TILTING-SPEAR : It is sufficient to blazon this weapon as a *Spear* (fig. 265). When a plain Spear is intended, it must be blazoned as a *Javelin*. A *Broken Spear* often appears as a charge, and means the lower half.

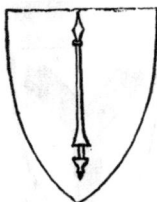

Fig. 265.

Fig. 266.

TRELLIS : This differs from *Fretty*, inasmuch as the pieces of which it is composed are not interlaced, but are continued throughout, and nailed at the points of contact (fig. 266).

TRUMPET : This instrument generally appears straight, with the end rather distended. A very ancient form is *flexed*, in the shape of the letter S.

TURRET : A small tower commonly set upon a Castle, as shown at fig. 232.

VAMBRACE : Armour for the arm (fig. 192).

VAMPLATE : A Gauntlet.

VANNET : The Escallop is so named when the ears are wanting.

WATER-BOUGET : A leathern vessel formerly used by soldiers and pilgrims to contain water. It may be represented in either of the forms shown in fig. 267, but that in base is more generally adopted.

Fig. 267.　　　　　　　　Fig. 268.

Another form is that in which the Arms of DE ROOS are usually depicted (fig. 268), *Gules ; three Water-bougets argent.* The fancy of Armorists has represented this Charge in a variety of forms, as may be seen by the accompanying examples.

WATER BOUGETS.—Figs. 269-274.

WINNOWING-BASKET : See FAN.

WREATH : A circular fillet of twisted silk upon which the Crest is placed (fig. 347). Wreaths also appear as en

circling the heads of human figures, particularly those of
Saracens and Moors.

DISPOSITION OF SMALL CHARGES

When there are several small Charges of the same kind
blazoned on a shield, the position they occupy, as well as
their number, must be mentioned. The method of arranging
them in the form of an Ordinary has already been noticed at
page 72. They may likewise be disposed as in the following
Blazons of Arms.

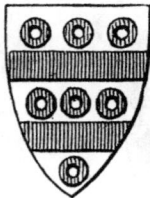

*Argent; two Bars between seven Annulets, three, three,
and one gules.* SEAFORTH (fig. 275).

*Azure; eleven Billets, four, three, and four
argent.* LAVARDIN.

*Argent; three Escutcheons sable, on each
nine Bezants, three, three, two and one.* LUD-
HAM.

Fig. 275.

*Azure; ten Étoiles or, four, three, two
and one.* ALSTON (fig. 276).

*Argent; six Crosses fitché sable, three, two and one; on
a Chief azure two Mullets or.* CLINTON (fig. 277).

Fig. 276.   Fig. 277.

Unless some other disposition be specially noted in the
Blazon (as in the Arms of the County of MIDDLESEX, (fig.
262), three Charges are always to be placed *two and one*, as
in the Arms of CHIDLEY, of DEVONSHIRE : *Ermine ; three
Lions rampant gules* ; and of RYDER, EARLS of HARROWBY :

Azure; three Crescents or, on each an Ermine spot (fig. 278).
When, however, the escutcheon is traversed by a Bend or
Bend sinister, and three Charges are on either side, this
arrangement may be with propriety disregarded, as in the
Arms of DE BOHUN (fig. 179), on page 89. Charges on a

Fig. 278.   Fig. 279.   Fig. 280.

Fess or Bend are always disposed at length, and never two and
one, unless specially so directed. *Sable ; on a Fess between
three Owls or, as many Crosses-crosslet of the first.* PYM (fig.
279). It should also be noticed that Charges on Ordinaries
are always placed in the position of those Ordinaries : thus
in fig. 279 the Crosses being on a Fess are upright ; but in
fig. 280, the Lions being in Bend, are disposed bendwise,
as though they were on a Bend. That example would be
blazoned, *Or ; three Lions passant in bend sable, between two
Bendlets vair,* for GAPE.

CHAPTER VIII

MISCELLANEOUS DESCRIPTIVE TERMS

THE following list of descriptive Terms does not include those which have been previously mentioned in treating of Charges. Any Term not set down in this place may be readily found by reference to the Index at the end of the volume.

ABAISÉ : Lowered. This term is applied when a Charge which usually occupies the centre of a shield, such as a Fess, is depressed below it. When the wings of an Eagle displayed are inverted, they are sometimes described as *Abaisé*.

ABSCONDED : Covered by a superimposed Charge. In *Argent ; in Chief three Roses gules ; a Canton azure*, the Canton would completely cover, or *abscond* the first Rose.

ADUMBRATED : Shaded, or under shadow.

AIGUISÉ, or URDÉ : Used by French and the early English Heralds to signify pointed, as a *Cross aiguisé*.

AMBULANT : Walking : commonly applied to Beasts of the Chase.

ANNODATED : Curved somewhat in the form of the letter S.

ANNULATED, or ANNULY : Charges are thus blazoned when they terminate in Annulets : as a *Cross annuly*, which means that an Annulet is affixed to the end of each limb.

ARCHED, or ENARCHED : When an Ordinary, such as a Fess or Bend, is slightly curved, it is blazoned as *Arched*. (See Arms of PRINCE of WALES.)

ARMED AT ALL POINTS : This term is used in blazoning a Knight who is completely encased in Armour—sometimes described as *Cap-à-pie*.

ARONDÉ : Rounded off.

ARRASWAYS : A rectangular Charge, such as a Book or a Cushion, is thus described when it is placed on its side, with one corner towards the spectator.

ASPERSED : See SEMÉ.

ASSURGENT : Rising from the sea.

AT BAY : Used in describing a Stag with its head depressed, as if it were butting with its horns.

BANDED : When a Charge, such as a Garb or Sheaf of Arrows, is bound together with a band of a different tincture, it is said to be *Banded* of that tincture.

BARDED : Caparisoned.

BEZANTÉ : *Semé* or covered with Bezants.

BI-CORPORATED : Having two bodies conjoined to one head. Animals, more particularly Lions, are occasionally so represented, and, sometimes, TRI-CORPORATED. Such a device was borne by EDMUND CROUCHBACK, EARL of LANCASTER, brother to King EDWARD the FIRST.

BILLETÉ : *Semé* of Billets.

BLADED : When the blade or stalk of corn is borne of a different tincture from the ear, it is described as *Bladed* of whatever tincture it may be.

BLEMISHED : See REBATED.

BOLTING : Applied to Hares and Rabbits when *courant*.

BRACED : Interlaced.

BRINDED, or BRINDLED : Spotted. Applied only to animals.

CANTONED : A Cross is *Cantoned* when it is between four Charges, or groups of Charges, as in the Arms of WODEHOUSE of HERTINGFORDBURY :—*Gules ; a Cross between* (or *Cantoned by*) *twelve Crosses-crosslet or* (fig. 281).

Fig. 281.

CLOUÉ : Studded with nails.   A Portcullis, or a Gate, is sometimes thus described.

CORDED : Bound round with cord,—as, *a Bale gules, corded or.*

CORNED : Horned.

CONJOINED : Joined together.   When hollow Charges, such as Annulets, are linked together, so as to form a chain, they are sometimes blazoned as *Conjoined* ; they would, however, be better described as *Braced.*

COUNTER-CHANGED : See page 81.

CRUSILLÉ : *Semé* of Crosses ; usually of Crosses-crosslet.

DECOLLATED : Decapitated.   Rarely used.

DILATED : Opened or extended.   Applied to a pair of Compasses, Barnacles, &c.

DISARMED : Beasts and Birds of prey are thus blazoned when they are deprived of their claws and teeth, or beaks.

ENALURON, ENTOYRE, and ENURNY : Terms formerly used to express Bordures severally charged with Birds, Inanimate Objects, and Animals.   (See page 68.)

ENGOULED : Being swallowed or devoured.   It also signifies being pierced through the mouth with a weapon.

ENHANCED : Any Ordinary set above its usual position.   The BYRONS bear : *Argent ; three Bendlets enhanced gules* ; and the CITY of MANCHESTER emblazons the same Charges *Or*, on a field *gules* (fig. 282).

ENSIGNED : Ornamented, or garnished.

ENVELOPED : Entwined.

FLEXED : Bent.

Fig. 282.

FLIGHTED : An arrow is *flighted* of its feathers.

FLOTANT : This term is usually applied to Flags when displayed as if by the wind.   It may, also, be used to express anything floating or swimming.   (See JESS, page 92.)

FORCENÉ, or FRESNÉ : Applicable only to Horses when in a rampant position.

FUMANT : Emitting smoke.

FUSILLÉ : *Semé* of Fusils.

GERATED : See SEMÉ.

GARNISHED : See PURFLED.

GENUANT : In a kneeling posture.

GLIDING, or GLISSANT : Used to describe Serpents when moving forwards in Fess.

GUARDED : Trimmed, or turned up with. Commonly applied to a Mantle or Chapeau.

HABITED : See VESTED.

HACKED : An indented Charge is thus described when the notches are curved upon both sides, similar to the Teeth of Barnacles. (See fig. 219.)

INTERCHANGEABLY POSED : When Charges are placed in parallel lines, so that the head of each appears between the tails of two others,—in the manner that mackerel are usually served at table,—they are said to be *Interchangeably posed.*

LAMINATED : Scaled. Applied only to reptiles, and to them but rarely.

LINED : Attached by a line, usually affixed to the collar of an Animal. This term is also applied to the lining of a Mantle, Chapeau, &c., when borne of a different tincture from the garment itself.

MASONED : As though built with stone, like a Castle. (See fig. 218.)

MORNÉ : Disarmed.

OVER-ALL : See SURTOUT.

POWDERED : See SEMÉ.

PURFLED : When applied to a Mantle, implies that it is lined or guarded with fur ; and when to Armour, that the studs and rims are of another metal,—as, an *Arm vambraced ppr., purfled* or *garnished or.*

REBATED : When the head of a Cross, Weapon, &c., is broken or cut off.

REFLEXED : Bent, or turned backwards, as the chain of the sinister Supporter of the Royal Arms.

REMOVED : Depressed.   (See ABAISÉ.)

RENVERSÉ, or REVERSED : Turned contrary to the usual direction.

SCINTILLANT : Emitting sparks.

SEMÉ, ASPERSED, GERATED, SANS NOMBRE, and POWDERED : These terms are used to signify that a Shield or Charge is covered with an indefinite number of minor Charges promiscuously scattered over the surface. *Powdered, Gerated, Sans Nombre,* and *Aspersed,* however, commonly imply that the Charges are to be smaller, and more thickly distributed than *Semé.*   It will be seen by reference to the Shield on the following page,—which is FRANCE ANCIENT, *Azure ; semé de Lys or,*—that the Fleurs-de-lys occurring at the extremities are cut through, as if the Field were covered with a Diaper pattern.   When the other terms are employed, the small Charges are represented complete.

STRINGED : Used in specifying the tincture of the string or ribbon by which a Bugle-horn is suspended (fig. 243). It is also employed in describing the strings of musical instruments,—as in the Arms of IRELAND, which are : *Azure ; a Harp or, stringed argent.*

SUR-TOUT, SURMOUNTING, or OVER-ALL : These terms are synonymous, and signify that a Charge—usually an Inescutcheon—is to be placed in the centre of the Shield, partially concealing whatever may have been previously emblazoned thereon, as shown at fig. 311.   When on such an Inescutcheon a second is charged, it is described as SURTOUT-DE-TOUT.   (See also fig. 122, and the examples given on page 86.)

SUSTAINED : Usually applied to a Chief or Fess when a narrow fillet or fimbriation occupies the base of the Charge.

This term is seldom used in modern Armory, nor, indeed, is it necessary, for a Chief or Fess sustained would be better described in the one case as a *Chief fimbriated,* and in the other as a *Fess fimbriated on its lower side,* or *base.*

TREFLÉ : Ensigned with Trefoils. The Arms of SAXONY,

borne by the PRINCE of WALES, afford an example of a *Bend treflé.* In a *Cross treflé,* each of the limbs terminates with a single Trefoil.

VESTED : Clothed. Usually applied in blazoning a part of the body,—as a *dexter Arm couped, vested gules, hand proper.* When an entire Figure is clothed, it is commonly described as HABITED.

Fig. 283.

France Ancient.

CHAPTER IX

KNOTS, BADGES, REBUSES, AND MERCHANTS' MARKS

KNOTS of silk cord entwined in various manners were adopted as Armorial Bearings at a very early date. As far back as the fifteenth year of the reign of Edward the Third, we read of the STAFFORD knot being the Badge of the DUKE of BUCKINGHAM; and the BOURCHIER knot, that of FITZWARREN. Knots seldom appear as Charges upon shields, but serve for the most part as Badges and Crests. These Devices are known in Armory by the names of the Families to whom they severally belong; the principal of which are the following:

Fig. 284.

The Bowen Knot.

Fig. 285.

The Wake and Ormond Knot.

Fig. 286.

The Lacy Knot.

Fig. 287.

The Stafford Knot.

Fig. 288.

FAST THOUGH UNTIED.

The Heneage Knot.

Fig. 289.

The Bourchier Knot.

Figs. 287 and 289 are taken from monuments in St. Edmund's Chapel, Westminster : the former from that of JOHN, EARL of STAFFORD ; and the latter from that of HUMPHREY BOURCHIER, who was killed at the Battle of Barnet, in 1471. It will be observed that, in the last mentioned, one strap is pierced with holes, to receive the tongue of the buckle. The example in the margin occurs on the tomb of ARCHBISHOP BOURCHIER, in Canterbury Cathedral, A.D. 1486.

Fig. 290.

The Family of HARRINGTON also bears a knot, called by their name, which should justly be known as the VERDON knot, that family having previously adopted it. This knot is not represented as composed of cord, but is flat, and may be described as a Fret, with the extremities of the Saltire couped (fig. 128).

BADGES, or COGNISANCES, were Devices adopted by Families as certain distinctive marks, which cannot be strictly regarded as Armorial Bearings (although they were to some extent employed as such), but rather as subsidiary Arms. They were intended to be borne on military equipments, caparisons, articles of domestic use, &c. ; and also on the breasts of common soldiers, attendants, and household servants. As the bearing of Crests was restricted solely to their individual possessors, and as Coats of Arms were frequently of too elaborate a description to be embroidered on the garments of retainers, &c., Badges, consisting of a single figure, were employed to designate the family to which such dependents belonged. None but the private Herald bore the Arms of his lord upon his dress. In many instances, such tenants of the great Baronies as were entitled to Armorial distinction assumed the Badge of their superior lord as Arms ; hence the prevalence of the PELHAM Buckle in the Arms of Sussex families, and the Garb in those of Cheshire.

A Badge may readily be distinguished from a Crest, from the circumstance that the former is complete by itself, while the latter is always placed either on a *Wreath, Crest-coronet,* or *Cap of Maintenance.* The string-course which passes beneath the windows and connects the trusses in WEST-

Fig. 291.

MINSTER HALL is enriched along its entire length with the Crest and Helmet of RICHARD the SECOND, placed between two Ostrich-feathers, alternating with his favourite Badge—*a white Hart, lodged, gorged, and chained.* In these examples, the distinction between the Crest and the Badge is plainly marked ; for although there is a variation in each, as to position and accompaniments, yet the former — *a crowned Lion statant-guardant*—is in every instance placed upon a Cap of Maintenance.

The origin of Badges may be traced to a period coeval with, if not antecedent to, that of regular Coats of Arms. Thus, we find King STEPHEN bearing two separate Devices as Badges, which have been sometimes, though erroneously, regarded as his Arms. These were a Sagittarius, and a Plume of three Ostrich-feathers, with this Motto : ' VI NULLA INVERTITUR ORDO '—*By no force is their form altered ;* alluding to the fold and fall of the Feathers, which, however shaken by the wind, recover their original form.

The *Planta genista* of the PLANTAGENETS ; the *Ostrich-feathers* of EDWARD, PRINCE of WALES ; and the *Red* and *White Roses* of the LANCASTRIAN and YORKIST factions, are examples of Badges familiar to every student of English History. Some of the Kings and the Nobles of the Fourteenth and Fifteenth Centuries adopted several Badges which they used indiscriminately : HENRY the FOURTH, for example, had no less than twelve ; which were, a *Gennet*

(Ermine or Weasel) *passant between two sprigs of Broom*— thus forming the word PLANTA-GENET ; the *Monogram S.S.; three Ostrich-feathers ; the stump of a Tree*, for WOODSTOCK ; a *Fox's tail ;* a *Crescent ;* a *silver Swan, ducally gorged*, for BOHUN ; a *red Rose ;* a *Panther ;* an *Antelope ;* an *Eagle displayed ;* and a *Columbine-flower.* The *Portcullis* was a favourite device of HENRY the SEVENTH, as may be seen in the Chapel at WESTMINSTER, where it repeatedly occurs. This was the Badge of the DUKES of BEAUFORT, descendants of JOHN of GHENT, through whom HENRY was anxious to exhibit his Lancastrian origin : he was also equally desirous of showing his connection with the House of York ; for, besides the White and Red Roses conjoined, is to be seen a *Falcon standing on a Fetterlock*, which was the Cognisance of EDMUND LANGLEY, DUKE of YORK. A more extended account of the Royal Badges of England will be found in Chapter xvii.

As in many historical records, particularly in ballads, Nobles are referred to by the Badges which they bore, and not by their names, it is important that we should know to whom such Badges belonged. The following list, chiefly compiled from *Harl. MS. No.* 5910, *Part II., Mus. Brit.*, and *2d M.* xvi., *Coll. Herald*, contains the names of the principal Nobles who were distinguished by Badges :

ARUNDEL : An Acorn.

ASTLEY : A Cinquefoil ermine.

AUDLEY : A Butterfly argent ; a Saracen's head.

BEAUFORT, DUKE of : A Portcullis.

BEAUMONT : An Elephant.

BOLEYN : A Bull's head, couped, sable, horned gules. (See *Harl. MS.* 303, first page.)

BOOTH : A Boar's head erect, erased, sable.

BOROUGH : An Arm vambraced, embowed, and gauntleted proper, suspended by a golden cord, in the manner of a Bugle-horn (*MS. No.* 1121, *Ash. Coll.*).

BOTTRELL : A Bundle of Arrows argent, within a sheaf sable, garnished or, the straps gules (*Harl. MS. No.* 4632).

BRANDON : A Lion's head erased or.

BRAY : A Coney sable.

BUCKINGHAM, DUKE of : Stafford knot.

BURLEIGH : Wheat-sheaf or.

CASSELL : An Anchor gules, bezanté, ringed or, corded of the first.

CHENEY : Two Horns argent.

CHICHESTER, EARL of : A Buckle or.

CLIFFORD : An Annulet or.

CLINTON : A Mullet or.

COBHAM : A Saracen's head sable.

COMPTON : A Beacon or, fired proper.

COURTENAY (EARL of DEVON) : A Boar argent.

CUMBERLAND, EARL of : A Raven argent.

CURSON : A Cockatrice displayed gules, armed azure.

DENNY : Two Arches supported on columns argent, capitals and bases or.

DESPENCER : An Annulet per pale or and argent (*Ash. Coll. MS. No.* 1121).

DE VERE (EARL of OXFORD) : A Boar azure (Stowe's *Survey of London*). The Earls of Oxford also used a bottle argent, suspended by a cord azure, in right of their hereditary office of Lords High Chamberlain ; or possibly this Badge was only a Rebus, and was intended to represent *verre*—a glass bottle. Over the west window of the church at CASTLE HEDINGHAM, ESSEX, this Badge appears as in the margin.

Fig. 292.

DOUGLAS : A Heart proper.

DRAYCOTT : A Serpent's head erased gules.

EDGECOMB : A Boar's head couped argent, the neck encircled with a wreath of leaves proper (*Harl. MS. No.* 4632 *fol.* 217).

FAUCONBERG, LORD : A Fish-hook.

FITZWARREN : A Bourchier knot.

GREY : A Scaling-ladder argent.

HASTINGS : A Bull's head erased sable, gorged and crowned or.

HOLLAND (DUKE of EXETER) : A Cresset fired.

HOWARD : A Lion rampant argent.

HUNGERFORD : A Sickle (*Tomb of Walter, Lord Hungerford, in Salisbury Cathedral*).

KENT, EARL of : A Bear argent.

KNOWLES : An Elephant.

LANGFORD : Two Wings argent.

LINCOLN, EARL of : A Plume of Feathers.

MAINWARING : An Ass's head sable.

MARMION : An Ape passant argent, ringed and chained gold (*Harl. MS. No.* 1453, *fol.* 158*b*).

MARCH, EARL of : A white Lion ; a Rose.

MONTACUTE, LORD : A Roebuck.

MORLEY, LORD : A Boar's head muzzled.

MOWBRAY : A Mulberry-tree proper ; a white Lion.

MUNFORD : A Fleur-de-lys gules.

NEVILLE : A dun Bull ; a Fret or ; a Bear and ragged staff ; a Fish-hook.

NEWCASTLE, DUKE of : A Buckle or.

NORFOLK, DUKE of : A Lion passant argent.

NORRIS : A Fountain.

OGLE : A Bull's head erased argent.

PELHAM : A Buckle or.

PEMBROKE, EARL of : a Dragon vert.

PERCY : A Crescent argent.

RICH : A Greyhound courant.

RIVERS : A Magpie proper ; an Escallop argent.

RUTLAND, EARL of : A Peacock.

SANDES : An Elephant.

SCROPE : A Plume of Feathers azure ; a Cornish Chough proper.

SIDNEY : A Hedgehog.

STANLEY : A Hart's head argent.

ST. LEGER : A pair of Barnacles erect gules, ringed or.

SUFFOLK, DUKE of : A Lion rampant, queue fourché or.

TALBOT : A Talbot or Hound.

TREVILLIAN : A Cornish Chough.

WALSINGHAM : A Tiger's head (*Harl. MS. No.* 5910, *Part II., fol.* 167) ; a Boar's head couped sable, holding in the mouth a walnut vert (*Harl. MS. No.* 4031, *fol.* 162).

WHARTON : A Bull's head erased argent.

WILLS, LORD : A Bucket and Chain.

WINCHESTER, MARQUESS of : A Falcon.

WINSOR : A Unicorn argent.

WIATT : A pair of Barnacles erect argent, ringed or.

WILLOUGHBY : A Mill-sail, or Wind-mill.

WORCESTER, EARL of : A Camel.

YARBOROUGH, EARL of : A Buckle.

Preserved in the British Museum (*Cott. MS. II.* 23) is a Political Song referring to the Wars in France, written about the year 1449. It is full of personal allusions, which, unless we knew the Badges of the Nobles referred to, would be entirely lost to us :—

> ' The Rote [1] is ded the Swanne [2] is goone
>   The firy Cressett [3] hath lost hys lyght
> Therfore Inglond may make gret mone
>   Were not the helpe of Godde almyght.
> The Castelle [4] is wonne where care begowne
>   The Porte colys [5] is leyde adowne
> Iclosed we haue our welevette hatte [6]
>   That kiveryd us from mony stormys browne.
> The white Lionn [7] is leyde to slepe
>   Through envy of the Ape clogge [8]

---

[1] John Plantagenet, Duke of Bedford, died 1435.
[2] Humphrey Plantagenet, Duke of Gloucester, died 1446.
[3] John Holland, Duke of Exeter, died 1446.   [4] The Castle of Rouen.
[5] Edmund Beaufort, Duke of Somerset.
[6] Cardinal Beaufort, died 1447.
[7] John de Mowbray, Duke of Norfolk, died 1432.
[8] William de la Pole, Duke of Suffolk.

And he is bownden that our dore should kepe
    That is Talbott [9] our good dogge.
The Fishere [10] hathe lost his hangulhooke
    Gete theym agayne when it wolle be
Our Mylle-saylle [11] will not abowte
    His hath so longe goone emptye.
The Bere [12] is bound that was so wild
    For he hath lost his ragged Staffe
The Carte-nathe [13] is spokeles
    For the Counseille that he gaffe.
The Lily [14] is both faire and grene
The Coundite [15] rennyth not I wene
The Cornysshe Chough [16] offt with his trayne
    Hath made oure Egulle [17] blynde
    The white Harde [18] is put out of mynde
Because he wolle not to him consente
    Therfore the Commyns saith is both trew and kynde
Both in Southesex and in Kent.
    The Water Bowge [19] and the Wyne Botelle [20]
With the Vetturlockes [21] cheyne bene fast
    The Whete-yere [22] wolle theym susteyne
As longe as he may endure and last.
The Boore [23] is farre unto the west
    That shold us helpe with shilde and spere
The Fawkoun [24] fleyth and hath no rest
Tille he witte where to bigge hys nest.'

It was frequently the practice at Tournaments for a Knight to exhibit two shields, one charged with his hereditary Bearings, and the other with his Badge or *Impress*. Before the commencement of the Tournament, if anyone was desirous of an encounter with him whose two shields were thus

[9] John Talbot, Earl of Shrewsbury.
[10] William Nevile, Lord Fauconberg.
[11] Robert, Lord Willoughby.   [12] Richard Nevile, Earl of Warwick.
[13] Humphrey de Stafford, Duke of Buckingham.
[14] Thomas Daniel.   [15] John Norris.   [16] David Trevillian.
[17] The king.   [18] William Fitz-Alan, Earl of Arundel.
[19] Henry, Lord Bourchier.   [20] James Butler, Earl of Ormond.
[21] Richard Plantagenet, Duke of York.
[22] Henry Holland, Duke of Exeter.
[23] Thomas Courténay, Earl of Devon.   [24] Edward, Duke of York.

exposed, he signified whether he wished it to be simply a trial of skill or a *combat à outrance* by touching either the Badge or Arms. EDWARD the BLACK PRINCE, in his Will, in which he gives directions for his funeral obsequies, specially mentions both kinds of shields which were to be carried in the procession—'l'un pur la guerre, de nos armes entiers quartellés ; et l'autre pur la paix, de nos bages des plumes d'ostruce.' Another mode of challenging—and that most generally adopted—was for Knights to exhibit their Shields of Arms, and for their opponents to signify their intention by touching them with *Sharps* or *Blunts*.

From the Fourteenth to the Sixteenth Centuries, Badges were commonly depicted on the friezes, entablatures, and stained-glass windows of Mansions and Churches, many fine examples of which are still preserved.

In the historical plays of Shakespeare, frequent allusions are made to Badges. CLIFFORD, in his quarrel with the EARL of WARWICK, exclaims :

> ' I am resolved to bear a greater storm
> Than any thou canst conjure up to-day ;
> And that, I'll write upon thy Burgonet (*helmet*),
> Might I but know thee by thy Household Badge.'

To which threat WARWICK replies :

> ' *The rampant Bear, chained to a ragged staff,*
> This day I'll wear aloft my Burgonet.'
>   *King Henry VI.*, Part ii. Act v. Sc. 1

In the ancient ballad entitled 'The Rising of the North Countrie,' we read :

> ' Now spreade thine Ancyent (Banner), Westmorland,
>   Thy *Dun Bull* faine would we spye ;
> And thou, the Earle of Northumberland,
>   Now raise thy *Half-Moone* up on hye.'

NEVILLE, EARL of WESTMORELAND, carried a *Dun Bull* as a Badge, and a *Dun Bull's head and neck erased* for Crest. The Badge of PERCY, EARL of NORTHUMBERLAND, was a

Crescent, which is again referred to in 'The Hermit of Warkworth':

> 'The minstrels of thy noble House
> All clad in robes of blue,
> With *silver Crescents* on their arms,
> Attend in order due.'

About the time of QUEEN ELIZABETH, the custom of wearing Badges began to fall into disuse : there are at the present day but few of our noble families which retain it. In Scotland, however, the custom still in a great measure survives ; a branch of a tree, a sprig, or a flower, in every instance constituting the distinguishing Badge of the various Clans, as exemplified by the following list :

BUCCLEUCH	Heather.
BUCHANAN	Birch.
CAMERON	Oak.
CAMPBELL	Myrtle.
CHISHOLM	Alder.
COLQUHOUN	Hazel.
CUMMING	Common Sallow.
DRUMMOND	Holly.
FARQUHARSON	Purple Fox-glove.
FERGUSON	Poplar.
FORBES	Broom.
FRAZER	Yew.
GORDON	Ivy.
GRAHAM	Laurel.
GRANT	Cranberry Heath.
GUNN	Rose-wort.
LAMONT	Crab Apple-tree.
MAC ALLISTER	Five-leaved Heath.
MAC DONALD	Bell Heath.
MAC DONNELL	Mountain Heath.
MAC DOUGAL	Cypress.
MAC FARLANE	Cloud-berry Bush.
MAC GREGOR	Pine.

K

MAC INTOSH	Box.
MAC KAY	Bullrush.
MAC KENZIE	Deer Grass.
MAC KINNON	St. John's Wort.
MAC LACHLAN	Mountain Ash.
MAC LEAN	Blackberry.
MAC LEOD	Red Whortle-berries.
MAC NAB	Rose Buck-berries.
MAC NEIL	Sea Ware.
MAC PHERSON	Variegated Box.
MAC QUARRIE	Black Thorn.
MAC RAE	Fir-Club Moss.
MENZIES	Ash.
MURRAY	Juniper.
OGILVIE	Hawthorn.
OLIPHANT	Maple.
ROBERTSON	Fern.
ROSE	Brier-rose.
ROSS	Bear-berries.
SINCLAIR	Clover.
STEWART	Thistle.
SUTHERLAND	Cat's-tail Grass.

The chief of each Clan, in addition to his family Badge, wears in his bonnet two Eagles' feathers : only the members and dependents of the house of MUNRO are entitled to bear Eagles' feathers as a Badge.

The last personal Royal Badge was that devised by Queen ANNE, in which the Rose of ENGLAND and the Thistle of SCOTLAND appeared growing from one stem, and Imperially crowned. The Rose, Thistle, and Shamrock, however, still constitute the national emblems of ENGLAND, SCOTLAND, and IRELAND ; and the custom of emblazoning devices upon the *Colours* of Infantry Regiments, and *Standards* of the Cavalry, is continued to the present day. As examples, it may not be out of place to enumerate the Badges displayed by a few of our Infantry Regiments :

1ST REGIMENT : (*Lothian*). V.R. within the Collar of the Order of the Thistle, surmounted by an Imperial Crown.

2ND   ,,   (*Royal West Surrey*). A Paschal Lamb. V.R. within the Garter, surmounted by a Crown. *Motto* : Pristinæ virtutis memor.

3RD   ,,   (*East Kent*). A Red Dragon. The Tudor Rose. *Motto* : Veteri frondescit honore.

4TH   ,,   (*Royal Lancaster*). A Lion of England. V.R. within the Garter.

5TH   ,,   (*Northumberland Fusiliers*). St. George and the Dragon. The Tudor Rose ensigned with the Crest of England. *Motto* : Quo fata vocant.

6TH   ,,   (*Royal Warwickshire*). Antelope. The Tudor Rose ensigned with the Crest of England.

7TH   ,,   (*Royal Fusiliers*). The Tudor Rose within the Garter, beneath a Crown, proper. A White Horse courant.

8TH   ,,   (*The King's*). A White Horse courant within the Garter. V.R. and Crown. *Motto* : Nec aspera terrent.

9TH   ,,   (*The Norfolk*). Britannia.

      &c.   &c.   &c.

THE REBUS was a fanciful combination of two or more figures, whereby the name of the adopter was usually formed, and was frequently borne by those who possessed both Arms and Crest. Sir WILLIAM DUGDALE quaintly observes, that 'they who lackt wit to expresse their conceit in speech, did use to depaint it out (as it were) in pictures, which they called *Rebus*, by a Latin name well fitting their device.'

Rebuses were very generally adopted by Ecclesiastics, as

K 2

is evinced by the number which are still to be seen carved
in Churches and Monastic Edifices.   On the tombs of the
Abbots WHEATHAMSTEAD and RAMRYGE in ST. ALBAN'S
CATHEDRAL, *Ears of Wheat*, and *Rams* with the syllable
'*rydge*' carved on their collars, are introduced in a variety
of forms ; and in a window of ST. PETER'S CHURCH,
GLOUCESTER, contributed by THOMAS COMPTON, Abbot of
CIRENCESTER, is a Rebus in which the donor's name is ex-
pressed by a *Comb* above a *Tun*, or Barrel.   The Rebus of
WILLIAM BOLTON, Prior of ST. BARTHOLOMEW'S, SMITHFIELD,

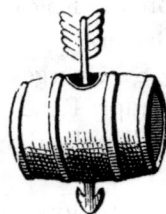

Fig. 293.

is similarly devised, as shown by the annexed
cut.   In a stained-glass window in the Chapel
at LULLINGSTONE, KENT, appear the Arms of
Sir JOHN PECHÉ,—*a Lion rampant*, surrounded with a Garland of Peach-branches ;
and on the fruit is inscribed the letter **f**,
which in French would form PÉCHE-É.   A
Shell over a *Tun* still remains on the Par-
sonage-house of GREAT SNORING, NORFOLK, placed there by
its builder, whose name was SHELTON.   .

In a similar manner, a member of the GRAFTON family
devised a Rebus of his name, composed of a *Graft* issuing
from the favourite *Tun*.   This device appears in a stained-
glass window of the Hall of the Rectory-house in BUCKLAND,
GLOUCESTERSHIRE.

ADDISON writes in the *Spectator* : ' When Cæsar was
one of the masters of the Roman Mint, he placed the figure
of an Elephant upon the reverse of the public money, the
word Cæsar signifying an Elephant in the Punic language.
This was artificially contrived by Cæsar, because it was not
lawful for a private man to stamp his own figure upon the
coin of the Commonwealth.   Cicero, who was so called from
the founder of his family, that was marked on the nose with
a little wen, like a vetch (which is *Cicer* in Latin), instead
of Marcus Tullius Cicero, ordered the words Marcus Tullius,
with a figure of a vetch at the end of them, to be inscribed

on a public monument.' We thus see that the adoption of Rebuses dates from a remote period of antiquity, long anterior to the time of Armory.

The Reader is referred to the chapter on ARMES PAR-LANTES, where other forms of Rebuses will be found treated of.[1]

It commonly occurred that Knights who, on entering the Lists, wished to conceal their identity, would assume a Device with an allusive Motto, which was designated an IMPRESS. Dallaway defines an Impress as 'a painted metaphor, or rather an enigma inverted.' There was a difference between the Household Badge and the Impress, as appears from the quotation from *Richard the Second* at page 37, where both are mentioned. The Impress belonged exclusively to the Knight's person, and was usually relinquished after having been once exhibited. The following incident aptly illustrates the nature of Impresses, and the circumstances under which they were frequently adopted.

At a Tournament held in London in the year 1390, an English Knight, Sir PIERS COURTENAY, chose for an Impress a Falcon, with this legend :

> ' I beare a Falcon, fairest of flighte ;
> Whoso pinches at her, his deth is dight,
>   In graith.'

Sir WILLIAM DALZELL, a Scotch Knight, who wished to provoke a challenge from Sir PIERS, parodied his Impress,

---

[1] Rebuses, other than heraldic, are often alluded to in the writings of some of the old authors. Ben Jonson puts the following words into the mouth of his ' Alchemist ' :

> ' He shall have *a bell*, that's *Abel ;*
> And by it standing one whose name is *Dee,*
> In a *rug* gown — that's *D* and *rug*, that's *Drug ;*
> And right anenst him a dog snarling *er,* —
> That's *Drugger*, ABEL DRUGGER.   That's his sign.'
>   *The Alchemist.*

and appeared the following day bearing a Magpie, beneath which was inscribed :

> ' I beare a Pye, picking at a peice ;
>   Whoso picks at her, I shall pick at his nese (*nose*),
>   In faith.'

As may be supposed, Sir WILLIAM DALZELL attained his object, and a trial of skill was the result. A narration of the manner in which he outwitted his opponent is given in Sir Samuel Meyrick's *Ancient Armour :* which, though highly entertaining, is too long to recount here.[1]

Another class of Badges, of great antiquity, is that commonly known as MERCHANTS' MARKS. When the right of bearing Arms was restricted exclusively to *Nobiles*, and any infringement of this ordinance was visited by severe punishment and heavy fines, citizens were permitted to adopt certain devices, which were placed upon their merchandise. These were not strictly armorial, but were employed, for the most part, by Merchants to whom Arms were denied, in much the same manner as Trade-Marks are at the present day. In one of the Harleian Manuscripts, preserved in the British Museum, we read : 'Theys be none armys but a marke as merchaunts use, for every man may take hym a marke, but not armys, without a herawde or purcyvante.'

Those by whom such Marks were principally adopted were the WOOL-STAPLERS, or MERCHANTS OF THE STAPLE. At an early period of England's history, wool formed an important article of commerce ; and Spelman, in his *Icenia*, asserts that half the wealth of EDWARD the FIRST was derived from that source. About the middle of the Fourteenth Century, the Wool-staplers were associated into a Guild ; and during the reigns of HENRY the FIFTH and SIXTH, stringent

---

[1] For further notes on Impresses, the reader is referred to Nichols's *History and Antiquities of Leicestershire*, vol. iii.

enactments were passed for their protection. Many of them accumulated immense fortunes, and some of our present noble Families date their origin from Merchants of the Staple. The Devices which they adopted were generally a combination of a Cross and their own Initials, as in the Marks of GEORGE HUCKLEY and JOHN WALDRON, carved in ST. PETER'S Church, TIVERTON, to the Restoration of which, during the Sixteenth Century, they were contributors (figs. 294–5). In many other churches,

Fig. 294.

notably in those of ST. JOHN THE BAPTIST, in BRISTOL, and the parish churches of HULL, DON-CASTER, and HITCHIN, are to be seen similar records of those who contributed towards their endowment. So thoroughly identified were the adopters with their peculiar Marks, that they practically fulfilled every function of legitimate

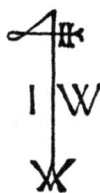

Fig. 295.

Arms, and, as PIERS PLOWMAN expresses it, were '*ymedeled* (painted) *in glass*,' and engraven on monuments.

The Marks here given are from HITCHIN Church, HERT-FORDSHIRE :

Merchants' Marks.—Figs. 296, 297, 298.

Leaden seals, similar to those here engraved, are frequently found in and around Hitchin. These seals are identical with the *plombs* of Continental Custom-houses, and were so affixed to bales of wool, and other merchandise, that it was impossible to open the packages without breaking the seal or cutting the string by which it was fastened.

Fig. 300.

Occasionally we find examples of the lawful bearers of Arms assuming a Mark, as in the case of WILLIAM GREVEL, A.D. 1401, on whose Brass, in CHIPPING CAMPDEN Church, are represented both his Arms and mercantile Device, bespeaking that, although a merchant, he was of gentle blood. WILLIAM CANYNGE also, who was the founder—or at least the restorer—of the church of ST. MARY REDCLIFFE, BRISTOL (*temp.* HEN. VI.), as Gentleman and Merchant, used both Arms and. Mark, which are sculptured on his Tomb.

In STANDON Church, HERTFORDSHIRE, is a remarkably fine Brass, which I have engraved in my History of that County, to Alderman JOHN FIELD (A.D. 1477) and JOHN FIELD, Esquire, his son. The father is in his civic robes, with the Arms of the City of London above him, and his Mark beneath him. The son is in armour, his Arms emblazoned on his Jupon ; the same Arms on a shield at his feet, and the Arms of the STAPLE of CALAIS :—*Barry nebulé of six, argent and azure ; on a Chief gules a Lion passant guardant or,* above him.

Similar Devices were early adopted by Printers ; and

Fig. 301.

Fig. 302.

their use, under a somewhat modified form, is still continued by many Publishers. All Books issuing from the Press of

ROBERT COPLAND, who died in 1548, bore his Mark (fig. 301), within a garland of Roses ; and ROBERT WYER (A.D. 1527–1542) adopted a Device, of which fig. 302 is a copy.

The ALDINE MARK is too well known to need an Illustration.

For other examples of printers' marks, the reader is referred to ' Collectanea de Arte Typographia,' *Harl. MSS. No.* 5910, *Part II. fol.* 166 *et seq., Mus. Brit.*

Fig. 303.

Rebeus of ABBOT ISLIP, from his chapel in WESTMINSTER ABBEY

CHAPTER X

MARKS OF CADENCY, OR DIFFERENCES

ATERNAL Arms being by right borne by all the sons of a Family, it is highly important that there should be some means by which the various members may be distinguished. For this purpose Heralds have instituted certain devices called MARKS OF DIF-FERENCE, or BRISURES, which, when charged upon a shield, clearly indicate to which branch of a Family their Bearers belong.

In the early days of Heraldry, Differences were effected by a variety of arbitrary arrangements—such as changing the tinctures of the Coat ; adding, or suppressing, some minor Charge ; substituting one Ordinary for another ; enclosing the Shield within a Bordure, &c. ; but as, by these methods, a Coat of Arms, after a few generations, frequently became so changed in appearance as to lose all resemblance to the original, much confusion and uncertainty were necessarily engendered. A simpler plan was subsequently devised— that of adding certain recognised figures to the Coat—which in no way, however, changed its identity.

The initial letter is taken from the Monument to PETER RAMSDEN, Abbot of SHERBOURNE, DORSETSHIRE (A.D. 1500), in the Church of that place.

The first of these Marks of Cadency is the LABEL, or FILE, which is borne by the eldest Son during the lifetime of his Father, at whose death, of course, it is removed from the Son's Escutcheon. Some authorities assert that the eldest Son should bear a Label with three *Lambeaux*, or *Points*, while his Father lives ; and if his Grandfather should survive, it should have five *Lambeaux ;* but, in many instances, we find both forms of the Label in use by one person at the same time. On the seal of EDWARD PLANTAGENET, afterwards EDWARD the FIRST, bearing date 1267, his Arms are differenced with a Label of five points, and on the counter-seal with three points ; which example was followed by his Son and Grandson. Occasionally we find a Label of four points employed—as in the effigy of CROUCHBACK, first EARL of LANCASTER, son of HENRY the THIRD, who thus differences the Lions of England. Guillim mentions an example—that of HOWELL DE MONNEMOTH—in which a Label was borne with two points ; but, in modern Armory, the Label is invariably represented with three. The Illustration at the end of this chapter is an example of the Label of five points, and is taken from the Tomb of EDWARD the BLACK PRINCE, in CANTERBURY CATHEDRAL.

Fig. 304.

It was not until the Fourteenth Century that *Cadency*, as the word is now understood, became general, for although, as has been said, Edward I., before he was king, assumed a Label to mark his position towards his father, then living, we find in the *Roll of Caerlaverock* (A.D. 1300), the two systems, one of changing Charges, the other of adopting Marks of Cadency, in vogue at one and the same time.

> ' E l ij frere Basset ausi
> Dont le ainsnez portoit ensi
> De ermine au chef rouge endenté
> De trois molettes de or entré
> Li autres de cokilles trois.

E Morices de Berkelée
Ki compaigns fu de cele alée
Baniere ot vermeille com sanc
Croissillie o un chievron blanc
Ou un label de asur avoit
Por ce que ses peres vivoit.'
                    Cott. MS. Calig. A. xviii. *Mus. Brit.*

Thus Englished by the late Thomas Wright :—

'And the two brothers Basset likewise
Of whom the eldest bore thus :
Ermine, a red chief indented
Charged with three gold mullets,
The other with three shells.

And Maurice de Berkeley
Who was a partaker in this expedition
Had a banner red as blood
Crusilly with a white chevron
On which there was a blue label
Because his father was (fathers were ?) living.'

In case the eldest son should die without issue during the lifetime of his Father, the second Son is permitted, as Heir expectant, to bear his Label ; and on succeeding to his estate would bear his paternal Arms, without any Mark of Cadency, the same as his Brother would have done, had he survived.   In other words, the Label is the Mark of the eldest surviving son.

FIG. 305.

A CRESCENT, in like manner, constitutes the Mark by which the Second Son distinguishes his Arms (fig. 305).

The Third Son differences his paternal Coat with a MULLET.

The Fourth Son differences his Arms with a MARTLET.

An ANNULET indicates the Fifth Son.

The Arms of the Sixth Son are differenced by a FLEUR-DE-LYS.

The Seventh Son has a ROSE.

A CROSS-MOLINE distinguishes the Eighth Son ; and a DOUBLE QUATREFOIL (fig. 306) the Ninth. No provision is made for further Sons.

Should the eldest son himself have a Son, the latter would, during his Grandfather's lifetime, bear his paternal Arms, differenced by a Label, to show that he was of the first 'House' ; and on that Label there would be charged another, showing that he was the first

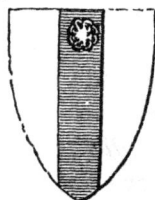

Fig. 306.

Son of that House. On the death of his Grandfather, his Arms would of course be differenced by a single Label, in the manner that his Father's had been previously. Again : the fourth Son bears, as we have seen, a Martlet for Difference ; his fifth Son, therefore, would charge an Annulet on his Father's Martlet, thereby implying that he was the fifth Son of the fourth House.

All the members of the Royal Family—the Sovereign excepted—difference their Arms with a silver Label of three points, charged with some distinguishing mark, specially assigned to them by the Crown. Thus, the DUKE of EDINBURGH bears on the first and third points of his Label *an Anchor azure*, and on the middle point a *Cross humetté gules*. The DUKE of CONNAUGHT : *a Cross gules between two Fleurs-de-lys azure*. The PRINCESS ROYAL : *a Rose, between two Crosses gules*, &c. The DUKE of CAMBRIDGE bears on the first and third points *two Hearts in pale*, and on the middle point *a Cross, all gules*. The PRINCE of WALES, as the eldest son, of course, bears his Label uncharged.

It is extremely doubtful when this system of differencing came into universal practice ; for though we find DE QUINCY, EARL of WINCHESTER, differencing his seal with a Label about the year 1215, yet long subsequent to that date the arbitrary methods before alluded to were commonly adopted. In a window of the Collegiate Church of ST. MARY's, WARWICK, erected in 1361, the Arms of the six Sons of THOMAS BEAUCHAMP, fifteenth EARL of WARWICK, appear differenced

with a Crescent, Mullet, &c., in the manner I have described ; yet, as late as 1486, instructions are given in the
Boke of St. Albans for differencing Arms by *Gerattyng*, or
powdering the Shield with *Crosslets, Fleurs-de-lys, Roses,
Primroses* (quatrefoils), *Cinquefoils, Escallops, Chaplets,
Mullets,* and *Crescents.*   In the reign of HENRY the EIGHTH,
however, the system of Differencing, as practised at the
present day, seems to have been firmly established in England, as frequent and systematic reference is made to it in
the Visitations of the Heralds of that period.

The Arms of Ladies—Princesses excepted—are not
charged with Marks of Cadency, as all the daughters of a
Family rank alike.   If, however, their paternal grandfather
were still living, they would each bear the same mark over
their Arms as their Father.

Not only should the distinctive marks of the various
Houses be borne upon the Shield, but they should also be
represented upon the Crest and Supporters.   It is much to
be regretted that this method of indicating the seniority
of the different branches of a Family should have recently
fallen so much into disuse ; for its neglect is productive of
much uncertainty in deciding to which House any particular
member of a Family belongs, besides being in absolute defiance of Heraldic usage ; for, as Sir Henry Spelman writes,
'it is not lawful for several persons to bear one and the
same Arms without a Difference, not even to those of the
same Family, though they be Brothers thereof.'

In some few instances we find Labels represented upon

Fig. 307.

Shields as Charges, as in the case of the
family Arms of HENLINGTON, which are,
Argent ; a Label of five points azure.
The BARRINGTONS bear a similar Coat,
viz. :—*Argent ; three Chevronels gules, and
a Label azure* (fig. 307).   It is probable that
Labels were originally designed as Marks of
Cadency, and allowed to remain on the

Shield after their purpose was accomplished, and thus became permanent Charges ; or else, that they were intended to indicate two different Families who had inadvertently assumed the same Arms.

As a Label is merely an accidental Difference, and is not an integral part of the armorial composition, the rule which forbids charging Colour on Colour, and Metal on Metal, may be legitimately violated, as in the Arms of the first two EDWARDS, both of whom, while Heirs-apparent, differenced their Shields gules, with a Label of five points azure.

As with the *Cadets*, or younger branches of a Family, so with the Illegitimate there formerly existed no fixed rule to determine the fashion of the Brisure imposed upon their Arms. Sir JOHN DE CLARENDON, for instance, the natural Son of EDWARD the BLACK PRINCE, bore : *Or ; on a bend sable, three Ostrich-feathers, the quill fixed in a scroll argent.* JOHN BEAUFORT, eldest natural son of JOHN of GHENT, DUKE of LANCASTER, bore : *Party per pale, argent and azure, on a Bend gules the Lions of England, over all a Label of three points argent, each charged with as many Fleurs-de-lys of the second ;* which Arms were subsequently changed for those of *France ancient and England, quarterly, within a Bordure compony argent and azure,* as borne by the Family of the DUKE of BEAUFORT at the present day.

It is commonly supposed by many persons, that the Brisure to be charged upon the arms of Illegitimate Children is the Bend sinister. This is not the case, for this Ordinary is as honourable as any of the others.[1] It is its Diminutive, the Bâton, which is sometimes so employed.

According to some old authorities, this Mark should be borne by the descendants of the natural son until the third generation, when they are permitted to relinquish it, and

---

[1] Ignorant people often speak of the *Bar-sinister* as the Mark of Illegitimacy. A Bar-sinister or dexter is a simple impossibility. As well may one speak of two parallel straight lines which, meeting, form an isosceles triangle.

assume the original paternal Coat. When there are more natural Sons than one in the same family, their seniority is ndicated by the tincture of the Bâton being varied. The Arms of the numerous sons of CHARLES the SECOND afford examples of differencing in this manner. The Bâton is never composed entirely of Metal, except for those who are of Royal blood.

Fig. 303.

Arms of EDWARD the BLACK PRINCE, taken from his Tomb
in CANTERBURY CATHEDRAL.

CHAPTER XI

BLAZONING

'Plain Coates are noblest, though y⁰ vulgar eye
Take Joseph's for the best in Herauldry.'
(From Epitaph to George Walton [1662]
in Little Burstead Church, Essex.)

IT has been already mentioned that Heraldry was probably
reduced to the limits of a Science by the Germans
during the Eleventh and Twelfth Centuries, when Jousts
and Tournaments held a similar place amongst the Nobles
of that period that the maiming of tame pigeons does
amongst many gentlemen of this. At these trials of military
skill, it was the custom for the directors of the contests to
examine and publicly proclaim the Armorial Bearings and
achievements of such competitors as presented themselves
for the first time, before they were permitted to engage in
the Lists ; while an attendant Esquire would BLASEN, or
blow a horn, to attract attention to the ceremony. The
antecedents of a Knight having been thus once openly
proclaimed, he was permitted thenceforth to bear on his
helmet two Horns, which signified that his Arms had been
duly *blasened*, thereby rendering a subsequent examination unnecessary : and thus
we find that the Crests of German Nobles
are frequently placed between two Horns,
as in the accompanying example.

Blazoning has consequently become to
mean, in a general sense, a public pro-

Fig. 309.

L

claiming ; and, more particularly, a description of Armorial Bearings, according to the established rules of Heraldry. Iden, after killing Jack Cade, the rebel, is thus made by Shakespeare to apostrophise his sword :

> ' I will hallow thee for this thy deed ;
> Ne'er shall this blood be wipèd from thy point ;
> But thou shalt wear it as a Herald's coat,
> To emblaze the honour that thy master got.'

In Blazoning, all tautology must be particularly avoided. A tincture must never be mentioned twice in the same Blazon : should it occur again, it must be expressed as *of the first* (or *field*), *of the second, of the last*, &c., as the case may be.[1] At the same time, everything should be described with the utmost minuteness, so that a person, by reading the Blazon, may be enabled to delineate the Shield and its Charges with unerring precision.

I have, in a former place, alluded to a few recent grants of Arms, in which the Charges are of such a nature that it is almost impossible to emblazon the Coat correctly from any written description.   In the Arms of SIR JOHN HERSCHEL, for example, the imagination of the emblazoner is seriously taxed ; they are : *Argent ; on a mount vert, a representation of the forty-feet reflecting Telescope,* WITH ITS APPARATUS *proper ; on a Chief azure, the astronomical symbol of ' Uranus,' or ' Georgium Sidus,' irradiated or.* Such Armorial monstrosities are, however, extremely rare ; and to the credit of the Science be it said, that no such composition is to be found of an earlier date than the Seventeenth Century.

---

[1] In using the words 'in the same Blazon,' I mean in describing the Arms on a single shield. Fig 311, for example, gives the Arms of five distinct families. Each quarter and the Inescutcheon are, therefore, treated separately, and though the tincture Argent is mentioned in the first quarter, it is quite right when that quarter is disposed of, to start off afresh with the second quarter as Argent, and not as ' of the first.'

In blazoning a Coat of Arms, the tincture of the field must be first stated ; and if it be not of a simple tincture, whether it be *party of any of the Ordinaries ;* such as *Lozengy ; Chequé ; Semé ;* &c. : then the principal object charged upon it, *which lies next the Shield ;* and if that Charge be formed of any irregular lines, such as *invected, ragulé,* &c., it must be stated ; its attitude and position on the Shield follow next : then the Tincture ; and, lastly, any peculiar features, such as *armed, gorged,* &c. ;—for example : *Argent ; three Greyhounds courant in pale sable, collared or ;* borne by MOORE. Having described the principal Charge (or that which occupies the centre of the field), the subordinate Charges, also lying on the Shield itself, follow. Should any of the before-mentioned Charges be themselves charged, the secondary Charges, so lying on them, must not be mentioned until every object in direct contact with the field has been described.

Although Cotices, Bendlets, Barrulets, &c., are Charges in themselves, they are but Diminutives, and yield in precedence to Perfect Charges. Thus, in the arms of KAY, the Martlet takes precedence of the Bendlets. Fig. 310 should be blazoned as *Argent ; in the dexter chief point a Martlet, between two Bendlets sable,* and not as *Argent ; two Bendlets, and in the dexter chief a Martlet sable.* I confess that this is somewhat of a refinement, but nevertheless it is strictly correct ; and when there are two ways, equally easy, of doing a thing, it is as well to do it right.

Fig. 310.

Having enumerated the principal rules to be observed in Blazoning, I shall now proceed to show their practical application, by reference to an apocryphal Coat of Arms.

QUARTERLY OF FOUR : 1. *Party per pale arg. and gu. ; on a Saltire, between four Herrings naiant, five Billets, all counterchanged.* 2. *Arg. ; six Trefoils slipped vert, three, two, and one ; on a Canton gu., a Lion of England.* 3. *Gu. ;*

L 2

a Sword in Bend or, pommelled and hilted arg., within a Bordure embattled of the last ; on a Canton az., a Crampette of the second.   4. Arg. ; on a Chevron engrailed gu., between

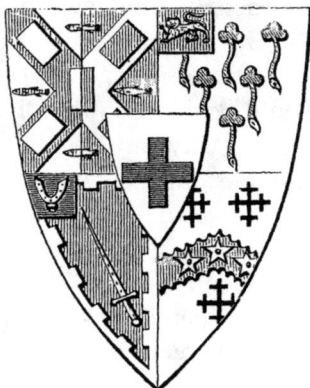

Fig. 311.

three Crosses-crosslet sa., as many Mullets of the first pierced of the second.   SURTOUT (or OVER ALL), *an Inescutcheon arg., on which a Cross humetté az.*

It will be seen that in blazoning this Coat of Arms we first describe its distinctive feature, which is *Quarterly of four.* We next proceed to blazon each Quarter, as we would a separate Shield.   The field of the first Quarter is party of two tinctures, and the principal charge thereon is a Saltire : the secondary charges on the field itself are the Herrings ; these, therefore, are blazoned before the Billets, which are charged on a Charge.

Charges, whether placed *in* or *on* an Ordinary, always incline in the direction of such Ordinary.

I print the last two lines in a separate paragraph and in slightly larger type, so that it may be impressed on the student.

The four Billets, therefore, on the limbs of the Saltire, are each posed in a different manner from the one in the centre.   An explanation of *Counterchanging* will be found at page 81.   In the second Quarter, only five Trefoils appear the Diagram, though six are mentioned in the Blazon — the ·st is *absconded*, or covered, by the Canton. It will be bserved that the Lion, being *passant-guardant or*, on a field *ules*, is blazoned as a Lion of England. In the third)uarter, the Canton and its Charge are not mentioned until ıe last, being the farthest removed from the Shield ; and in ke manner the Mullets in the fourth Quarter are not .escribed until after the Crosses-crosslet, which are in direct ontact with the Shield. We do not say '*three Mullets*,' but *as many*,' as the number *three* has already occurred, in .escribing the Crosses : neither do we blazon them as *Argent*, hat tincture having been before mentioned. *Of the field* ;ould have been equally as correct as *of the first*.

The *Inescutcheon*, or *Shield of Pretence*, being an exraneous addition, and, consequently, the farthest removed rom the surface of the Shield, is blazoned last.

In blazoning a Coat of Arms in which two or more ?harges of the same Tincture immediately follow each other ı the Blazon, it is not necessary to mention he Tincture until all the Charges of such ?incture have been specified. Thus, in the \rms of FINDLAY, of AYRSHIRE, the Chevron, {oses, and Eagle being all of the same Tincture, hey would be blazoned as follows : *Argent ; on ₁ Chevron between two Roses in chief, and a* *ouble-headed Eagle displayed in base, gules,* *wo Swords, points downwards, of the first, pommelled and* *iilted or.*

Fig. 312.

It is a fundamental law of Heraldry that Metal should ıever be charged on Metal, nor Colour on Colour. Thus, a ield azure, charged with a Lion gules, would be false Heraldry ; though Sir William Dugdale instances several ıncient Coats in which this rule is violated. The Arms of he CRUSADER KINGS OF JERUSALEM afford a notable example. Γhey bore : *Argent ; a Crosse pommé* (subsequently *potent*), ·antoned by four Crosses humetté or. This rule does not

apply when Charges are blazoned in their natural colours,
termed heraldically *Proper* (*ppr.*). It would, therefore, be
perfectly correct to blazon a Tree *proper*, on a field *gules*.
Should a Charge be ensigned with a Crown *or*, it is unnecessary to mention the Tincture : the terms, *Imperially* or
Ducally crowned, or *gorged*, imply that the Crown or Coronet
is to be emblazoned *proper*.

There is, perhaps, no detail in connection with the science
of Armory which demands greater attention, and in which
greater diversity of practice occurs, than in Punctuation.
The late Mr. Boutell usually placed a comma after each
item of every descriptive clause, as in the following example,
being the Arms of JOHN DE CORNWALL, K.G., LORD FANHOPE :
*erm., within a bordure, sa., bezantée, a lion rampt., gu. :
crowned, or, and charged for difference with a mullet, arg.*   In
the following Blazon of the Arms of SIR JOHN LUBBOCK, BART.,
taken from Burke's *Peerage and Baronetage of the British
Empire*, three commas, at least, might have been omitted :
*Arg. ; on a mount, vert, a heron, close, erm., a chief, gu.,
charged with three estoilles, of the field.*   Papworth, on the
other hand, in his *Ordinary of Arms*—a most useful book to
the Herald—went to the opposite extreme, and blazoned
Coats of Arms including many Quarterings without using
any stops whatever.   This omission may seem to be of no
great importance—neither, indeed, is it in the majority of
instances ; but, occasionally, a point misplaced, or left out,
may totally change the Coat.   The plan which I have
adopted can be readily understood by reference to a Blazon
of Arms.

Fig. 313.—Arms of HUME.

CHAPTER XII

MARSHALLING

BY MARSHALLING is meant the grouping together of two or more Coats of Arms on one Escutcheon, whereby the family alliances or official dignity of the bearer are indicated.

The most ancient method of Marshalling two Coats on the same Shield was by DIMIDIATION, which was effected by simply dividing both Coats per pale, and joining the Dexter half of one to the Sinister half of the other. The Arms of the Borough of GREAT YARMOUTH are compounded in this manner. By a seal affixed to an ancient Charter, the Arms appear to have been originally *Three Herrings naiant in pale*, to which were subsequently added, by dimidiation, *Three Lions of England ;* producing the curious combination represented in the annexed diagram. The city of Chester impales in a like manner the Lions of England with the arms of the Earldom : *Azure ; three Garbs or.* In this

Fig. 314.

case the dexter Garb in chief is completely *absconded* from the shield.

This method of Marshalling, however, was very unsatisfactory ; for, in many instances, the general features of both coats were lost. For example, if we wished to combine, by Dimidiation, *Party per pale, gules and azure ; two Lions combattant or ;* with *Gules ; a Male Griffin passant or*, we should produce, on a field gules, a *Lion rampant contourné*, and the sinister half of a *Lion passant ;* thus losing the azure field, and the rampant Lion charged upon it, of the first coat ; and transforming the Griffin of the second coat into a Lion passant.[1]

On the seal of ROBERT FITZHARDING, the founder of the BERKELEY family, *circa* 1180, is represented a grotesque figure, apparently formed by combining by Dimidiation a Bird and an Animal.

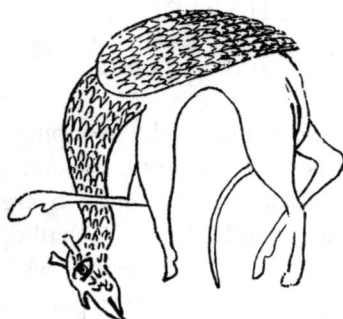

Fig. 315.

Again, if a SERLE, whose coat is simply *per pale, or and sable*, without any charge, were to marry a FAIRLEY, who bears *per pale, sable and or*, the compound shield, if mar_ shalled by Dimidiation, would be plain gold.[2]

Marshalling by Dimidiation was, towards the close of the Fourteenth Century, superseded by IMPALEMENT, although instances of dimidiated coats are occasionally to be met with

---

[1] It was probably by uniting two Coats by Dimidiation, one charged with an Eagle and the other with a Lion, that the Griffin was devised.

[2] This objection would, perhaps, hardly hold good at the present day, when it is customary to define Impalements and Quarterings by a fine sable line ; but it was formerly the practice to make no such division between the different compartments, as appears, among other examples which might be quoted, from the shield on the monument to EDMUND, DUKE OF YORK, at KING'S LANGLEY (A.D. 1399), in which *France ancient* and *England* are quartered (see fig. 308). In such a case, the combined SERLE and FAIRLEY coats would be, as stated above, plain gold ; but, as it would now be blazoned, it would be, *Or ; impaling another of the same ;* or, *Party per pale ; both or*.

at a much later period ; as on the seal of MARY QUEEN OF SCOTS, on her marriage with the DAUPHIN, where *France modern* (three Fleurs-de-lys) is dimidiated with the entire shield of Scotland. The Arms of WILLIAM the FIRST appear on the cornice of Queen Elizabeth's tomb, as impaled with those of MATILDA, daughter of BALDWIN, fifth EARL OF FLANDERS ; but this is evidently an anachronism, for the system of Impalement did not obtain in England until nearly three centuries after the Conqueror's death.

Marshalling by Impalement is effected by slightly compressing the two Coats of Arms, and placing them in their entirety side by side on one Escutcheon. In this manner the Arms of a husband and wife are usually combined, those of the Husband—or, in Heraldic phraseology, the *Baron*— toward the dexter, and those of the *Femme* on the sinister, as shown at fig. 316, which would be blazoned, *Argent ; a Fess gules : Impaling, Gules ; a Chevron argent, within a Bordure or.* As these are the arms of two separate families, the Blazon must be kept totally distinct. It would be incorrect to blazon the wife's arms as, *of the last ; a Chevron of the first ;* for each is complete without the other.

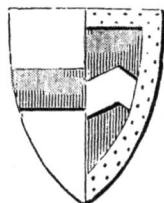

Fig. 316.

When two coats are combined by *Impalement*, and one of them is surrounded by a Bordure, the system of Dimidiation is retained with regard to the Bordure ; thus, in the example here given the Bordure is not represented complete ; but in *Quartered* shields, as in the third quarter of fig. 311, and in the second quarter of the Royal Arms of England, the Bordure is always rendered complete.[1]

Kings-of-arms and Bishops bear their official Arms im-

---

[1] Formerly, when the wife was of a higher rank than her husband, her Arms were frequently placed on the dexter side ; which Arms were sometimes assumed by the husband, and his own abandoned. Several instances of this practice are mentioned in the *Sussex Archæological Collection*, vol. vi. p. 75.

paled on the same shield with their hereditary Insignia, the latter being placed on the sinister side.

Impaled Arms are not hereditary; a widow, however, may bear her deceased husband's Arms, with her own, charged upon a Lozenge, but is not permitted to display Crest, Helmet, or Motto.

In the case of a man marrying an Heiress, or Co-heiress (heraldically called Heir or Co-heir), he would, after her father's death, impose her Armorial Bearings upon his own shield, charged on an Inescutcheon, or Shield of Pretence, thereby intimating that he has a *pretence* to her hereditaments. This, however, he cannot do, unless his wife has actually succeeded to her inheritance. During her father's lifetime, or while there is a possibility of an heir male being born—however remote the probability of that event may be—her husband only *impales* her Arms.

All the issue of a marriage with an heir female are entitled to bear both their paternal and maternal coats quartered, together with all the quarterings to which their mother may have been herself entitled. Thus, an Escutcheon may be charged with the bearings of an unlimited number of families.

The earliest known example of a quartered shield occurs on the monument of ELEANOR, daughter of FERDINAND the THIRD, KING OF CASTILE, and wife of EDWARD the FIRST, in WESTMINSTER ABBEY, whereon are sculptured, in the first and fourth Quarters, the *Castle* of Castile, and, in the second and third quarters, the *rampant Lion* of Leon (see fig. 323). Quartering, however, was not generally adopted until the end of the Fourteenth Century.

The manner in which various coats are *brought in*, and marshalled by Quartering, will be readily understood by reference to the accompanying diagrams. I have selected, for the sake of simple illustration, the Coats of families which possess few and plain Charges, the Alliances being entirely fictitious.

HENRY ST. JOHN = MARY BOYLE.　　　JOHN STEWART = JANE BUTLER.

WALTER WEST = EMMA ST. JOHN.　　JAMES STEWART = EDITH SHERRARD.

ALFRED WEST = ANNIE STEWART.

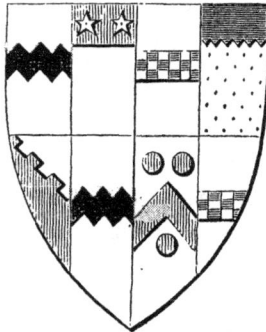

Figs. 317-321.

In the first place, HENRY ST. JOHN, whose paternal Arms are, *Argent ; on a Chief gules, two Mullets of the field*, marries MARY BOYLE, an Heiress. He therefore charges an Inescutcheon containing the Boyle Arms upon his shield (fig 317). Their daughter EMMA, also an Heiress, is entitled to bear both her Father's and her Mother's Arms quarterly : which Coat her husband, WALTER WEST, imposes on a Shield of Pretence over his own. Their son, ALFRED, in the right of his Mother, marshals with his paternal Arms those of ST. JOHN and BOYLE, in the manner exemplified on the dexter side of Fig. 321. It may be mentioned here, that when there is an uneven number of Quarterings to be marshalled on one shield, the paternal arms may be repeated in the last Quarter or a *Secondary* or *Tertiary* Quartering may be omitted. In this instance the secondary Quartering is that of St. John.

On the other side of the Chart we see how ANNIE STEWART becomes the possessor of the BUTLER and SHERRARD Coats in addition to her own. Now, if ALFRED WEST were to marry ANNIE STEWART—who is *not* an Heiress—he would Impale her Arms with his (fig. 321) ; but his children would have no right to bear either the STEWART, BUTLER, or SHERRARD Arms, their Mother not being an Heiress. If a Clive, not entitled to any Quarterings, had married ANNIE STEWART, the same arrangement would be adopted ; that is, the Arms of both would be impaled and blazoned as follows : *Argent, on a Fess sable, three Mullets or,* for CLIVE ; IMPALING, *Quarterly of four :* 1 *and* 4. *Or ; a Fess chequé,* for STEWART. 2. *Or ; a Chief indented azure,* for BUTLER. 3. *Argent ; a Chevron gules, between three Torteaux,* for SHERRARD. Supposing Annie Stewart to have been an Heiress, and married to Clive, her husband would set her quartered Arms on an Inescutcheon over his Fess, as we have already seen ; but the Arms of their children would assume a new aspect. They would bear on a quartered shield the Arms of the Clives, Stewarts, Butlers, and Sherrards, as at fig. 322, which would be thus briefly blazoned : QUARTERLY OF FOUR ; *First and Fourth,* CLIVE : *Second and Third grand Quarters, quarterly quartered :* 1 *and* 4, STEWART ; 2, BUTLER ; 3, SHERRARD.

Should a man marry two heirs female he might impale their respective paternal Arms on an Inescutcheon. His children, however, would only be entitled to quarter the Arms of their real mother.

Fig. 322.

By observing the foregoing rules, it can readily be known by a Coat of Arms whether the possessor be unmarried, married, or a widow.[1] The Arms of a bachelor consist either of a single Coat, or quartered ; but never of two Coats impaled, except in the instance before mentioned, in which a gentleman impales his official arms, and a few families whose party shields are referred to at p. 56. The same arrangement applies to the Arms of unmarried Ladies, with this difference, that they are borne on a Lozenge, and are not ensigned with Crests, &c. A husband impales his wife's

[1] This statement, perhaps, requires some modification ; for a married man is not *compelled* to impale his wife's Arms. It is no uncommon thing to see on old Brasses the Arms of *Baron* and *Femme* on two separate shields, and the combined Arms on a third. On leases granted by noble families at the present time, the paternal Arms only of the Lessor are frequently lithographed on the deed, though he may be legally entitled to impale. There is just another point that may arise. A man entitled to Arms marries a woman who is not. What then ? To impale his Arms with a simple *Diapering* is a studied insult to her. Should he occupy such a position as High Sheriff or Lord Mayor, in which he *must* display his Arms, it is still a worse insult to her to use his paternal coat only. In such a case he should obtain a grant of Arms for his wife. In the granting of Leases, there is no slur on the wife if the Earls of Derby and Sefton have their paternal coats only engraved on the deed ; for in that case it is the family, not the man, who is the lessor.

Arms, or bears them on a Shield of Pretence. A widow bears the same impaled Arms as her late husband, blazoned on a Lozenge ; the Helmet, Crest, and Motto being omitted.

If a Peeress in her own right should marry a Commoner, the respective Arms are not impaled, but are placed on two separate shields side by side, the husband's charged with an Inescutcheon containing his wife's Arms, ensigned with her Coronet, towards the Dexter ; and on the other shield the Arms of his wife alone. As, however, she retains, even after marriage, not only her title, but her maiden or widow name, she bears her Arms upon a Lozenge, together with all the Insignia to which her rank entitled her before such marriage. The position of Peeresses is, under certain circumstances, rather anomalous. All the daughters of a Peer take the same rank as that of their eldest brother during the lifetime of his father. Thus, the son and daughter of a Duke would be styled Marquess and Marchioness respectively. Now, supposing one of two daughters were to marry a Baron—the lowest order of the nobility—she would lose three grades ; but, should the other daughter marry her footman, she would still retain her titular rank, and actually take precedence of her sister, though the wife of a Peer.

It is the general custom for a widower, on marrying the second time, to divide his shield *in tierce*, that is, in three equal divisions in pale, and to emblazon the Arms of his first wife in the centre, and those of his second wife towards the sinister : or, to divide the shield per pale, and the sinister half again per fess, placing his deceased wife's Arms in chief, and the Arms of his second wife in base. These arrangements are, however, opposed to the true purposes of Armory ; for, unless his first wife were an Heiress, and had issue by him, her Arms ought not to appear in the same Escutcheon with those of his second wife.

Should a gentleman marry an Heiress, and have issue but one daughter, and subsequently marry again, and have a son, the latter would be heir to his Father, and the daughter heir to her Mother. In this case, the daughter would be entitled to bear her Mother's arms, surmounted by those of her Father, charged upon a Canton. If an *Ignobilis*, that is, one without Armorial Bearings, were to marry an Heiress, he could make no use whatever of her Arms ; for, having no Escutcheon of his own, it is evident that he could not charge her Shield of Pretence ; neither would their issue—being unable to quarter—be permitted to bear their maternal Coat. By 'an Heiress' is not necessarily implied an inheritrix of landed or other property. A Lady is an Heiress when she is the sole issue of any gentleman bearing Arms ; and Co-heiress (or, more correctly, Co-heir, which in Heraldry is equivalent to Heiress), when she has other sisters, but no brother.

A Knight of any of the Orders is not permitted to surround his shield, on which his own and his wife's Arms are combined, with the Motto of the Garter, Bath, or any other distinction essentially pertaining to himself. The respective Arms must be blazoned on two separate Shields placed side by side ; that on the Dexter containing the Knight's paternal Coat, ensigned with the Insignia of the Order to which he may belong ; and that on the Sinister bearing his own and his wife's Arms impaled, or in pretence, as she may happen to be an Heiress or not.

Fig. 323.

Quartered Shield of ELEANOR of CASTILE ; from her tomb in EDWARD the CONFESSOR'S Chapel, Westminster Abbey (A.D. 1290).

CHAPTER XIII

AUGMENTATIONS AND ABATEMENTS OF HONOUR

AUGMENTATIONS are certain honourable Addenda to hereditary Arms, specially granted by the Sovereign to individuals in recognition of some extraordinary public service. The Arms ascribed to EDWARD the CONFESSOR — *Azure ; a Cross Patonce between five Martlets or*—and granted by RICHARD the SECOND to THOMAS, EARL of SURREY, and THOMAS MOWBRAY, DUKE of NORFOLK—are probably the earliest examples of Augmentations to Arms upon record. These Arms were impaled with those of the noble recipients ; but subsequently Augmentations were, for the most part, charged on an Ordinary, and that Ordinary usually a Quarter or Canton.

Augmentations generally bear an allusion to the particular act by which the grantee distinguished himself. Thus, DUNCAN KEITH, of Dunotter Castle, Kincardineshire, who, during the usurpation of Cromwell, safely preserved the Regalia of Scotland, received, as an acknowledgment of his services, permission to blazon in the first and fourth quarters of his Coat, *Gules   a Sceptre and Sword in saltire ; and in chief, a regal Crown, all proper, within an Orle of Thistles or ;* with the Motto, *Quæ amissa salva.*

In commemoration of SIR JOHN RAMSEY having killed RUTHVEN, EARL of GOWRY, when, in the year 1600, he attempted to assassinate JAMES the SIXTH, the King granted the following additional Arms to Sir John, to impale with his paternal coat : *Azure ; a dexter Hand holding a Sword in pale argent, pommelled and hilted or, piercing a human Heart proper, and supporting on the point an Imperial Crown.*

CHARLES the SECOND, having little else to bestow, and certainly nothing of any value which cost him less, granted Augmentations to a great number of his subjects—they duly paying therefor—who remained faithful to his cause during the Interregnum. To the EARL of MACCLESFIELD he granted an Imperial Crown ; and Lions of England to SIR ROBERT HOMES ; ROBINSON, of Crauford ; MOORE, Lord Mayor of London ; and LANE, of Staffordshire. To PENDERELL, and CARELESS (or, as the King afterwards called him, CARLOS), who saved his life at Boscobel, he granted nearly similar Arms—those of the former being, *Argent; on a Mount vert, an Oak-tree proper ; over all, a Fess sable, charged with three Imperial Crowns :* and those of the latter, *or,* and the Fess *gules,* the other Charges remaining the same. To Captain TITUS, the faithful servant of his unfortunate father, who vainly attempted to assist him to escape from Carisbrooke Castle, was granted as an Augmentation, *Or ; on a chief embattled gules, a Lion of England.*

To the paternal Arms of SIR CLOUDESLEY SHOVEL were added, by QUEEN ANNE, as Augmentations of honour, two Crescents and a Fleur-de-lys, for victories gained over the Turks and French. The DUKE of WELLINGTON was permitted to charge upon an Inescutcheon the Union Jack, in commemoration of his distinguished services to the nation. SIR ROBERT HARVEY, K.T.S., bore as his paternal Arms, *Erminois ; on a chief indented gules, three Crescents argent,* but for his services at the battle of Orthes the centre Crescent was absconded, and in its place he was permitted to bear a representation of the gold medal presented to him by H.R.H. the PRINCE REGENT, pendent from a ribbon gules, *fimbriated* azure, beneath it the word ORTHES, and the addition of a Canton ermine, charged with the Insignia of a

M

Knight of the Royal Portuguese Order of the Tower and
Sword, pendent from a ribbon. The Augmentations granted
to LORD NELSON and other Naval and Military Commanders
have already been noticed at page 39. To SIR HUMPHRY
DAVY, the inventor of the safety-lamp, was conceded, as an
Augmentation, *A Flame proper, encompassed by a Chain,
issuant from a Civic Wreath or ;* with the Motto, *Igne con-
stricto, vita secura.*

An Augmentation of honour is not restricted solely to
the Shield of him to whom it was granted, but is transmitted
with the hereditary Arms to his descendants.

ABATEMENTS, at one time rigorously enforced, have long
since fallen into disuse. At the present day, when the
bearing of Arms is entirely optional, it seems strange that
men should not have renounced all claim to Armorial distinction, rather than bear about with them such palpable
marks of disgrace. But in former times this was impossible,
for every man who claimed to have inherited gentle blood
was obliged to bear Arms if he would maintain his position ;
and the knowledge that any action which he might commit
unworthy of his knighthood would, if detected, be made
patent to the world, undoubtedly tended, in no small degree,
to make him show at least an outward respect to the
amenities of Society, to which otherwise he might be inclined
to pay but scant regard. Shakespeare thus alludes to the
restraining influence which a fear of public degradation
might exercise over the mind of one who respected no higher
tribunal than that of men's opinions :

> ' Yea, though I die, the scandal will survive,
>   And be an eyesore in my golden coat ;
>   Some loathsome dash the Herald will contrive
>   To cipher me.'

Abatements, which were represented upon the Escutcheon
by voiding certain parts thereof, were liable to be imposed
for any of the following misdemeanours : a knight revoking
his challenge ; deserting the banner of his sovereign ; vainly

boasting of martial achievements ; ' demeaning himself not well in battle ; ' killing a prisoner with his own hands, when not justified by self-defence ; uttering a lie to his sovereign ; effeminacy ; drunkenness and licentious conduct ; acting as a traitor towards his King and Country. For this last crime, the most disgraceful of all, the Escutcheon was condemned to be borne reversed. (See *Harl. MS. No.* 6079, *ff.* 11*b et seq., Mus. Brit.*)

As an instance of Abatements, I need only suggest to the reader the Black Knight, in *Ivanhoe* and his remarks on the subject.

Helm of Richard, Earl of Arundel, from his seal (A.D. 1346).

CHAPTER XIV

CORONETS AND HELMETS

CORONETS are Crowns worn by Princes and Nobles on state occasions, and are always represented above their Coats of Arms. To every grade of Nobility is assigned a Coronet of a peculiar form, by which the rank of the possessor is readily apparent. The original purpose which Coronets were intended to serve appears to have been simply as fillets to confine the hair, and, as such, they were adopted at a very early period. During the reign of EDWARD the THIRD, they were ornamented with leaves, but were not then used as marks of distinction of rank, as at the present day ; for they are to be seen on the monumental effigies of Nobles of every degree. They were also worn by ladies, as appears by illuminations and monumental effigies of the Fourteenth and Fifteenth Centuries. In ARUNDEL CHURCH, BEATRICE, COUNTESS of ARUNDEL (*temp. Henry V.*), is represented with a coronet, as on next page ; and in EWELME

CHURCH, Co. Oxford, ALICE, DUCHESS of SUFFOLK, appears with a Coronet very similar to that of JOHN of ELTHAM. (See heading of Chap. XV.)

Coronets, however, were not devised and worn solely as ornaments ; for, although they did not by their form distinguish the various grades of Nobility, yet they were employed in the ceremony of conferring such dignities ; as appears from the will of LIONEL, DUKE of CLARENCE (A.D. 1368), whereby he bequeaths 'two golden circles,' with one of which he was created a Duke, and, with the other, the

Fig. 324.—Head-dress of Beatrice, Countess of Arundel, from her effigy in Arundel Church.

title of Prince was conferred upon his brother Edward. RICHARD, EARL of ARUNDEL, in his will, which bears date the 5th of December, 1375, devises to his eldest son, Richard, his *meliure Coronne ;* to his daughter, Lady Joan, his *seconde meliure Coronne ;* and to another daughter, Lady Alice, his *tierce Coronne,* or third best Coronet : from which it appears that they were formerly worn merely as ensigns of Nobility, arbitrarily assumed, and without any Royal warrant for the same, or restrictions as to their use or descent.

The Coronet encircling the Bascinet of EDWARD the BLACK PRINCE, as represented on his effigy in Canterbury

Cathedral (see Frontispiece), affords a good example of the ornamentation in vogue towards the close of the Fourteenth Century. Half an hour's attentive study of this and other effigies, which are so admirably reproduced in the Crystal Palace, would be of more practical service to the student of Arms and Armory, than a day's hard reading of a printed book.

The accompanying illustrations (figs. 325 and 326), are taken respectively from the effigies of JOHN of ELTHAM, EARL of CORNWALL, second son of King EDWARD the SECOND, in

Fig. 325.

Fig. 326.

Westminster Abbey (A.D. 1334), and of THOMAS, DUKE of CLARENCE, second son of HENRY the FOURTH, in St. Michael's Chapel, in Canterbury Cathedral (A.D. 1420).

The Coronet of HIS ROYAL HIGHNESS THE PRINCE OF

WALES differs from the Imperial Crown of England (fig. 361) in having a single, instead of a double, Arch ; and the Cap being of Crimson in the place of Purple velvet. The Ball on the top which supports the Cross is termed a *Mound*.

Fig. 327.

The younger sons of her Majesty possess Coronets resembling that of the Prince of Wales, except that they are not enarched, and that on the top of

the Crimson Cap is a golden tassel. The Coronet of the
DUKE of CAMBRIDGE has Strawberry-leaves substituted for
Fleurs-de-lys on the rim, the Crosses paté remaining unchanged. The various modifications in form to which Crowns
and regal Coronets have at different periods been subjected
will be found noticed at greater length in Chapter XVII.

A DUKE'S Coronet (fig. 328) is composed of a circle of
gold richly chased, and *guarded* with Ermine, having on the
rim eight Strawberry-leaves of equal height, five of which
are shown in illustrations. All the Caps of the Coronets of
the Nobility are of crimson velvet. A *Ducal Coronet* serving
as a *Crest Coronet* (figs. 236 and 339) is not furnished with
a Cap, and may exhibit but three Strawberry-leaves.

The Coronet of a MARQUESS (fig. 329) is *heightened* with

Fig. 328.

Fig. 329.

four Strawberry-leaves, and as many Pearls, or balls of
silver, set on low pyramidical points, which alternate with
the leaves, — all being of equal height. Two of the Pearls,
and three of the leaves, are to be seen in drawings.

An EARL'S Coronet (fig. 330) has eight Pearls set on as

Fig. 330.

Fig. 331.

many lofty rays or spikes, alternating with Strawberry-leaves of about one-fourth their height. Four of the latter, and five of the former, are represented in illustrations.

The Coronet of a VISCOUNT (fig. 331) is ensigned with fourteen or sixteen Pearls, which are placed close together, and rest on the circle. The privilege of wearing Coronets was accorded to Viscounts by James the First.

The MITRES of ARCHBISHOPS and BISHOPS—which in Episcopal Coats of Arms supply the place of Helmet and Crest—may justly be regarded as Coronets. A Mitre is a circle of gold, from which rises a high Cap cleft from the top

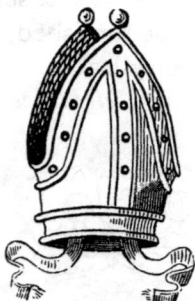

Fig. 332.

Fig. 333.

(fig. 332). From within the circle depend two *Vittæ*, or *Infulæ*, or ribbons of purple, fringed at the ends with gold. Before the Eighteenth Century, no variation in form was observed to designate the distinction between the Mitres of Bishops and Archbishops ; both alike rose from a plain circle of gold. In the north window of the Library of LAMBETH PALACE are displayed the Arms of a great number of the Archbishops of Canterbury. These Arms are ensigned with Archiepiscopal Mitres, which, prior to the year 1715 (with one exception), rise from a plain circle. The exception to which I allude is that of Archbishop JUXON (*ob.* 1662), whose Mitre rises from a circle having several pearls visible on the rim. The Arms of the same prelate (dated 1660) are also depicted in the Hall of GRAY'S INN, where the circle appears without the pearls. In the window at LAMBETH PALACE, the Mitre of

Archbishop WAKE (1715) rises from a Ducal Coronet, which manner of representation has been adopted by all succeeding Archbishops (fig. 333).

The illustration (fig. 334) is taken from the Mitre of Archbishop LAUD (beheaded 1645), sculptured over a door in the 'post-room' at LAMBETH PALACE. In this example, it will be observed that the arches of the Mitre spring directly from the circle.

Fig. 334.

The Bishops of DURHAM, as former EARLS of the PALATINATE, and the Bishops of MEATH, ensign their Shields of Arms with an Archiepiscopal Mitre ; from that of the first-named prelate there issues from the sinister cleft a plume of feathers, as a mark of their temporal dignity. Mitres do not appear to have been actually worn (except by Bishops of the Roman Catholic Church) since the Coronation of Queen Elizabeth. Subsequently to that period they have been considered only as heraldic insignia. Much valuable information on the subject of Mitres will be found in the *Gentleman's Magazine*, vol. xlviii. p. 209 ; and in *Notes and Queries*, Second Series, vol. ix. p. 67.

A BARON'S Coronet is fashioned in the same manner as a Viscount's, except that it has no Jewels set around the circle, and is ornamented with but six pearls, of which four are seen in profile. Previous to the reign of CHARLES the SECOND, Barons wore simply a Crimson Cap guarded with *miniver*—a

Fig. 335.

plain white fur. Sir Symonds d'Ewes, in a letter giving an account of the Coronation of Charles the First, expressly states that, when the higher grades of Peers put on their Coronets, the Barons sat bareheaded. The wives of Nobles are entitled to the same Coronets as their husbands. Although the Coronets of British Nobles are all furnished with Caps of velvet, they are not absolutely essential. The Coronet, strictly speaking, is the circle, and the distinguishing ornaments upon its rim.

In addition to the before-mentioned Coronets, there are others which should more properly be considered but as common Charges, inasmuch as they do not constitute the recognised insignia of any particular rank, but may be borne by either Peer or Commoner. They are frequently employed as *Crest Coronets*—that is, Coronets from which the Crest issues.

The EASTERN, or ANTIQUE, Crown (fig. 336) is of gold, and is composed of a circle, from which rise an indefinite number of rays.

The CELESTIAL Crown differs from the Eastern in having its rays somewhat slighter and higher, and each charged on the top with a small Étoile, or star.

The MURAL Crown (fig. 337)—also of gold—has the

Fig. 336.

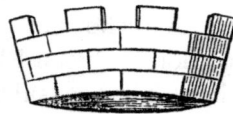

Fig. 337.

circle *masoned* and the top *embattled*. It was conferred by the Romans on the soldier who first scaled the walls of a besieged town.

The NAVAL Crown (fig. 338) bears, on the rim of the circle, the sterns of vessels, alternating with masts, on each of which is affixed a large sail.

Fig. 338.

Fig. 339.

The VALLERY Crown is represented by a number of stakes or pales—usually six to eight—sharpened at the points, rising from the rim of the circle. When the stakes appear as though they were nailed to the outer side of the circle, the Crown is known as a CROWN PALLISADO.

A DUCAL Coronet (fig. 339), when placed beneath a Crest, or around the neck of an Animal, is represented without a Cap, and as exhibiting but three leaves.

The CHAPEAU, or CAP OF MAIN-TENANCE, formerly worn by Dukes, and even by Kings, has long since ceased to be regarded as an emblem of dignity. A few families bear it as a Charge ; but it is generally to be seen supporting the Crest in the place of a *Wreath*.

Fig. 340.

The HELMET—one of the most important pieces of defensive armour—has at various times undergone many altera-tions of material and form, according to the different methods of warfare which have rendered such changes ex-pedient. It is not, however, necessary in this place to con-sider the various modifications to which it has been subjected in an *Armourial*, but simply in an *Armorial*, point of view. As with Coronets, so with Helmets, there appears formerly to have existed no specific regulation by which the form was changed according to the rank of the bearer. The assign-ment of particular forms to the various grades of the greater and lesser Nobility is of comparatively recent institution, certainly not anterior to the reign of Queen Elizabeth.

Every Achievement of Arms is ensigned with a Helmet. Baronets', Knights', Esquires', and Gentlemen's rest on the upper part of the shield ; those of Peers are placed over their respective Coronets.

The ROYAL HELMET (fig. 341) is of gold. It stands affronté, and is guarded with six *Bars, Bailes,* or *Grilles.*

The Helmet of DUKES and MARQUESSES also stands affronté, and is made of steel, guarded with five bars of gold.

The Helmets of EARLS, VISCOUNTS, and BARONS are of silver, garnished with gold. They are always represented in profile, and guarded with ten steel bars, half of which number is visible.

Fig. 341.

BARONETS and KNIGHTS have their Helmets of steel, garnished with silver. They are placed affronté ; and, instead of bars, are furnished with a Visor, or Beaver, which is raised, exhibiting the crimson lining within.

The Helmet assigned to ESQUIRES and GENTLEMEN is of steel. It is represented in profile, with the Visor closed (fig. 342).

Fig. 342.

The BASCINET was a Helmet without a Visor, which fitted close to the head, and is sometimes, though rarely, used as a Charge.

A very effective and becoming form of Helmet, adapted for any Achievement of Arms, is that which was generally used at Tournaments, styled a TILTING-HELMET. This was a second Helmet, which was attached to the armour by a ring and chain, or a buckle (see Title-page). The inner Helmet was usually a Bascinet, or Coif of Mail. In the *Romance of Guy of Warwick* we read :

> ' An helm he had upon his head yset,
> And ther-under a thick basnet.'

When not actually engaged in the Field, the Knight commonly carried the outer Helmet slung over his back by a chain ; and is so represented in several old Illuminations. For a full description of the various defensive coverings for the head, the reader is referred to Sir Samuel Meyrick's *Critical Inquiry into Ancient Armour,* Hewitt's *Ancient Armour and Weapons,* and Planché's *Cyclopædia of Costume.*

Fig. 343.

Crest, Coronet, and Helmet of RICHARD BEAUCHAMP, EARL OF WARWICK, from his Effigy in St. Mary's Church, Warwick (A.D. 1439).

Coronet, from effigy of Alice, Duchess of Suffolk A.D. 1475.

CHAPTER XV

CREST, WREATH, MANTLING, SUPPORTERS, MOTTO, ARMES PARLANTES, ETC.

THE adoption of CRESTS, as a ready means of distinguishing military leaders when engaged in battle,
is of very ancient origin : anterior, probably, to the period
in which escutcheonal Arms were instituted, and certainly
earlier than when such Arms became hereditary.   The right
of bearing a Crest was considered even more honourable than
that of Coat Armory ; for to the latter a Noble would succeed by birth, but to obtain the former he must have been a
Knight in actual service.   The earliest recorded Royal concession of a Crest was by EDWARD the THIRD, who, in the
year 1335, conferred upon WILLIAM DE MONTACUTE, EARL of
SALISBURY, an Eagle ; and ' that he might the more decently
preserve the honour of the said Crest,' the King bestowed
upon him, at the same time, the Manors of WODETON,

FROME, WHITFIELD, MERSHWODE, WORTH, and POLE ; which Crest and Estates MONTACUTE, by the permission of the King, subsequently conferred upon his godson, PRINCE LIONEL of ANTWERP.

The Crest was generally composed of leather, but sometimes of metal ; and towards the end of the Thirteenth Century, not only appeared on the Helmet of the Knight, but was affixed to the head of his charger ; thus rendering both horse and rider conspicuous to the soldiers.   The Seal of PATRICK DUNBAR, EARL of MARCH (A.D. 1292), engraved in Laing's *Ancient Scottish Seals*, affords a fine example of a Fan Crest thus borne.

Crests belonging essentially to the *person* of a military commander—in this respect differing from the Badge, which all his dependents and retainers were permitted to bear—it necessarily follows that Ladies were not allowed to display them over their Arms, which prohibition still obtains.

The Crest appears originally to have been taken from the principal Charge in the Shield ; sometimes the Coat

Fig. 344.

Fig. 345.

Fig. 346.

itself furnished the Crest, as in the instance of Sir GEOFFREY de LOUTERELL, *circa* 1340 (fig. 345).   ROGER de QUINCY,

EARL of WINCHESTER, whose Arms were Mascles, bore a
Wyvern for a Crest (fig. 344) ; and a Lion statant guardant
was the Crest of EDWARD the THIRD (fig. 346).

Among the French Nobility, the Crest is generally
neglected ; but its adoption by the Germans is carried to an
absurd extent.   They ensign a Shield of Arms with as many
Crests, supported by Helmets, as there are families whose
Armorial Bearings appear on the Escutcheon.   When the
number is even, the helmets are placed in profile, *respecting*
each other : and when uneven, the middle one is *affronté*, the
others being in profile on both sides, as before.   In England
we occasionally see two or more Crests placed over a Shield ;
but if we consider the purpose which they are designed to
serve, this practice is manifestly incorrect.   Some writers
have asserted that if a man should marry an Heiress, he and
his descendants are permitted to bear her paternal Crest as
well as Arms ; but this can scarcely be ; for a lady is not
entitled to a Crest, and she surely cannot confer on another
that to which she has no right herself.   The various branches
of a family should always *difference* their Crests with the same
Marks of Cadency that they may bear upon their Escutcheon.

The Helmet was formerly encircled with a Coronet, or

Fig. 347.

a WREATH, which was composed of two
strands of twisted silk, on which the Crest
appeared to be supported, and it is so represented in modern Heraldry.   The Wreath,
Bandeau, or Torse (sometimes, though
improperly, styled a Chaplet), was probably adopted from
the Saracens by the Crusaders, who found that it afforded an
additional defence to the head from the heat of the sun,
as well as from the blows of the enemy.   It is composed of
six twists, and derives its tinctures from the Shield and
Charges which it ensigns.   The predominant metal and
colour appear alternately, the metal towards the Dexter.
In the case of a quartered Shield, the tinctures are derived
from that Coat of Arms to which the Crest appertains.

Furs are never employed in the composition of a Wreath. When the predominant tincture of a Field is a fur, the Wreath is formed by combining either the metal or colour of which such fur consists with the tincture of the principal Charge, or *vice versâ*. Thus, if a Coat of Arms were *Ermine ; a Fess gules*, the Wreath would be *argent*, and *gules* ; if the Coat were *Ermine ; a Fess or*, the Wreath would be *or*, and *sable*—the sable, in this case, being taken from the ermine.

From Monumental Effigies which still exist, we learn that, during the Middle Ages, it was customary to enrich the

Fig. 348.

Wreath with embroidery, and sometimes with precious stones. The Bascinet of RALPH NEVILLE, EARL of WESTMORLAND (fig. 348), who died during the reign of King HENRY the SIXTH, is thus adorned in his effigy in STAINDROP Church DURHAM. Around the Bascinets of SIR EDMUND DE THORPE, in ASHWELTHORPE Church, NORFOLK, and of WILLIAM PHELIP, LORD BARDOLPH, K.G. (A.D. 1440), in DENNINGTON Church (fig. 349), similar wreaths are to be seen. The Helmet of SIR THOMAS DE ST. QUENTIN is represented on his brass in HARPHAM Church, YORKSHIRE (A.D. 1420), as encircled by a wreath composed of feathers.

N

Although Crests are sometimes borne upon Chapeaux, Ducal Coronets, and Mural and Naval Crowns, yet they are always supposed to rest upon Wreaths, unless otherwise

Fig. 349.

specified : it is, therefore, superfluous to blazon a Crest as *upon a Wreath of the colours*, as is sometimes done.

The MANTLING, LAMBREQUIN, or COINTISE is the ornamental accessory which generally appears behind and around the Escutcheon. It was probably devised to protect the Helmet from the rain and sun, in the same manner that the Surcoat protected the Armour.

Fig. 350.

In the accompanying illustration, taken from the Helmet of THOMAS, EARL of LANCASTER, the Cointise is flotant, as it would appear when the bearer was on horseback and galloping swiftly. In heraldic compositions the Mantling is always represented as hanging in graceful folds.

One of the earliest examples in England of a Mantling occurs on the Brass to JOHN of INGHAM, engraved in plate 66 of Stothard's *Monuments*. When the Shield has Supporters, it is usual to represent the Mantling as a Cloak

Fig. 351.

(*Manteau*), or robe of estate. The Royal Mantling is of gold, and that of Peers of crimson velvet, both being lined with ermine. Some authorities, however, insist that the Mantling should derive its colour from the predominant tinctures contained in the Arms, in the same manner as the Wreath. As originally worn, it was of the same tincture as the *Livery Colours*. The Mantlings of Knights and Esquires are commonly depicted as depending from the helmet ; and the curls and other fantastic shapes they are made to assume are supposed to indicate that they have become thus mutilated from service in the Field. The Brass to SIR JOHN SAY in BROXBOURNE Church, HERTFORDSHIRE (A.D. 1473), affords an admirable example of a Mantling (see Title-page), which may be advantageously imitated by the modern Armorist. Another excellent design occurs in the Garter plate of HUMPHREY, EARL of STAFFORD (A.D. 1460), in St. George's Chapel, Windsor (fig. 351). In fact there is scarcely a Knightly effigy of the Fourteenth and Fifteenth Centuries that does not furnish an example of a Helmet and Crest, ensigned with a Lambrequin.

SUPPORTERS are figures of Men, Beasts, Birds, or Imaginary Creatures, which, standing on the Motto-scroll, seem to support the Escutcheon, which is placed between them. Of their origin and period of introduction there exist no authentic records. They probably date from about the time of EDWARD the THIRD ; but what purpose they were originally intended to serve, it is impossible to determine with precision. Menestrier inclines to the belief that they deduce their origin from the Shields of Knights being supported at Tournaments by attendants grotesquely habited, so as to represent Saracens, Lions, Dragons, &c. That Shields were so supported during Tournaments appears from an illuminated manuscript of the Froissart Chronicles, in which a figure disguised as a Lion, having on its head a Tilting-helm, is represented as holding a Shield, paly of six, surmounted by a Bend. In another place, a Sagittarius, armed with a Falchion, is seen guarding a Shield charged with three Piles ; and in the third example, a figure with the body of a Fish and the legs of a Lion (?), habited in a doublet, with a plain Helmet on his head, appears holding a Banner. Anstis, in a Manuscript preserved in the British Museum, attributes the origin of Supporters to the fancy of seal-engravers, ' who, in cutting on seals Shields of Arms, which were in a triangular form, and placed in a circle, finding a vacant space at each side, thought it an ornament to fill up the spaces with vine-branches, garbs, trees, lions, wiverns, or some other animal, according to their fancy.' This is, I think, the most probable hypothesis ; for in some early impressions of seals, the Arms are flanked by Supporters, which in subsequent seals are omitted, or entirely changed. Their number, also, frequently varies ; one, two, or three, indifferently, being borne at short intervals of time, for members of the same family. Again : in examining a

Fig. 352.

collection of ancient seals, the student cannot fail to be struck by the frequent occurrence of creatures resembling Wyverns as Supporters. Now, if these figures were of any material importance to the Achievement, those who adopted them would certainly not have exhibited such extraordinary paucity of invention as to have copied, in almost every instance, the Supporters of others, when so many figures blazoned as Charges were open to their selection. The accompanying outline of the impression of a seal (fig. 352) supposed to have belonged to HUGH O'NEILL, KING of ULSTER, and formerly in the possession of Sir Robert Walpole, exhibits two of these conventionalised animals.   But, granting that these figures legitimately belonged to those families on whose seals they are engraved, it is strange that no such Supporters are borne by their descendants at the present time.   On the seal of ROBERT DE QUINCI, second EARL of WINCHESTER (A.D. 1219–60), engraved in Hewitt's *Armour*, a Wyvern is placed beneath his charger, evidently inserted to fill the vacant space ; and on the counter-seal is a similar figure, and a Fleur-de-lys, for the same purpose. As a further proof that Supporters did not form a distinguishing feature of an Achievement, as they do now, Sir Henry Spelman makes mention of a paper addressed to Pope Boniface the Eighth, in the year 1301, in which the Arms on the seals of twenty-seven nobles are supported by Wyverns ; and of seven others, by Lions.

In Smith's *Antiquities of Westminster*, drawings are given of thirty-five grotesque monsters, employed as Supporters to the Shields, on the lower frieze around St. Stephen's Chapel.   One of these figures is represented at the end of this chapter.

In some of the early impressions of seals, particularly in those of Scotland, the Shield appears to rest on the ground, the Helmet being guarded by either one or two figures ; and sometimes the Shield is suspended by a *Guige*, or belt, around the neck of the Animal which supports it.   (See initial letter, page 19.)   Double Supporters were not generally adopted until the Fourteenth Century.

Over the entrances of regal residences— as at Buckingham Palace—and the lodge-gates of the Seats of the Nobility, we frequently see the Supporters divided, one being placed on either side, each holding an Escutcheon, charged with the Armorial Bearings of the occupant.   On the tomb of MARY QUEEN of SCOTS, in WESTMINSTER ABBEY, her Supporters— two Unicorns—are represented *sejant, affronté,* and each supporting a Shield ; that on the Dexter being charged with a *Thistle, Imperially crowned ;* and that on the Sinister with a *Rose*, similarly ensigned. The golden Lion and red Dragon of Elizabeth are represented in the same manner on her monument, supporting the Cognisances of England and Ireland.

Although Supporters are generally transmitted unchanged from father to son, yet their use cannot be strictly considered as hereditary ; the regal Heraldry of England affords numerous instances of their arbitrary assumption. HENRY the EIGHTH, for example, on different occasions, ensigned his Arms with no less than five various Supporters.

Regarding the right of bearing Supporters, Dallaway, quoting from a manuscript of Wingfield, York Herald, writes : ' There is little or nothing in precedent to direct their use, . . . which is now chiefly in the greater Nobility, and Knights of the Garter, and persons that were of the Privy Council, or had some command whereby they had the title of Lord prefixed to their style, as Lord Deputy of Ireland, Lord Warden of the Cinque Ports, &c.' At the present day, the use of Supporters is restricted to Peers of the Realm, and Peeresses in their own right ; Knights of the Garter ; Knights Grand Cross of the Bath ; Baronets of Nova Scotia ; and the Heads of the Scottish clans. Their use is also accorded to those sons of Peers who by courtesy are titular nobles. Besides these, there are many families amongst the Gentry who ensign their Escutcheons with these honourable additamenta ; which right they derive either by special grant from the Sovereign, or by prescription— their Ancestors having borne them from time immemorial. Amongst such may be mentioned CAREW, of Surrey ; CHUDLEIGH, HELE, and POMEROY, of Devon ; HILTON, of Durham ; PIERREPONTE, of Notts ; and STAPLETON, of York. Among Scottish families, the use of Supporters is very general.

Robson states that Supporters are granted by Garter King-of-Arms. This is not so : the prerogative rests solely with the Crown ; Supporters being granted as a peculiar

mark of royal favour for eminent services rendered to the
State. Thus, in 1867, her Majesty was pleased to grant
Supporters to BENJAMIN GUINNESS, Esquire, in recognition
of his munificence in restoring the Cathedral of St. Patrick,
in Dublin. In Scotland, Lord Lyon, who occupies a similar
position in that Country to that which Garter holds in
England, is permitted to grant Supporters to such families
as he may deem fit. For information on all subjects connected with Scottish Heraldry, the reader is referred to Seton's
Law and Practice of Heraldry in Scotland ; 8vo, 1863.

The MOTTO is an expressive word, or short, pithy sentence,
which accompanies a Crest, or Coat of Arms. It usually
embodies some sentiment of a religious, warlike, or patriotic
import ; as, *Corona mea Christus,* inscribed by BARON CHET-
WODE ; *Virtutis præmium honor,* by the EARL of DENBIGH ;
and *Pro rege et patriâ,* by EARL LEVEN. Mottoes, however,
very frequently have an allusion to the Arms or Crest of the
bearer : thus, the BULLERS, of Devonshire, bear on their
shield four Eagles displayed, with the Motto, *Aquila non
muscas captat ;*—and a Serpent issuing from a Garb, with the
Motto, *In copiâ cautus,* is the Crest of the DODS, of Shrop-
shire. By far the greatest number of allusive Mottoes is
derived from the family name of the bearers ; thus, the
VERNONS inscribe for Motto, *Ver non semper viret ;* which
may be translated either as 'The Spring is not always
green,' or 'Vernon always flourishes.' The NEVILLE family
have, *Ne vile velis*—'Desire no evil thing,' or 'Desire
Neville.' *Festina lente*—'Hasten slowly,' or 'On slow,' is
the Motto of the ONSLOW family; and *Doe no yll, quoth D'Oyle,*
that of DOYLEY. The family of CORBET inscribes *Deus pas-
cit corvos*—'God feeds the Ravens' (Ravens are heraldically
termed *Corbeaux* or *Corbies*). The Motto of FAIRFAX is
Fari fac. Forte scutum salus ducum is the well-known
Motto of the FORTESCUES, and may mean either, 'A strong
shield,' or 'Fortescue is the safeguard of generals.' The
Scotch family WIGHTMAN bears for a Crest, *A demi-savage*

holding over the dexter shoulder a Club proper ; with the Motto, *A wight man never wanted a weapon.*

The family of DIXIE, of Bosworth, bears for Motto, *Quod dixi, dixi ; Vero nihil verior* is the Motto of the DE VERES ; and *Pollet virtus* of the POLES. The MYPONTS, of Burgundy, emblazoned on their shield a Bridge, for Arms, beneath which they inscribed, *Mi pont est difficile à passer ;* the PIERRE-PONTES, of Nottinghamshire, in allusion to their name, have adopted, *Pie reponete ;* and the Motto of HOLDEN is *Teneo et teneor* ' I hold and am holden.'

Sometimes Mottoes seem to be chosen on account of the harmonious jingle of the words ; thus, the EARL of BALCARRAS has *Astra castra, numen lumen*—'The Stars my canopy, Providence my light.' *Think and thank*, is the Motto of the MARQUESS of AYLESBURY ; and the PEYTONS have adopted *Patior potior.* The SALTERS' COMPANY have for their Motto, *Sal sapit omnia*, and to the Merchant Tailors has been ascribed—probably by some wag, for I can find no authority for it—the admirable motto, *Sit merita laus.* The *merry tailors* of to-day repudiate the motto, and use *Concordiâ parvœ res crescunt*, which may be freely rendered as *A coat is built up of its component parts, deftly cut out, and skilfully sewn together.*

The origin of the Mottoes of some families appears totally inexplicable. *Strike, Dakyns, the Devil's in the hemp*, is the Motto of the DAKINS, of Derbyshire ; *Furth, fortune, and fill the fetters*, of the DUKE of ATHOL ; *Posse, nolle, nobile*, of WINGFIELD of Tickencote ; *If you look at Martin's ape, Martin's ape will look at you*, of the MARTINS, of Gloucestershire. Examples of many similar Mottoes are to be found.

There seem to have formerly existed two classes of Mottoes—the *Cri-de-guerre*, or War-cry, used by the Knight's retainers in the Field ; and the Motto proper, as the word is now understood, which accompanied his personal Arms. Anyone entitled to armorial distinction was permitted to adopt the latter, but the Cri-de-guerre was forbidden to

those below the degree of Knight-Banneret. We sometimes
find, in ancient records, Nobles described as *Nobles d'armes*,
and others as *Nobles-de-cri*.   To such an extent did these
war-cries foster the spirit of partisanship, that, on the
termination of the wars between the rival houses of York
and Lancaster, it was deemed expedient to pass an act of
Parliament, by which it was declared penal for a Noble or
Villein to use any cry except *The King*, or *St. George for
England*. In all ages, and in all countries, warriors, on rush-
ing to a charge, have employed peculiar shouts or *Slogans*,
analogous to the war-whoop of the American Indians.   In
Europe, the *Montjoye St. Andrew* of the Dukes of Burgundy ;
the *Au Lion*, of the Counts of Flanders ; the *Dieu aide au
premier Chrétien*, of the Montmorencies ; and the *Boo*, of
the Irish Chieftains, are of great antiquity. *A Home* was
the slogan of the Earls of Dunbar, to which Sir Walter
Scott refers in the following passage :

> ' Beneath the Crest of old Dunbar
> And Hepburn's mingled banners come,
> Down the steep mountain, glittering far,
> And shouting still, A Home ! A Home !

Though generally transmitted with the family Arms,
Mottoes are not strictly hereditary. An individual is at
liberty to affix to his Escutcheon whatever Motto his fancy
may dictate. It was not until the Fifteenth Century that
Mottoes were considered as important adjuncts to Armorial
Bearings. Before that period, Nobles (except Knights of
the Garter) very rarely ensigned their Achievements with a
Motto. The Seal of Sir John de Byron, appended to a
deed bearing date 1292, and inscribed with the words, *Crede
Beronti*, affords, perhaps, the earliest example of the custom
of adding a Motto to the Arms.

In Achievements of Arms, the Motto is placed below
the Shield, unless it bear direct reference to the Crest, in
which case the Motto usually surmounts it. There are many
ancient families who, though bearing Arms, possess no

Motto ; and its use is in all cases forbidden to Ladies, the Queen excepted.

Arms and Crests frequently deduce their origin from the family name in the same manner as Mottoes ; and when such is the case, they are styled ARMES PARLANTES, or CANTING HERALDRY.   The families of SALMON, STURGEON, LAMB, LUCY, HERRING, SHELLEY, TALBOT, WOLF, RABBETT, FALCONER, &c., bear respectively *Salmons, Sturgeon, Lambs, Lucies* (pike), *Herrings, Whelk-shells, Talbots, Wolves, Rabbits,* and *Falcons.*   The CARDINGTONS bear three *Wool-cards ;* and the HARROWS, as many implements of that name. In the *Lay of the Last Minstrel,* we read :

> ' dancing in the sunny beam,
> He marked the Crane on the Baron's Crest ; '

alluding to BARON CRANSTOUN, whose Crest was a *Crane* holding a *stone* in its foot.   BARON FERMOY, whose family name is ROCHE, bears for Crest, *a Sea-eagle standing on a rock* (roche), *holding in its claw a Roach ;* with the Motto, *Mon Dieu est ma roche.*   The Crest of the HERONS is a bird of that name, subscribed with the Motto, *Ardea petit ardua.* The Motto of the EASTWOODS—*Oriens sylvâ*—is a literal rendering of their name : it likewise has a punning reference to the Crest—a Stag—which may be said to be *rising from the wood.*   Why, however, the family of WOTTON, of Marlay, Co. Kent, should bear for Crest, Satan's head sable, with azure wings, is not easy to determine.

A Weir-basket filled with fish appears on a seal of WILLIAM WEARE, of Wear Gifford, Devonshire (*temp.* Hen. IV.), with the Motto, *Sumus*—'We are.'

A good example of allusive Arms, though, perhaps, scarcely coming under the denomination of Armes parlantes, was the Device of MARY QUEEN of SCOTS, assumed after the death of her husband, the Dauphin ; which was, *a Stalk of Liquorice,* 'duquel la racine est douce, mais tout le reste, hors de terre, amer ; ' with the Motto, *Dulce meum terra tegit ;* 'The Earth covers my sweetness.'

We have seen how Armorial Bearings are sometimes taken from family names : but it is very probable that in many instances this order was reversed ; and that the Scutal Device furnished a name to its possessor.   Of the many Nobles who accompanied the Conqueror to England, but few, if any, were distinguished by surnames; they were described simply by their Christian names, followed by the locality whence they came; as, ROBERT DE COURÇON, JOHANNES DE BOURGOGNE, &c.   Even the Conqueror's sons, WILLIAM and HENRY, were distinguished by such names as RUFUS and BEAUCLERC.   Hereditary surnames were not generally adopted in England, even amongst the Nobility, until the Fourteenth Century ; yet long anterior to that period we find Nobles designated by the name of the Charge which they bore upon their shields, which names and bearings have descended to their posterity.   (See DR. E. NARES, and M. A. LOWER, on SURNAMES.)   HUGH, first Earl of CHESTER, undoubtedly derived his appellation, DE LOUPE, from his device, which was a Wolf's head : and in an old manuscript attributed to William de Brito (A.D. 1170), the poet thus sings the praises of one of the ancestors of the ARUNDEL family, whose bearing was then, as it has since continued, a Swallow—in French, *Hirondelle:*

' More swift than bird hight Arundell,
   That gives him name, and in his shield of Arms emblazoned well,
   He rides amid the armèd troops.'

Fig. 353.—Supporter to a Shield, from the lower frieze around St. Stephen's Chapel, Westminster.   From Smith's ' Antiquities of Westminster.'

CHAPTER XVI

DEGREES OF THE NOBILITY AND GENTRY

BEFORE treating of the various grades of Rank as they now exist, it will be necessary to give a short account of the origin of those degrees, and to explain by what right they continue to be enjoyed.

One of the first official acts of WILLIAM of NORMANDY, after his accession to the throne of England, was to assume actual possession of nearly all the land, which he divided into 700 BARONIES, or great fiefs, and these were subdivided into about 60,000 KNIGHT'S FEES. The Baronies were apportioned amongst his Norman followers who had assisted him in his enterprise, on condition of their performing certain offices,—such as giving personal service when required ; providing and equipping men for the Field ; and executing other duties connected with the Royal Household.[1]

---

[1] Sir William Hale, in his *Pleas of the Crown*, asserts that no Englishman was permitted by the Conqueror to retain any landed property in England ; and that it was nearly three centuries after William's death before a Saxon held any higher dignity than that of a Knight's Fee. This assertion, however, is refuted by the pages of *Domesday Book* ; and I recently examined a Charter preserved in the library of the City Corporation, whereby William granted to one Dereman, an Englishman, considerable tracts of land in the Counties of Essex and Hertford. Several other instances might be cited of similar concessions being made to Englishmen. Turchill, for example, —the ancestor of the Ardens of Warwickshire,—as early as the Eleventh Century, was lord of a great portion of that County.

The tenants-in-chief from the Crown, who held lands of the annual value of four hundred pounds, were styled BARONS ; and it is to them, and not to the members of the lowest grade of the Nobility (to whom the title at the present time belongs), that reference is made when we read of the Barons of the early days of England's history.

Many of the Baronies conferred by the Conqueror were of immense extent, and frequently comprised *Baroniæ in Baroniis*, by the original tenants *in capite* from the Crown making concessions to some of their vassals, in the same manner as they themselves held their possessions from the King. These secondary Lords afterwards came likewise to be styled Barons—as appears from a Charter of WILLIAM of GLOUCESTER (*temp.* Hen. II.), which is addressed, *Dapifero suo, et omnibus Baroniis suis.* Hence arose the titles, GREATER and LESSER BARONS.[1]

At the death of WILLIAM the FIRST, there were about 400 Baronies in England ; but so generally did the process of subinfeudation prevail, that during the succeeding century the number was enormously increased. King JOHN, fearing that the Barons would become too powerful in the kingdom,

---

[1] 'About this time' (the Twelfth Century), 'it is observed that those who were either menial attendants or else feudatories to any Noble personage, or which held any lands of them, did usually assume to themselves for their Armes the Device of ye Coate of ye Lord, either changing the colours retaining the Charge, or by adding something to ye Charge—as, for example, Albayne, Lord of Belvoir, bore Or, two Cheverons and a Cantone gules ; from him, Staunton of Staunton, a gentleman of Nottinghamshire, bears Argent, two Cheverons and a bordure sable, and held his lands of ye said Albayne by the tenure of Castleward, by keeping and defending a tower in the Castle of Belvoir,' &c. (*Harl. MSS. No.* 4630). This Manuscript also contains : 'The originall and beginning of sirnames : ' 'Names varied according to ye dwelling of ye partys, and changed upon entry into religion ; ' 'The meanes of our Ancestors attaining unto the rank of Nobility ; ' 'The first using of seales to Charters and Deeds here in England ; ' 'Punishments inflicted for counterfeiting another's seale ; ' 'Armes, when first hereditary.'

attempted to check the practice ; but he was too irresolute, or too weak, to accomplish it. EDWARD the FIRST vigorously carried out the intentions of his predecessor, and by the most severe enactments abolished the continuance of a custom which from experience he had learned was fraught with so much danger to the Crown. HENRY the THIRD, however, had some years before struck a fatal blow at the power of the Barons, all of whom, hitherto, had been privileged to assemble for the purpose of assisting the King in the affairs of state ; but HENRY determined that that privilege should be accorded but to certain whom he selected. WRITS were therefore despatched, in the King's name, to a chosen number of the Barons, including some of the lesser degree, or those who did not hold *in capite* from the Crown ; and the Writ thus issued constituted the receiver, and his heirs general, Peers of the Realm, to the exclusion of many of those who had hitherto enjoyed that privilege ; and proof of tenure *per baroniam* was no longer required.

It would appear that the issue of a Writ of Summons was not sufficient of itself to elevate him to whom it was addressed to the rank of Baron, unless he actually fulfilled the duties to which he was called ; for in the reign of JAMES the FIRST, one of the descendants of EDWARD NEVILLE—who had been summoned to Parliament by QUEEN MARY, but died before taking his seat—claimed the hereditary Barony. The decision at which the Council arrived was, that 'the direction and delivery of the Writ did not make him a Baron or Noble until he came to Parliament, and there sat, according to the commandment of the Writ.' The custom of issuing Writs is now disused, except when a Barony, which has been in *Abeyance* (of which more hereafter), is terminated by the Crown in favour of a Commoner, and occasionally to the eldest sons of Dukes, Marquesses, and Earls, in their fathers' Baronies. A Writ of Summons, however, in the latter case, does not create an hereditary peerage, but becomes null as soon as the receiver succeeds to his father's title.

Of all the original Baronies by feudal tenure, not one remains.[1]   Several families have at various times attempted to revive Baronies, alleging that they held estates in tenure *per Baroniam* from the Crown ; but these applications have invariably been resisted.   In the year 1669,—when the Barony of FITZWALTER was revived in favour of Benjamin Mildmay, the heir general, in opposition to Robert Cheeke, who claimed it by right of tenure,—the King and Privy Council passed a resolution that, 'as no such Baronies had for many ages existed,' it was not expedient to bring them again into force ; and the House of Lords has in every instance, when called upon, confirmed this Order of the Council.

In the reign of RICHARD the SECOND, Barons were created not only by Writ of Summons, but by PATENT, by which the succession was restricted to the male heir of the grantee ; and in this manner Commoners are usually elevated to the Peerage at the present day.

The Earldom of WILTS—the succession to which was recently claimed—was created by letters patent bearing date the 27th September 1397, in the person of Sir William Scrope, to hold the same to him and his heirs male for ever.   Sir William died the following year without issue, since which time the title had never been claimed by any of his representatives.   The Earldom of OXFORD was also conferred by Richard II. with a similar limitation.   At the time that Sir William Scrope was created a Peer, King Richard raised six Earls to the rank of Dukes, the EARL of SOMERSET to the rank of MARQUESS of DORSET, and three Barons to the rank of Earls ; in each instance limiting those honours

---

[1] The Earldom of Arundel, belonging to the DUKE of NORFOLK in right of his tenure of Arundel Castle, may, perhaps, be quoted as an exception.   His Grace, however, holds the Earldom by favour of a special Act of Parliament, passed in the reign of Charles the First.

to the heirs male of the grantees. Subsequently, King Henry the Sixth created Sir Thomas Hoo, Lord Hoo and Hastings ; Sir Thomas Percy, Lord Egremont ; and Sir Thomas Grey, Lord Richmont Grey ; with limitations to their heirs male. No other grant of dignity, with a distinction to the heirs male, has since been conferred in England, with the sole exception of the Earldom of Devon, granted by Queen Mary. Of the above-mentioned Peerages, Oxford and Devon only exist, the others having become extinct. The House of Lords, in 1625, declared Robert de Vere entitled to the Earldom of Oxford ; and in 1831, their Lordships allowed that William, Viscount Courtenay, had made out his claim to the title, honour, and dignity of Earl of Devon, and thereby established that the grant of a dignity to the grantee and his heirs male was valid, and that the succession was thereby lawfully and effectually limited to the collateral heirs male.

Besides that of succession, there is another difference between a Writ and a Patent. When a barony is conferred by Patent, the title—both personal and hereditary—is complete as soon as the official seal is affixed to the document, although the baron thus created may have never taken his seat in Parliament.

Should a Noble, holding his Barony by Writ, die leaving two or more daughters and no son, the title would fall into Abeyance ; for, there being no distinction of primogeniture amongst daughters, as there is with sons, they would each be entitled to an equal division of their father's estate ; but the title being imparticipable, it must necessarily remain unattached so long as both co-heirs female, or their descendants, remain alive. A Barony, held by virtue of a Writ, having fallen into Abeyance, cannot revive naturally until but one branch remains to represent the Family : the Crown, however, possesses the power of determining an Abeyance at any time—a prerogative seldom exercised. When an Abeyance is terminated in favour of a Commoner,

o

he receives the Barony by a Writ of Summons ; but if in favour of a Peer, by a Patent. A Barony held by Patent can never fall into Abeyance ; for, the title descending to heirs male, and not to heirs general, when such heirs fail it becomes extinct—as in the case of the late VISCOUNT PALMERSTON.

The terms ' IN ABEYANCE ' and ' DORMANT ' are, by many persons, considered as synonymous. This, however, is not the case. A title is necessarily in Abeyance while co-heirs survive, each having an equal claim : it is Dormant when the rightful possessor, for any reason, such as inability or disinclination to support his dignity, neglects to assume the rank to which he is entitled.

The hereditary possessor of a Peerage title, notwithstanding he may be a minor, is *de facto* a Peer of the Realm, although he is ineligible for some of the higher privileges of his order, such as sitting in Parliament.   Ladies also may sometimes be Peeresses of the Realm in their own right, as in the case where dignities descend to heirs general.   Every Peer in Parliament is possessed of equal privileges irrespective of his rank.

' All Noblemen were Barons, or had a Barony annexed, though they had also higher dignities. But it has sometimes happened that when an ancient baron has been raised to a new degree of peerage, in the course of a few generations the two titles have descended differently ; one, perhaps, to the male descendents, the others to the heirs general ; whereby the Earldom or other superior title has subsisted without a Barony ; and there are also modern instances where they have been created without annexing a Barony.   So that now the rule does not hold universally, that all Peers are Barons.'—*Robson.*

The ARCHBISHOP of CANTERBURY enjoys the highest rank in the British Peerage, immediately following that of the Royal Dukes. To him succeed the LORD HIGH CHANCELLOR, and the Archbishops, in the following order : YORK, ARMAGH, and DUBLIN. The ARCHBISHOP of CANTERBURY is

'Primate of all England,' and subscribes himself, 'By Divine Providence.' It is his duty to officiate at Coronations, and all religious ceremonies connected with the Royal Family, the members of which have always been considered as his Parishioners. His principal officers are Bishops : the Bishop of London is his Provincial Dean ; the Bishop of Winchester, his Chancellor ; the Bishop of Lincoln, his Vice-Chancellor ; the Bishop of Salisbury, his Precentor ; and the Bishop of Rochester, his Chaplain. The Archbishop of York is ' Primate of England,' and is styled ' By Divine Permission.' An Archiepiscopal Mitre is shown at page 180, and a Crosier at page 114. The Arms of the See of Canterbury are : *Azure ; an Archiepiscopal Staff in pale or, ensigned with a Cross paté argent, surmounted by a Pall of the last, fimbriated and fringed gold, charged with four Crosses paté and fitché sable.* The Arms of York are : *Gules ; two Keys in saltire argent ; in Chief, an Imperial Crown of England.* It will be remembered that Bishops impale the Arms of their Sees with their own.[1] Archbishops are styled ' Most Reverend ; ' and are addressed as ' Your Grace ; ' but their wives derive no title from the official position of their husbands.

The next in order are Dukes. The title, derived from the Latin *Dux*, signifies a leader, and is employed in that sense by old writers. Sir John Ferne (A.D. 1586) describes the Israelites as ' pitching their tents in the wildernesse, vnder the conduct of their captaine, Duke Moyses.' The first English subject who was created a Duke was Edward Plantagenet, by his Father, Edward the Third, in the year 1335, under the title of Duke of Cornwall. Anterior to this date, the nobility consisted entirely of Barons, and a few Earls. The title of Duke was for some time confined

---

[1] One Archbishop and three Bishops represent the spiritual Peers of Ireland in Parliament. The Archbishops of Armagh and Dublin sit alternately from session to session ; and the Bishops in the following rotation : Ossory, Cork, Killaloe, Meath, Kilmore, Cashel, Tuam, Derry, Limerick, and Down.

exclusively to members of the Royal Family, and was but sparingly conferred ; but by HENRY the SIXTH this restriction was not so particularly observed. On the accession of QUEEN ELIZABETH to the throne there existed but one Duke in England—THOMAS HOWARD, of NORFOLK ; the other Dukedoms having become extinct through failure of male issue, or on attainders of Treason, during the Wars of the Roses. In 1572, the DUKE of NORFOLK himself suffered at the hands of the executioner. From that time until 1623, when JAMES the FIRST created George Villiers DUKE of BUCKINGHAM, the title was extinct. CHARLES the SECOND restored the dignity in several families, and created others, including the Dukedoms of GRAFTON, ST. ALBANS, and RICHMOND, which he conferred upon three of his illegitimate sons. The Order received several further additions during the reigns of WILLIAM and MARY and of ANNE. The present number of English Dukes is twenty-two ; of Scotch, eight ; and of Irish, two. A Duke is styled ' Your Grace,' and ' Most Noble ;' his eldest son takes his second title, which is usually that of Marquess. This title, however, is only accorded by courtesy : thus, the DUKE of ATHOLE's eldest son would be officially described as ' John George Stewart-Murray, Esquire, commonly called Marquess of Tullibardine.' [1] The younger sons and the daughters of a Duke are addressed as ' Lords ' and ' Ladies,' with the addition of their Christian names, as Lord Henry, Lady Mary.

The next degree in the Peerage is that of MARQUESS. This order was instituted by RICHARD the SECOND, who, in the year 1386, created Robert de Vere, Earl of Oxford,

---

[1] It sometimes occurs that the second title of a Duke or Marquess is not the next lowest in the scale of the peerage. In this case, although their eldest sons would not enjoy the titular ranks of Marquess or Earl respectively, they are equally entitled to the station and Coronet of those degrees. Thus, the eldest son of the Duke of Manchester, though only a Viscount, takes precedence of Earls, and bears the Coronet of a Marquess.

Marquess of Dublin; and, subsequently, Duke of Ireland. In 1388, his Grace was attainted for High Treason, and banished; when the dignity became extinct, until revived, in 1397, in the person of John Beaufort, Earl of Somerset, who was created Marquess of Dorset. A Marquess is addressed personally as 'My Lord Marquess;' and is styled, 'The Most Honourable the Marquess of ——.' The children of a Marquess bear the same courtesy-titles as those of a Duke—the eldest son taking his father's second title: he is therefore styled Earl or Viscount of a place; as Earl of Yarmouth, Viscount Raynham, who are respectively the eldest sons of the Marquess of Hertford, and the Marquess Townshend. The younger sons of a Marquess have no official title of Peerage, although by courtesy such titles are usually accorded, as in the case of the sons of Dukes. Thus, the eldest son of the Marquess of Bath would be officially described as 'Thomas Henry Thynne, Esquire, commonly called Viscount Weymouth.'

The title of Earl is the most ancient of any of the Peerage, dating its origin from the Saxon Kings. Until the close of the Twelfth Century, nobles of this dignity seldom used any other addition than *Comes* to their Christian names; but about the time of Richard the First, they added to their names that of their shire. An Earl is styled 'Right Honourable,' and his eldest son is commonly a Viscount, that being his father's second title. His younger sons have no title of Peerage, and are by courtesy styled 'Honourable;' but all his daughters are 'Ladies.' The wife of an Earl is a Countess.

Viscounts succeed Earls. The title of *Vice-comes* is probably as ancient as that of *Comes*, but it did not constitute an order of the Peerage until the year 1440, when Henry the Sixth conferred the title, by Patent, upon John, Baron Beaumont. A Viscount is 'Right Honourable,' and his sons and daughters are 'Honourable.'

The next in succession are Bishops. The Bishop of

LONDON, as Provincial Dean of Canterbury, takes precedence
of his brethren.   To him succeed the BISHOP of DURHAM,
as formerly holding the rank of Count Palatine, and Earl of
Sedberg ; and the BISHOP of WINCHESTER, as Prelate of the
Most Noble the Order of the Garter ; then the remaining
Bishops, according to the priority of their consecration.[1]
All Bishops are styled 'Right Reverend Father in God ; '
and subscribe themselves, ' By Divine Permission.'

BARONS constitute the lowest grade of the British Nobility.
The origin of this dignity has already been noticed. Barons
are addressed as ' My Lord ; ' and are styled ' Right
Honourable.' All their sons and daughters are 'Honourable.'

The various Coronets of the Nobility are described at
pages 178-181.

The title of *Lord*, although it cannot be said to constitute
a degree of Nobility by itself, has a more general application
than any other, for it is commonly employed in addressing
Peers of every rank.   The Judges, when on the Bench, are
ex-officio Lords; and so, likewise, are the Mayors of London,
Dublin, York, and Belfast, during their terms of office. The
title of *Lady* is used equally indiscriminately, for not only
are the wives and daughters of certain Peers thus addressed,
but also the wives of Baronets and Knights. These last,
although permitted by courtesy to bear the title of Lady, are
not allowed to prefix their Christian to their Family name,
for this is the peculiar privilege and mark of distinction of
the daughters of Peers. Lady Smith may be the wife of
John Smith, who was knighted because he presented an

---

[1] When, during the course of the present reign, the Episcopate was
increased in numbers, it was settled from the first that no addition
should be made to the number then entitled to sit in the House of
Lords.   The Bishops now succeed to a seat by seniority, except the
Archbishops and the Bishops of London, Durham, and Winchester,
who are always to be in the House.   Hence it follows that the seven
junior Bishops—St. Albans, Worcester, Rochester, Peterborough,
Lichfield, Truro, and Carlisle—have not at present a seat in the
Upper House.   The Bishop of Sodor and Man has a seat but no vote.

address on an opportune occasion ; and although her Christian name may be Mary, she must not call herself Lady Mary Smith, for by so doing she would appear to be the daughter of a Peer, and not the wife of a Knight.

It was not until the reign of HENRY the EIGHTH that Kings' daughters were styled Princesses. Previous to that date they were simply designated as 'Lady.' Thus, we find the daughters of HENRY the SEVENTH were styled, 'The Lady Margaret' and 'The Lady Mary.' Even the daughters of HENRY the EIGHTH were occasionally styled 'The Lady Mary' and 'The Lady Elizabeth :' and in a Tract on the Marriage of the daughter of JAMES the FIRST with Prince Frederick, she is spoken of as 'The Ladie Elizabeth.'

Amongst the Gentry, BARONETS take the highest place. The origin of this dignity was as follows : Queen ELIZABETH having succeeded, towards the end of her reign, in reducing Ireland to some degree of order, JAMES the FIRST determined, on his accession to the throne, to continue the work of his predecessor ; but as economy was a distinguishing characteristic of JAMES, he contrived to obtain an army of occupation, and at the same time to enrich the Treasury, by a novel expedient. He directed that the hereditary title of Baronet should be conferred on every gentleman possessed of an estate of the annual value of one thousand pounds who would undertake to maintain, in the Province of Ulster, thirty soldiers for three years, at the rate of eightpence per day for each man, and remit the first year's pay to the Royal Treasury : in return for which service he should have the privilege of bearing the Arms of Ulster (fig. 352), either on an Inescutcheon or Canton, in his paternal shield. These constituted the BARONETS OF ENGLAND.

In 1619, the King instituted a second Order, in every way similar to the former, except that the grantees were styled BARONETS OF IRELAND ; and that they paid their fees into the Treasury of that country.

King JAMES having instituted Baronetcies of England

and Ireland, was desirous of extending the Order to his
native Country, having for his immediate purpose the im-
provement of the Province of Nova Scotia ; but his death
prevented his carrying the project into execution. His son
CHARLES, in 1625, fulfilled his father's intentions ; and he
subsequently directed that the BARONETS OF NOVA SCOTIA
should be distinguished by a Jewel, charged with the Arms
of that Province, viz. *Argent ; a Saltire azure ; on an
Inescutcheon, the Arms of Scotland; above the Shield, an
Imperial Crown:* supported by the Royal Unicorn on the
Dexter side, and by a Savage proper on the Sinister : for
Crest, *A Laurel-branch and Thistle issuing between a naked
and a mailed Hand conjoined ;* with the Motto, *Munit hæc,
et altera vincit.* This Jewel was suspended to the necks of
the Baronets of the Province by an orange ribbon.

Since the Union, no Baronets have been created of Scotland or Ireland, both Institutions having been superseded
by the title of BARONETS OF THE UNITED KINGDOM, who
are distinguished by the Badge of Ulster. Baronetcies are
always conferred by Patent : and the succession is usually
restricted to the heirs male ; though special conditions are
sometimes attached. There is no service required of Baronets
at the present day ; neither is there any money actually paid,
as formerly (except for Heralds' fees, on creation) ; but a
fictitious receipt is issued by the Treasury for the amount
of twelve months' pay for thirty soldiers. For KNIGHTS
BANNERETS, see 'Banner,' Chap. xix.

Baronets have the title of 'Sir' prefixed to their Christian names ; their surnames being followed by their dignity,
usually abbreviated, *Bart.* Their wives are addressed as
'Lady,' 'Madam,' or 'Dame.' This last title, however,
has now become obsolete, except in official documents. Their
sons are possessed of no title beyond 'Esquire.' The rights
and privileges of KNIGHTS are identical with those of
BARONETS, except that they are not hereditary.

The eldest son of a Peer above the dignity of Baron, who

is also a Baronet of Scotland, is styled ' Honourable Master ' of his family Barony ; as, THE HONOURABLE THE MASTER OF FORBES. In the case of a Baron, the Honourable is omitted ; as, THE MASTER OF LOCHMAN.

In 1840, a number of Baronets assembled under the direction of the late Sir Richard Broun, Bart., and formed a *Committee of the Baronetage for Privileges*, wherein were adopted several important resolutions, which, though not officially recognised by the Heralds' College, demand a passing notice. The members of the Committee resolved that all Baronets should take for Supporters, two armed Knights ; for Coronet, a plain circle of gold, with four pearls resting on the edge – which is engrailed—two of them appearing in drawings ; and that the Helmet should be affronté, and open, guarded with four grilles of gold ; and, besides these exterior ornaments, that they should surround their Escutcheons with a Collar of S.S. They likewise determined to prefix to their title that of ' Honourable.' These were the principal modifications suggested ; but they have not been generally adopted.

The office of ESQUIRE formerly constituted a kind of honourable apprenticeship to the profession of Arms, through which all classes of the Nobility were obliged to pass. At the age of fourteen, a youth, having previously served in the capacity of Page, was eligible to be admitted as an Esquire. There were several degrees of this order, as *Esquires of the Stable ; Esquires of the Chamber ; Carving Esquires*, who waited in the Hall, carved the dishes, and served the guests ; and *Esquires for the Body*, who attended their lords in the Field.

In the *Romance of Ipomydon* (*Harl. MS.* 2252, *circa* A.D. 1325), we read how, as a boy, the young prince was instructed in the duties of an Esquire. The king, his father, sought out for him a learned and courteous knight as preceptor ; accordingly,

> ' Tholomew a clerke he toke,
> That taught the child uppon the boke

> Both to synge and to rede ;
> And after he taught hym other dede,
> Afterward to serve in halle
> Both to grete and to smalle ;
> Before the kynge mete to kerve,
> High and low fayre to serve.
> Both of howndes and hawkes game,
> After he taught hym all ; and same
> In sea, in feld, and eke in ryvere ;
> In woode to chase the wild dere,
> And in feld to ryde a stede ;
> That all men had joy of his dede.'

The title of Esquire does not seem to have been adopted in England earlier than the time of RICHARD the SECOND, although the duties connected with the office date from a period far anterior.

Three centuries ago, Sir John Ferne thus speaks of the indiscriminate manner in which the title of Esquire was then applied : 'The title has been very much abused and profaned, whereunto I wish that the Lord Earle Marshall, with the advice and consultation of a learned heralde, would add some sharpe correction and punishment.' See also *Tatler*, No. xix. If, during the Elizabethan Era, the title was applied in too promiscuous a manner, what shall be said of that of the Victorian, when the difficulty is not so much to determine to whom it should be accorded, but to whom it should be denied ?

Wealth alone cannot constitute the slightest claim to this honourable degree. The title is, strictly speaking, confined to the eldest sons of Baronets and Knights ; the youngest sons of Peers and their eldest sons ; Kings-of-Arms, and Heralds who are Esquires by creation ; Esquires of the Bath, on an Installation ; Lords Lieutenant (when not Peers), Deputy Lieutenants and Sheriffs of Counties, Justices of the Peace, and Mayors of Towns, while holding office. There are several other degrees which give the title of Esquire by courtesy : as, Counsellors at Law ;

Bachelors of Divinity, Law, and Physic ; Secretaries of Legation, Consuls, Royal Academicians, &c.

The distinction between a Profession and a Trade, though difficult to define, is tolerably well understood. Modern usance requires that a professional man should be addressed as ' Esquire ' : but a tradesman, however large his establishment may be, is simply Mr. when written to at his place of business. It may happen that that same tradesman *at home*, is a County Magistrate, and keeps up a better estate than the Lord Lieutenant of his County. In such a case there is no impropriety in addressing him as Esquire.

GENTLEMEN are all those who, lawfully entitled to Armorial distinction, are not included in any of the before-mentioned degrees. An interesting paper on GENTLEMEN, too long to quote, will be found in the *London Chronicle*, 31 December, 1771.

The subjoined TABLE OF PRECEDENCE is given to indicate the relative positions of the various ranks of Nobility ; many, therefore, of the Officers of State are omitted. For a complete Table of Precedence, both amongst men and women, the reader is referred to the pages of *Nicholas, Burke*, or *Thom*.

The Sovereign.
The Prince of Wales.
The Sovereign's younger sons.
The Sovereign's grandsons.
The Archbishop of Canterbury.
The Lord Chancellor (being a Baron).
The Archbishops of York, Armagh, and Dublin.
The principal Officers of State (being Barons).
Dukes, according to their priority of Patent.
Eldest sons of Dukes of the Blood Royal.
Marquesses, according to their priority of Patent.
Dukes' eldest sons.
Earls.

Younger sons of Dukes of the Blood Royal.

Marquesses' eldest sons.

Dukes' younger sons.

Viscounts.

Earls' eldest sons.

Marquesses' younger sons.

Bishops of London, Durham, and Winchester.

Other Bishops, according to seniority of consecration.

Irish Bishops.

Barons.

Viscounts' eldest sons.

Earls' younger sons.

Barons' eldest sons.

Privy Counsellors, Judges, &c.

Viscount's younger sons.

Barons' younger sons.

Baronets.

Knights of the various Orders.

Eldest sons of the younger sons of Peers.

Eldest sons of Baronets and Knights.

Esquires.

Gentlemen.

All the unmarried daughters of Peers are entitled to the same rank as their eldest brother usually enjoys during the lifetime of his father. Married ladies and widows take precedence according to the rank of their husbands, provided such rank be not merely official.

It is the generally received opinion that the title of 'Royal Highness' is the hereditary right of all members of the Royal Family. Such is not the case. Strictly speaking, it belongs solely to the immediate issue of the Sovereign. The first innovation made upon this rule was in the year 1816, when FREDERICK WILLIAM, DUKE of GLOUCESTER, grandson of GEORGE the SECOND, was styled 'Royal Highness' on the occasion of his marriage with his cousin, the

Princess Mary. Prior to this event, his title, and that of Princes of a like consanguinity, was simply 'Highness.' Prince Louis of Hesse, and Prince Christian, are styled 'Royal Highness,' not because they are personally entitled to the dignity, nor because they married daughters of her Majesty, for in the latter case the Marquess of Lorne would be so styled, but in virtue of a special grant from the Queen : nor would their issue, though grandchildren of her Majesty, enjoy any hereditary title of Royalty whatever ; for, as a recent authority justly observes, 'a Princess of England, though she transmits the right of succession, can confer no interim advantage of precedence or degree.' Even the eldest son of the Duke of Edinburgh would be legally entitled but to the qualification of 'Highness,' and, by an Act passed in 1399, would yield precedence to Dukes ; and his younger sons, by a subsequent Act, would give place to Earls. The issue of such younger sons, although by courtesy they would probably be addressed by a higher title, would be simply Esquires.

There is another class of *nobiles minores* of which I could say much if space permitted. I refer to the Untitled Aristocracy, who have been in possession of their ancestral estates for many generations An interesting letter on this subject will be found in the *Standard*, 21 February, 1888, signed ' a *Garb, or*,' which I have reason to believe was written by a cadet of the House of Spurway, of Spurway, Co. Devon.

Coronet of Arthur, son of Henry VII., from a window in
Great Malvern Church.

CHAPTER XVII

REGAL ARMORY

THERE is probably no branch of the Science of Heraldry more interesting and instructive than that which relates to the history of our Country ; much of which history is indelibly written, and plainly to be read, on the Seals, Monuments, and other similar Records of the different Sovereigns who have occupied the throne of England. The Arms attributed to the Saxon Monarchs are not sufficiently authenticated to demand any notice : even the authority for ascribing distinctive Arms to the Anglo-Norman Kings rests entirely on tradition ; no contemporaneous record exists of such Heraldic Insignia having been borne by the Sovereigns to whom they are attributed. It is not proposed, in the following summary of the Armorial Bearings of the English Monarchs, to notice all the various modifications and changes which they severally effected in the extra-scutal accessories—such as Badges and Mottoes—but only those which, from being most generally adopted, may be considered as historical.

WILLIAM the FIRST is *said* to have borne, *Gules ; two Lions passant-guardant in pale, or* : [1] and his wife MATILDA,

---

[1] We have strong presumptive evidence that William did *not* bear the two Lions assigned to him, either on his shield or person ; or he would certainly have been recognised by his son Robert, who, when he rebelled against his royal father in 1085, unwittingly encountered him, and would have despatched him, had he not discovered the king by his voice.

Gyronny of eight, or and azure ; an Inescutcheon gules, for FLANDERS.

WILLIAM the SECOND : *Two Lions of England in pale.* BADGE : According to Guillim, this King adopted for his Device or Badge, *an Eagle looking against the Sun,* with the Motto *Perfero.*

HENRY the FIRST : The same Arms as the foregoing ; and *Or ; a Lion rampant within a Tressure, fleury-counter-fleury, gules,* for MATILDA of SCOTLAND.

STEPHEN : The Lions of his father ; and for his wife, MATILDA of BOULOGNE, *Or ; three Torteaux.* Three golden *Centaurs* are sometimes ascribed to Stephen as Arms, but these—or rather one of them—constituted his BADGE. Guillim mentions another Badge borne by this Monarch—*a plume of Ostrich feathers,* referred to at page 134 ; but for this he gives no authority.

HENRY the SECOND : *Gules ; three Lions passant-guardant in pale, or* ; commonly known as ' *The Lions of England.*' His wife, ELEANOR of AQUITAINE and GUIENNE, bore, *Gules ; a Lion passant-guardant, or.* His BADGES were, the *Broom* of the Plantagenets (Qy. *Planta-Angevenista,* or Anjou plant ; and an *Escarbuncle.*

RICHARD the FIRST : The *Lions of England* ; and for his wife, BERENGARIA of NAVARRE, *Azure ; a Cross argent* ; for which was afterwards substituted, *Gules ; an Escarbuncle or.* BADGES : The *Plantagenista ; an Étoile issuing from a Crescent ;* and a *Sun over two Anchors.* MOTTO: *Christo duce.*

JOHN : The *Lions of England.* For ISABELLA of AN-GOULÊME, *Lozengy, or and gules.* No Arms are assigned to his first two wives. BADGES : The *Plantagenista ;* and the *Crescent beneath a Star,* of his brother Richard.

HENRY the THIRD : The *Lions of England.* His queen, ELEANOR of PROVENCE, bore, *Or ; four Pallets gules.* BADGE : The *Plantagenista.*

EDWARD the FIRST : The *Lions of England.* On the tomb of ELEANOR of CASTILE, his first wife, in WESTMINSTER

ABBEY, are sculptured shields bearing, *Quarterly :* 1 and 4. *Gules ; a Castle, triple-towered or ;* for CASTILE : 2 and 3. *Argent ; a Lion rampant gules ;* for LEON (fig. 323). His second wife, MARGARET of FRANCE, bore on one of her seals the Arms of England dimidiated with *France ancient,* which were *Azure ; semé of Fleurs-de-lys or.* BADGES : The *Broom* ; and a *Rose or, stalked vert.*

EDWARD the SECOND : The *Lions of England ;* and his wife, ISABELLA of FRANCE, *England,* dimidiating *France ancient ;* she also bore, *France ancient,* dimidiating, *Gules ; an Escarbuncle or ;* which latter she bore in right of her mother Joan, daughter and heiress of HENRY the FIRST, KING of NAVARRE. BADGE : *A triple-towered Castle of Castile.*

EDWARD the THIRD : In the year 1340, consequent upon

Fig. 354.

The Royal Arms of England, from the tenth year of the reign of Edward the Third until the seventh year of the reign of Henry the Fourth.

the claim of Edward to the Crown of France, the Arms of that country first appeared upon the shield of England, as in the annexed illustration (fig. 354). See *Rot. Parl.* 14 *Ed. III. No.* 9. It is curious, however, to note that the gold nobles and half-nobles of Edward III coined in 1351 bear only three Fleurs-de-lys in the first and fourth quarters, as represented in fig. 355. The coiner may have used only three Fleurs-de-lys, inasmuch as the space at his disposal was limited ; but we find that similar coins of Richard II. have the first and fourth quarterings *Semé-de-lys*, as in fig. 354. This is a small but very interesting point, which has, I believe, hitherto passed unnoticed.

The Arms of Edward, when combined with those of his wife PHILIPPA, exhibit *France and England quarterly*, impaled with, *Or ; four Lions rampant in quadrangle, the first and fourth sable, the second and third gules ;* for HAINAULT. In the Lansdowne Collection of MSS., No. 874, in the British Museum, the Arms of Philippa appear quartered with England only, in the first and fourth quarters. BADGES : *Sunbeams issuing from a cloud* was the favourite Badge of this monarch, though he sometimes displayed a *Griffin ; a Falcon ; and the Stump of a tree.* In No. 1471 of the Harleian MSS., *a Sword erect on a chapeau, the blade enfiled with three Crowns*, appears as a Badge. From a Cottonian MS. (*Titus, A. XX., fol.* 78, *Brit. Mus.*), it appears that Edward III. bore also a Boar as a Badge :—

> ' Tertius Edwardus, aper Anglicus et leopardus,
>   Rex tuus est verus.'

And again—

> ' Est aper Edwardus, flos regum, pistica nardus,
>   Sol solus lucens, rosa mundi, stella reduens.'

RICHARD the SECOND : *France ancient* and *England quarterly.* Richard impaled these Arms, on the dexter side, with *Azure ; a Cross fleurie between five Martlets or ;* the Arms attributed to the CONFESSOR. To this composition Richard added, also in pale, the Arms of AUSTRIA, for ANNE, his first wife ; which were, *Quarterly of four :* 1 and 4. *Argent ; an Eagle displayed sable ;* for GERMANY : 2 and 3 *Gules ; a Lion rampant, queue fourché, argent, crowned or ;* for BOHEMIA—thus forming a shield *tierce in pale :* First, the CONFESSOR ; Second, ENGLAND ; and Third, AUSTRIA. For ISABELLA, his second wife, he substituted for the Arms of

P

Austria, those of *France modern*. BADGES : Richard's favourite device was the *white Hart, lodged, ducally gorged and chained or* (fig. 291),which he is supposed to have adopted from his mother JOAN, ' *The fair Maid of Kent*,' daughter of the EARL of KENT, whose Cognisance was a *white Hind*. The Badge of this unfortunate King forms a conspicuous decoration of the string moulding which connects the trusses in WESTMINSTER HALL, being sculptured thereon no less than eighty-three times, alternating with his Crest. He also displayed, as Badges, the *Plantagenista ; Sun in splendour* (fig. 362) ; *a white Falcon ;* and several other devices.[1] SUP-PORTERS : *Two white Harts* have been attributed to Richard

Fig. 355.

The Arms of England, from the seventh year of the reign of Henry the Fourth until the accession of James the First.

as Supporters, and thus appear sculptured on the new Houses of Parliament ; but it is doubtful whether Supporters, properly so called, are to be found in Regal Heraldry before the reign of HENRY the SIXTH. The LIVERY COLOURS of the House of Plantagenet were *White* and *Red*.

HENRY the FOURTH : *France ancient* and *England quarterly*, until the year 1405 or 1406, when *three Fleurs-de-lys* were substituted for a Field *semé*, for the Arms of France.

[1] Dallaway and others give the Peas-cod as well as the Plantagenista. Is it not possible that the *Sun* and *Peas-cod* may bear some reference to Cresci (*crescit*) and Poictiers (*Pois-tiers*) ?

This alteration had been made by CHARLES the FIFTH about forty years previously, and constituted what is commonly known as *France modern.* Henry the Fourth impaled with his Arms those of JOANNA of NAVARRE, his second wife (MARY BOHUN, his first wife, died before his accession), which were, *Quarterly of four:* 1 and 4. *Azure ; three Fleurs-de-lys or ;* for EVREUX : 2 and 3. *Gules ; an Escarbuncle or ;* for NÁVARRE. BADGES : The various devices adopted by Henry the Fourth as Badges will be found enumerated at page 134. SUPPORTERS : Dexter : a SWAN ; Sinister : a HART,—*both argent, ducally gorged and chained or.* MOTTO : *Soverayne* was Henry's Motto while Duke of Hereford, which he seems to have retained after he became King. The Lancastrian LIVERY COLOURS were *White* and *Blue.*

Fig. 356.

HENRY the FIFTH : *France modern* and *England quarterly ;* impaled with France, for his wife KATHERINE. On the Reverse of the Great Seal of Henry the Fifth three shields are displayed, severally charged as follows : *Quarterly, or and gules ; four Lions passant-guardant, counterchanged ;* for the PRINCIPALITY of WALES : [1] *Argent ; a Lion rampant gules, ducally crowned or, within a Bordure sable, bezanté ;* for the DUCHY of CORNWALL : and *Azure ; three Garbs or ;* for the EARLDOM of CHESTER. BADGES : While

---

[1] These Arms are said by some authorities to be those of SOUTH WALES only ; those of NORTH WALES being, *Argent ; three Lions passant-reguardant in pale gules, their tails passing between their legs, and reflexed over their backs.* The latter Arms are enamelled on the hilt of the sword which was used on the occasion of Prince EDWARD, son of EDWARD the FOURTH, receiving the title of EARL of CHESTER.

Prince of Wales he used the *Swan* of the BOHUNS ; and after his Accession, a *Fire-beacon*, a *chained Antelope* and *Swan*, (fig. 356) [1] and a single *Ostrich-feather.* SUPPORTERS : Dexter : a *Lion ;* Sinister : a *white Hart.*

HENRY the SIXTH : *France and England quarterly ;* impaled with *Quarterly of six :* 1. *Barry of eight, argent and gules ;* for HUNGARY : 2. *Azure ; semé of Fleurs-de-lys or, surmounted by a Label of three points gules ;* for NAPLES : 3. *Argent ; a Cross potent, between four Crosses humetté or ;* for JERUSALEM : 4. *France ancient, within a Bordure gules ;* for ANJOU : 5. *Azure ; crusillé or ; two Barbels hauriant addorsed, of the last, within a Bordure gules ;* for DE BARRE : 6. *Or ; on a Bend gules, three Allerions displayed, argent ;* for LORRAINE. These Arms Henry impaled for his wife, MARGARET of ANJOU. BADGES : An *Ostrich-feather, in bend argent, surmounted by another in bend-sinister or ;* and a *spotted Panther.*[2] Margaret, his Queen, bore, in allusion to her name, a *Daisy (*Marguerite), with the Motto, *Humble et loial.* SUPPORTERS : *Two Antelopes argent.* MOTTO : *Dieu et mon droit*, which has since continued as the Motto of England.

EDWARD the FOURTH : *France and England quarterly.* For ELIZABETH WOODVILLE he impaled, *Quarterly of six :* 1. *Argent ; a Lion rampant, queue fourché gules, Imperially crowned ;* for LUXEMBURG : 2. *Quarterly quartered ;* i. and iv. *Gules ; an Étoile argent ;* ii. and iii. *France Ancient ;* for BAUX : 3. *Barry of ten, argent and azure ; over all a Lion rampant gules ; for* CYPRUS : 4. *Gules ; three Bendlets argent ; on a Chief per fess of the last and or, a Rose of the*

---

[1] The illustration is taken from the Frieze of Henry the Fifth's Chapel in Westminster Abbey.

[2] In a manuscript numbered 8448, preserved in the Bibliothèque Nationale at Paris, giving an account of an embassy from LEWIS de BOURBON to HENRY the SIXTH (A.D. 1444), it is said, ' the ambassadors were admitted to an audience of the king, and found him on a high pallet, without a bed, hung with tapestry diapered with the livery of the late king, that is, with Broom-plants, and this motto worked in gold, *Jamais.*'

first; for URSIUS : 5. *Gules ; three Pallets vairy, and a Chief or, surmounted by a Label of five points azure ;* for ST. PAUL : 6. *Argent ; a Fess and Canton conjoined gules ;* Elizabeth's paternal arms. BADGES : The *Rose-en-soleil ; a black Bull, armed and unguled or,* for CLARE ; and *a Falcon and Fetterlock.* SUPPORTERS : Dexter : a *Bull sable, armed and unguled or ;* for CLARE, or CLARENCE : Sinister : a *white Lion ;* for MARCHE. The LIVERY COLOURS of the HOUSE of YORK were *Murrey* and *Blue.*

EDWARD the FIFTH : *France and England quarterly.* SUPPORTERS : Dexter : a *Lion guardant or ;* Sinister : a *white Hart, ducally gorged and chained gold.*

RICHARD the THIRD : *France and England quarterly :* impaled with *Gules ; a Saltire argent ; surmounted by a Label of three points compony of the second and azure ;* for ANNE NEVILLE, his wife. BADGES : A *Boar argent, armed, unguled, and bristled, or ;* a *White Rose ;* and the *Sun in splendour.* The Badge of ANNE NEVILLE was a *Bear argent, collared, chained, and muzzled, or ;* the Cognisance of the noble House of WARWICK. SUPPORTERS : *Two Boars,* as the Badge. Richard sometimes used, as the dexter Supporter, a *Lion or.*

HENRY the SEVENTH : *France and England quarterly.* His wife, ELIZABETH of YORK, daughter of EDWARD the FOURTH, bore, *Quarterly of four :* 1. *France and England quarterly :* 2 and 3. *Or ; a Cross gules ;* for ULSTER : 4. *Barry of six, or and azure ; on a Chief of the first, a Pallet between two Gyrons of the second ; surmounted by an Inescutcheon argent ;* for MORTIMER (fig. 357).

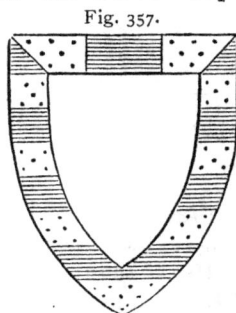

Fig. 357.

Arms of MORTIMER, from the seal of EDWARD MORTIMER (A.D. 1372).

BADGES : The *Portcullis,* of the BEAUFORTS ; *White Greyhound,* of the NEVILLES ; *Lancastrian and Yorkist Roses combined ;*[1] *Hawthorn-bush, fructed ppr., crowned and sur-*

---

[1] A *Rose quarterly argent and gules* ; commonly called a *Tudor Rose.*

mounted by H.R. ; Fleur-de-lys, Imperially crowned ; and *Red Dragon,* for CADWALLADER.[1] SUPPORTERS : Dexter : a *Dragon gules ;* Sinister : a *Greyhound argent, collared gules.* These figures, which were sometimes transposed, are to be seen at ST. GEORGE'S CHAPEL, WINDSOR, supporting a Portcullis, ensigned with a Rose. The TUDOR LIVERY COLOURS were *White* and *Green.*

HENRY the EIGHTH : *France and England quarterly.* The Arms of CATHERINE of ARRAGON, his first wife, were, *Quarterly quartered :* 1 and 4. Grand quarters, CASTILE *and* LEON, *quarterly :* 2 and 3. *Or ; four Pallets gules ;* for ARRAGON : *Impaling, per Saltire,* i. and iv. ARRAGON ; ii. and iii. *Argent ; an Eagle displayed sable, armed gules ;* for SUABIA. In the Base point of the Escutcheon, *Argent ; a Pomegranate slipped, proper ;* the Badge of GRENADA.

ANNA BULLEN, his second wife, bore, *Quarterly of six :* 1. *England, differenced with a Label of three points azure, charged on each point with as many Fleurs-de-lys or ;* for LANCASTER : 2. *France ancient, differenced with a Label of three points gules ;* for ANGOULÊME : 3. *Gules ; a Lion passant-guardant, or ;* for GUIENNE :[2] 4. *Quarterly of four :* i. and iv. *Or ; a Chief indented azure ;* for BUTLER ; ii. and iii. *Argent ; a Lion rampant sable, crowned gules ;* for ROCHFORT : 5. *England, differenced with a Label of three points argent ;* for BROTHERTON : 6. *Chequé, or and azure ;* for WARREN.

---

[1] A *Dragon with wings expanded gules, on a mount vert,* is still the Badge of the Principality of Wales.

Henry, shortly after the victory which placed him upon the Throne of England, proceeded in great state to St. Paul's, ' where he offered three Standards ; on one was the Image of *St. George* ; on the other was a *Red fiery Dragon,* beaten upon white and green sarcenet, the Livery Colours of the House of Tudor ; on the third was painted a *Dun Cow* upon yellow tartarn.'—*Baker's Chronicle.* The Dun Cow he probably assumed to bespeak his descent from Guy, Earl of Warwick.

[2] These three Quarterings were specially granted by the King to Queen Anna Bullen, as Augmentations, when she was created MARCHIONESS of PEMBROKE.

The Arms of JANE SEYMOUR were : *Quarterly of six :* 1. *Or ; on a Pile gules, between six Fleurs-de-lys azure, the Lions of England* (granted as an Augmentation) : 2. *Gules ; two Wings conjoined in lure or ;* for SEYMOUR : 3. *Vairy ;* for BEAUCHAMP, of HACHE : 4. *Argent ; three Demi-lions rampant, gules ;* for STINY : 5. *Party per bend, argent and gules ; three Roses bendwise, counterchanged ;* for MAC WILLIAMS : 6. *Argent ; on a Bend gules, three Leopards' heads or.* As ANNE of CLEVES, CATHERINE HOWARD, and CATHERINE PARR died without Issue, the Blazon of their Arms is omitted.

BADGES : The Badges most frequently displayed by Henry were : a *Portcullis ; Tudor Rose ; Red Dragon ;* and a *Cock argent, armed, crested, and wattled, gules.*[1] The Badges of CATHERINE of ARRAGON were the *Pomegranate,* already described, and a *Sheaf of Arrows argent.* ANNA BULLEN had a *Falcon argent, on the Stump of a Tree erased or, holding a Sceptre of the last : before him a bunch of Flowers issuing from the Stump of the first, and gules, stalked vert.* JANE SEYMOUR, a *Phœnix gules (or ?), between two Tudor Roses.* ANNE of CLEVES, a *Lion rampant sable, charged on the shoulder with an Escarbuncle, or.* CATHERINE HOWARD, uncertain. CATHERINE PARR, a *Maiden's head, crowned, proper, issuing from a Tudor Rose.*

SUPPORTERS : Dexter : a *Lion guardant or ;* Sinister : a *Dragon gules.* The *Dragon* sometimes forms the Dexter Supporter ; the Sinister being either a *White Greyhound* or a *Cock.*

EDWARD the SIXTH : *France and England quarterly.* BADGE : A *Sun in Splendour.* SUPPORTERS : The *Lion* and *Dragon* of his father ; the Lion being Imperially crowned.

---

[1] At a grand banquet given at Westminster in the first year of his reign, Henry is described as wearing a suit of 'shorte garments . . . . of blew velvet and crymosyne, with long sleeves, all cut and lyned with cloth of gould, and the utter parts of the garments powdered with Castles and sheaves of Arrows—the badges of Catherine, his queen—of fyne dokett (ducat) golde.'

MARY : *France and England quarterly ;* impaling the Arms of PHILIP of SPAIN, which were the same as those of CATHERINE of ARRAGON. BADGES : The *Sheaf of Arrows* of her mother, *impaling a Tudor Rose, beneath an Imperial crown ;* and a *Pomegranate, slipped proper.*

In Hearne's *Antiquarian Discourses,* by Sir Richard Cotton (vol. i. p. 112), Mary is said to have used as a Badge, an *Altar, thereon a sword erect ;* with the Motto, *Aræ et regni custodia.*

SUPPORTERS : Dexter : a *Lion guardant, gules, Imperially crowned ;* Sinister : a *Dragon gules ;*—after her marriage, an *Eagle* on the Dexter, and a *Lion* on the Sinister. MOTTO : Besides the national motto in use since the reign of Henry the Sixth, Mary adopted, *Veritas temporis filia.* Her arms, thus inscribed, are to be seen sculptured at WINDSOR.

Fig. 358.

The Royal Arms, from the accession of James the First until the year 1707.

ELIZABETH : *France and England quarterly.* On a Banner in the Tower of London, the Arms of Elizabeth are displayed as follows : *In a circle of her colours* (white and green) *three Shields, two and one :* 1. *Bend-sinisterwise ; France and England quarterly :* 2. *Bendwise ; Azure ; a Harp or, stringed argent ;* for IRELAND : 3. *In pale ;* WALES. BADGES : a *Falcon argent, holding a Sceptre or ;* and a *Tudor Rose,* with the Motto *Rosa sine spinâ,* were generally employed by Elizabeth, although she adopted at various times a great number of *Impresses.* SUPPORTERS : Dexter : a *Lion or* ; Sinister : a *Dragon gules.* MOTTO : *Semper eadem* seems to have been her favourite *personal* motto.

On the Accession of the STUARTS to the Throne, the Arms of Scotland and Ireland were combined with those of France and England, in the following manner : *Quarterly of four :* 1 and 4. Grand quarters, *France and England quarterly :* 2. *Or ; a Lion rampant, within a Bordure fleury-counterfleury, gules ;* for SCOTLAND : 3. *Azure ; a Harp or, stringed argent ;* for IRELAND (fig. 358.)

JAMES the FIRST marshalled the Arms of ANN of DENMARK, his wife, on a separate Escutcheon. They were : a *Cross gules, surmounted by another argent ; in the first quarter, or, semé of Hearts proper, three Lions passant-guardant azure, armed gules, crowned of the first ;* for DENMARK : *in the second quarter, gules, a Lion rampant, Imperially crowned, holding in its paws a Battle-axe argent ;* for NORWAY : *in the third quarter, azure, three Crowns ;* for SWEDEN : *in the fourth quarter, or, ten Hearts, four, three, two, and one, proper ; and in chief, a Lion passant-guardant azure ;* for GOTHLAND. In a compartment *gules,* at the Base of the Shield, beneath the Cross, a *Wyvern, tail nowed, and wings expanded or ;* the ancient Ensign of the VANDALS. *Over all an Inescutcheon, quarterly of four :* 1. *Or ; two Lions passant-guardant, in pale, azure ;* for the Duchy of SLESWICK : 2. *Gules ; on an Inescutcheon argent, three Holly-leaves, between as many Nails in triangle, all proper ;* for HOLSTEIN : 3. *Gules ; a Swan argent, membered sable, ducally gorged ;* for STORMERK : 4. *Azure ; a Chevalier armed at all points, brandishing his sword, all proper, upon a Charger argent, barded or ;* for DITZMERS : *Surtout-detout, an Inescutcheon of Pretence, party per pale, or ; two Bars gules ;* for OLDENBURG : and *Azure ; a Cross paté fitché or ;* for DALMENHURST. BADGE : a *Tudor Rose and Thistle, impaled by dimidiation, and Imperially crowned ;* with the MOTTO, *Beati pacifici.* SUPPORTERS : Dexter : a *Lion rampant-guardant or, Imperially crowned ;* Sinister : *a Unicorn argent, armed, unguled, and crined, or ; gorged with a Coronet composed of Crosses paté and Fleurs-de-lys, to which a Chain attached, passing between the fore-legs, and reflexed over the back, all gold.* These figures have ever since continued to form the Supporters of the Royal Arms.

CHARLES the FIRST : *England,* as borne by his father (fig. 358), impaling *France modern ;* for HENRIETTA MARIA, of FRANCE.   BADGE : *The Tudor Rose and Thistle, ensigned with a Crown ;* the same as JAMES the FIRST, but without the Motto.

The Arms of the COMMONWEALTH, although hardly coming under the denomination of *Regal* Heraldry, demand a passing notice in this place.   On the Great Seal, which was adopted within ten days of the execution of Charles, appears a shield blazoned as follows : *Quarterly of four : 1 and 4. The Cross of St. George : 2. The Saltire of St. Andrew : 3. The Harp of Ireland : Over all, on an Inescutcheon sable, a Lion rampant-guardant argent,* which were CROMWELL'S paternal Arms.   Beneath the Shield was the MOTTO, *Pax quæritur Bello ;* and around it, *Olivarius Dei gra : Reipub : Angliæ Scotiæ et Hiberniæ, &c., Protector.* The same Arms were engraved upon CROMWELL'S own seal, supported by the *Lion* of England, and a *Sea-horse ;* and further ensigned with all the extrascutal additions of Royalty.

CHARLES the SECOND : The quartered shield of the Stuarts, shown on page 228 ; impaling, *Argent ; on each of four Escutcheons in cross azure, as many Plates in saltire, within a Bordure gules, charged with eight Castles or ;* for PORTUGAL : borne by CATHERINE of BRAGANZA, his wife. BADGE : The same as his father.

JAMES the SECOND : The same as his predecessor.   For MARIE of ESTE : he impaled, *Quarterly of four : 1 and 4. Argent ; an Eagle displayed sable, Imperially crowned ;*

for ESTE : 2 and 3. *Azure ; three Fleurs-de-lys or, within a Bordure counter-indented gules ;* for FERRARA. His first wife, ANN HYDE, died before his Accession. BADGE : The same as that of CHARLES the FIRST.

WILLIAM the THIRD and MARY : WILLIAM retained the quartered shield of his immediate predecessors, charging it with an Inescutcheon, bearing his paternal Arms of NASSAU : *Azure ; billeté or, a Lion rampant of the last.* This composition he impaled with the Arms of JAMES the SECOND, for MARY his wife, daughter of JAMES : thus, the only difference between the Arms of WILLIAM and those of MARY was, that the former bore NASSAU in pretence.

ANNE : Until the year 1707, when the Union with Scotland was effected, Queen ANNE bore the same Arms as the preceding Sovereigns of the Stuart family : but in that year another change was made in their arrangement. This was by combining *England* and *Scotland*, by impalement, in the first and fourth Quarters, with *France* and *Ireland* in the second and third. The Arms of the Queen, thus emblazoned, and subscribed with the MOTTO, *Semper eadem*, are to be seen in the Church of ST. SAVIOUR'S, SOUTHWARK ; in the East window of ST. EDMUND the MARTYR, LOMBARD STREET ; and also on the pedestal of her statue in ST. PAUL'S Churchyard. The Arms of her husband, Prince GEORGE of DENMARK, were the same as those of ANN, wife of JAMES the FIRST. BADGE : *A Rose and Thistle proper, growing from the same stem, Imperially crowned.* ANNE was the last sovereign who adopted a personal Badge.

GEORGE the FIRST : The Arms of this King were the same as those of Queen ANNE, except that in the fourth Quarter he placed the Arms of HANOVER : which were, *Per pale and per chevron :* 1. *Gules ; two Lions passant-guardant in pale or ;* for BRUNSWICK : 2. *Or ; semé of Hearts proper, a Lion rampant azure, armed and langued gules ;* for LUNENBURG : 3. *Gules ; a Horse courant argent ;* for SAXONY : *Over all, on an Inescutcheon of pretence gules, the Crown of Charlemagne gold.*

The Arms of his wife, SOPHIA of ZELL, do not occur in the Royal Heraldry of England ; but, as both King GEORGE and SOPHIA were grandchildren of ERNEST AUGUSTUS, DUKE of BRUNSWICK, their Arms were probably the same.

Fig. 359.

The Arms of Hanover.

GEORGE the SECOND : Arms, the same as his father ; and so depicted on the West Window of WESTMINSTER ABBEY (A.D. 1735). For his wife, CAROLINE WILHELMINA of BRANDENBURG ANSPACH, he impaled: *Quarterly of fifteen :* 1. *Per fess, gules and argent ; a Bordure counterchanged ;* for MAGDEBURG : 2. *Argent ; an Eagle displayed sable, Imperially crowned :* 3. *Or ; a Griffin segreant sable :* 4. *Argent ; a Griffin segreant gules :* 5. As the last : 6. As 3 : 7. *Argent ; an Eagle displayed sable ;* for CROSSEN : 8. *Per pale, argent and gules ; a Bordure counterchanged ;* for HALBERSTADT : 9. As 7 : 10. *Or ; a Lion rampant sable, Imperially crowned, within a Bordure compony argent and gules ;* for NUREMBURG : 11. *Gules ; two Keys in Saltire or ;* for MINDEN : 12. *Quarterly, argent and sable ; a Bordure counterchanged :* 13. *Gules ;* for right of Regalia : 14. *Per fess, gules and argent :* 15. The same as 13 : *Over all, on an Inescutcheon of Pretence argent, an Eagle displayed gules ;* for BRANDENBURG.

GEORGE the THIRD : from his accession until the year

1801, GEORGE the THIRD bore the same Arms as GEORGE the FIRST ; but on the 1st of January in that year the *Fleurs-de-lys* were, by Royal Proclamation, removed from the shield of England. From that time, until the accession of our present Queen, the Royal Arms were : *Quarterly of four :* 1 and 4. *England :* 2. *Scotland :* 3. *Ireland :* in Pretence, *Hanover, ensigned with an Imperial Crown.* GEORGE the THIRD impaled the following Arms for CHARLOTTE of MECKLENBURG-STRELITZ : *Quarterly of six :* 1. *Or ; a Buffalo's head cabossed, sable, armed argent ; through the nostrils an Annulet of the last ; ducally crowned gules, the attires passing through the Crown ;* for MECKLENBURG : 2. *Azure ; a Griffin segreant or ;* for WENDEN : 3. *Per fess,* i. *Azure ; a Griffin segreant or ;* ii. *Vert ; a Bordure argent ;* for the Principality of SCHWERIN : 4. *Gules ; a Cross humetté argent, ducally crowned ;* for RATZBURGH : 5. *Gules ; a dexter arm embowed, vambraced, issuant from clouds, and holding between the thumb and index finger a gem ring, all proper ; round the arm a knot of ribbon azure ;* for the County of SCHWERIN : 6. The same as 1, except that the Buffalo's head is *couped ;* for ROSTOCK : *Over all, on an Inescutcheon of Pretence, per fess, gules and or ;* for STARGARD.

GEORGE the FOURTH : Arms, the same as those borne by GEORGE the THIRD since the year 1801. For Queen CAROLINE, daughter of the DUKE of BRUNSWICK, he impaled *Quarterly of twelve :* 1. *Or ; semé of Hearts proper, a Lion rampant, azure, armed and langued gules ;* for LUNENBURG : 2. *Gules ; two Lions passant-guardant in pale, or ;* for BRUNSWICK : 3. *Argent ; a Lion rampant azure, crowned gules ;* for EBERSTEIN : 4. *Gules ; a Lion rampant or, within a Bordure compony, argent and azure ;* for HOMBURG : 5. *Or ; a Lion rampant azure, crowned gules ;* for DIEPHOLT : 6. *Gules ; a Lion rampant or :* 7. *Gyronny of eight, argent and azure ; issuant from a Chief or, two Bears' paws addorsed sable :* 8. *Azure ; an Eagle displayed argent :* 9. *Barry of six, or and gules ; a Chief chequé :* 10. *Argent ;*

a Stag's attire in fess gules ; for REGENSTEIN : 11. *Argent ; a Stag tripping sable ;* for KLETTENBURG : 12. *Argent ; a Stag's attire in fess sable ;* for BLANKENBURG.

WILLIAM the FOURTH : *England, Scotland, Ireland,* and *Hanover,* as previously blazoned. The Arms of ADELAIDE of SAXE-MEINENGEN, his wife, were, *Quarterly of nineteen :* 1. *Azure ; a Lion rampant, barry of eight argent and gules, Imperially crowned ;* for THURINGIA : 2. *Gules ; on an Escarbuncle or, an Inescutcheon argent ;* for CLEVES : 3 and 4. *Or ; a Lion rampant sable, crowned gules ;* for JULIERS and MEISSEN : 5. *Barry of ten, or and sable, a Bend enarched, treflé, vert ;* for SAXONY : 6. *Argent ; a Lion rampant gules, Imperially crowned ;* for BERG : 7. *Argent ; an Eagle displayed gules, Imperially crowned ;* for WESTPHALIA : 8. *Or ; two Pales azure ;* for LANDESBERG : 9. *Sable ; an Eagle displayed or ;* for PFALZ : 10. *Or ; a Lion rampant sable, crowned gules ;* for ORLAMUNDE : 11. *Argent ; three Bars azure ;* for EISENBERG : 12. *Azure ; a Lion rampant or ;* for PLEISSEN : 13. *Argent ; a Rose gules, seeded and barbed proper ;* for ALTENBERG : 14. *Gules ;* for right of Regalia : 15. *Argent ; three Crampettes gules ;* for ENGERN : 16. *Or ; a Fess chequé, argent and gules ;* for MARCK : 17. *Gules ; a Column in pale argent, crowned or, the pedestal of the last ;* for ANHALT : 18. *Or ; on a Mount vert, a Cock sable, crested and jowlopped gules ;* for HENNEBERG : 19. *Argent ; three Chevronels gules ;* for RAVENSBERG.

VICTORIA : The Arms of HANOVER, which had appeared on the Shield of England from the year 1714, were relinquished on the Accession of VICTORIA ; as the *Salic Law,* which prevails in Hanover, precludes a Queen from reigning. The present Royal Arms are too well known to need an illustration.

His late Royal Highness the PRINCE CONSORT, instead of impaling, quartered the Arms of England with his own in the following manner : *Quarterly of four :* 1 and 4. *Grand quarters, quarterly ;* i. and iv. *England ;* ii. *Scotland ;*

iii. *Ireland ; differenced with a Label of three points argent,* *charged on the middle point with a Cross humetté, gules :* 2 and 3. *Saxony ;*—which arrangement is an Heraldic anomaly, for it would appear as though the Prince bore the quartered Arms of England by right of birth.

Since the Institution of the Most Noble Order, the Royal Arms have been encircled with the Garter and Motto.

PRINCE of WALES : From the year 1343, when EDWARD PLANTAGENET, the Black Prince, was created PRINCE of WALES, the title has served to distinguish the eldest son of the reigning Sovereign. He does not, however, inherit the dignity by birth,—as he does that of DUKE of CORNWALL,— but it is always conferred upon him by Patent—as is also the title of EARL of CHESTER. The eldest sons of the Kings of Scotland formerly bore the titles of DUKE of ROTHSAY, EARL of CARRICK, BARON RENFREW, &c. ; and in the year 1603, when the two kingdoms were united, these dignities were transferred to the Prince of Wales. The present Prince is the first who has enjoyed the title of DUKE of SAXONY, which was conferred upon him in 1841. In the event of there being no direct male heir to the Throne,—as was the case on the accession of George the Fourth,—the titles revert to the Crown.

The Arms of his Royal Highness ALBERT EDWARD, K.G., PRINCE of WALES, are, the *quartered Arms of England, differenced with a Label of three points argent ; over all, on an Inescutcheon of Pretence, Saxony.* Being by birth a Knight of the Garter, he encircles his shield with the Motto of that Most Noble Order. Above the Escutcheon is the Royal Helm (fig. 341), ensigned with the Prince's Coronet (fig. 327), supporting the Crest of England—*a Lion statant-guardant or, Imperially crowned.* This Crest, as well as the Royal Supporters, is differenced with a silver label. Beneath the Shield is the Motto, *Ich Dien.* Her Royal Highness ALEXANDRA, PRINCESS of WALES, bears for DENMARK, *Or ; semé of Hearts proper, three Lions passant-guardant azure,*

Imperially crowned. The Shield of the Prince of Wales would be rendered more complete by the addition of the less important Armorial Bearings to which he is entitled, and would be thus briefly blazoned : *Quarterly of four :* 1 and 4. *England ;* 2. *Scotland ;* 3. *Ireland : differenced with a Label of three points argent : over all, on an Inescutcheon, quarterly of six,* i. *Wales ;* ii. *Cornwall ;* iii. *Rothsay ;* iv. *Chester ;* v. *The Isles ;* vi. *Dublin : Surtout-de-tout, in pretence, Saxony.*

All the members of the Royal Family bear the quartered Arms of England, differenced with a Label specially charged, as described at page 153.

On the subject of setting up the Royal Arms in churches, Dr. Pegge writes as follows : ' The king's Arms are placed with great propriety in churches, the King of England being acknowledged to be the supreme head, in the temporal sense, of the National Protestant Church ; and yet I do not know of any express injunction for thus putting them up. However, they were very generally introduced at the Reformation.'

The earliest kind of Crowns worn by Kings was the diadem, which was no other than a fillet, primarily designed, doubtless, merely as a band to confine the hair. AURELIAN seems to have been the first of the Roman Emperors to wear a diadem enriched with jewels. Previous to his reign, only the Laurel and the Radiated Crowns were worn by the Emperors as ensigns of their dignity—the former being triumphal, and the latter bespeaking their affinity to the gods. In like manner was the fillet worn by the Saxon kings of England. ADULPH, King of the East Angles (A.D. 664), appears on his coins with his head bound with a plain band ; but when EGBERT, in 827, became sole monarch of the Heptarchy, he assumed, probably by way of eminence and as a mark of his distinction, a radiated Crown—the rays, however, being somewhat shorter than those of the Roman Emperors. EDWARD the CONFESSOR was the earliest

Saxon monarch who encircled his Helmet with a Crown, which he ensigned with crosses fleurie (see Fleur-de-lys, fig. 206). The Crown worn by WILLIAM the CONQUEROR was very similar to the Confessor's. The helmet was surrounded by a circle, ensigned on its rim with three lofty rays, terminating in crosses, having a pearl above each cross, and two fleurs-de-lys between the rays. From this period until the middle of the Fifteenth Century, the Crowns of our English Kings were for the most part open, the rim being ornamented with fleurs-de-lys, rays, or leaves. The sculptured Crowns on the effigies of RICHARD the FIRST, at FONTEVRAUD ; of JOHN, in WORCESTER Cathedral ; of HENRY the THIRD, in Edward the Confessor's Chapel, WESTMINSTER (fig. 360) ; of EDWARD the SECOND, in

Fig. 360.

GLOUCESTER Cathedral ; and of HENRY the FOURTH, in CANTERBURY Cathedral, afford good examples of the style of the Crowns worn during this period.

The first instance of an arched Crown occurring on the Great Seal is that of EDWARD the FOURTH, which consists of four trefoils between as many points, a pearl being placed between each ; from the trefoils spring four arches, which meet above, on the top of which is a small trefoil. HENRY the FIFTH had, however, previously worn an arched Crown, which was surmounted by a *Mound* and *Cross ;* the arches rising from four crosses on the rim, each between two small fleurs-de-lys, as appears from his monument in Westminster Abbey. The earliest coins struck by HENRY the SEVENTH bear an open Crown with fleurs-de-lys on the rim, alternating with pearls placed upon points ; but at a later date straw-berry-leaves seem to take the place of the fleurs-de-lys, sometimes with a single arch ensigned with little crosses placed saltirewise, and the circle adorned with crosses patonce (a larger and a smaller alternately) ; and sometimes they appear with the triple arch. Over the entrance of the screen or enclosure of HENRY the SEVENTH'S tomb at West-minster is a Crown heightened with alternate crosses paté and fleurs-de-lys. A similar Crown to this, but arched, appears upon his Great Seal, differing very slightly from that of RICHARD the THIRD.

Fig. 361.

From this period until the reign of CHARLES the FIRST no important change took place in the fashion of the Crown, except the introduction of the velvet cap, which first appears upon the Great Seal of HENRY the EIGHTH. On the second Great Seal of CHARLES, which was brought into use in the year 1640, the Imperial Crown assumed the shape it continued to bear until the accession of her Majesty— except that between the crosses and fleurs-de-lys on the rim there was placed a small ray having a pearl on the top ; a row of pearls surrounding the lower edge, in the place of the ermine.

The Crown worn by her Majesty retains all the features of the preceding, as may be seen by examining a two-shilling piece. The whole Crown is so studded with gems, that but very little of the gold is visible.

The Coronets worn by the Royal Princes of England are described at pp. 178, 179.

Fig. 362.

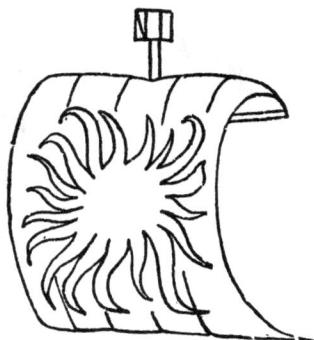

THE SUN IN SPLENDOUR, a Badge of Richard the Second, from an Illuminated Manuscript in the Harleian Collection, No. 1,319, containing an account, written in French verse, of the expedition of Richard the Second to Ireland, and the events which immediately succeeded it. The Illustration represents the sail of the ship in which the unfortunate King returned to England.

Fig. 363.—Queen Elizabeth in the habit of the Order of the Garter, from the print in Ashmole's History of that Order.

CHAPTER XVIII

ORDERS OF KNIGHTHOOD, COLLARS, ETC.

ONE of the most ancient and honourable Orders of Knighthood ever instituted in this country, and that in which some of the greatest personages recorded in history have been enrolled as members, is THE MOST NOBLE ORDER OF THE GARTER. The immediate cause which led to its institution, and even the date of its foundation, are alike uncertain: some authorities assigning the year 1344 as the period of its origin; while others, with probably less accuracy, fix the date five years later. The popular tradition as to Edward Plantagenet, Prince of Wales, and the Countess of Salisbury, is undoubtedly too frivolous to merit any serious attention. Froissart, who was attached to the Court of Edward the Third, in the account of the origin of the Order which he presented to Queen Philippa, makes no mention of the Prince picking up the garter of the Countess, and he assigns the year 1344 as that in which it was instituted. However much Chroniclers may be given generally to drawing on their imagination for their facts, it is not probable that Froissart would, in this instance, be guilty of any such indiscretion ; for discovery and exposure would have been certain. In the elaborate dissertation on the Order by Anstis, the subject of its origin will be found fully discussed : it is sufficient for our purpose to know that it was founded during the reign of EDWARD the THIRD, and that it is composed of twenty-five KNIGHTS COMPANIONS, exclusive of the Sovereign, members of the Royal Family, and foreign Princes.

The INSIGNIA worn by Knights of this Noble Order are, the GARTER, MANTLE, SURCOAT, HOOD, HAT, COLLAR, GEORGE, and STAR. Of these, the first four constituted the original decorations of the Order, the other Insignia being of more recent institution.

The GARTER is of dark-blue velvet, edged and buckled gold : the well-known motto—*Honi soit qui mal y pense*—

Fig. 364.

which is inscribed thereon is also of gold. Knights wear it below the left knee ; but it encircles the left arm of her Majesty.[1]

[1] 'It is curious that the motto of this Order should never have been properly translated ; for how few persons are aware that it has any other meaning than the almost unintelligible one of " Evil be to him who evil thinks." The proper version is, however, " Dishonoured be he who thinks evil of it." '—*Retrospective Review*, 1827.

Previous to the reign of George the Second, the colour of the Garter was a pale cobalt blue, and it is so represented on the large west window of Westminster Abbey (A.D. 1735).

The accompanying illustrations, showing the manner in which Knights of the Order wear the Garter, are taken from

Fig. 365.

Fig. 366.

the effigy of LORD BARDOLF, in DENNINGTON Church, and the brass of HENRY BOURCHIER, EARL of ESSEX, in LITTLE EASTON Church, ESSEX (A.D. 1483). It is somewhat singular that the effigy of EDWARD the BLACK PRINCE, in CANTERBURY Cathedral, should be represented without the Garter.

The MANTLE is of dark-blue velvet—so dark that, except in a strong light, it appears almost black—and lined with white taffeta. It is without sleeves, and reaches to the wearer's feet ; princes being distinguished by having a Mantle of greater length. It is fastened by a rich white cordon, with large tassels, which extend to about the middle of the body ; and it is further decorated on the shoulders with bunches of white ribbon. On the left side is attached the BADGE, which is a fimbriated Cross of St. George, enclosed within a Garter, precisely the same as the Star (fig. 367), but without the rays.

In an Illuminated Manuscript of the Fifteenth Century, preserved in the Royal Library (15, E. 6), JOHN TALBOT, EARL of SHREWSBURY, a Knight of the Order, appears presenting a book to Henry the Sixth. The Earl's Mantle is powdered with circular Badges, inscribed with the Motto, but without the Cross in the centre.

The SURCOAT is worn under the Mantle, and is fastened around the waist by a girdle. On it were formerly emblazoned the Arms of the wearer. It is of crimson velvet, lined with white ; though originally there existed no regulation to determine its colour, or that of its lining.

The HOOD is likewise crimson. It is no longer used as a covering for the head, but is allowed to fall over the right shoulder.

The HAT is of black velvet, and is decorated with a plume of white ostrich and black heron feathers.

The COLLAR is of gold, weighing thirty ounces, and is formed of twenty-six pieces, being the number of the Knights. These pieces represent knots of cord—*lacs d'amour*, or true-lovers' knots—alternating with combined Lancastrian and Yorkist Roses, surrounded with a buckled Garter, charged with the Motto.

From the Collar depends the GEORGE, which is a representation of the Patron Saint of England, on horseback, piercing the Dragon with a lance.

The STAR was devised in the second year of King CHARLES the FIRST, by surrounding the Badge with rays of silver.

Fig. 367.—Star of the Order of the Garter.

Knights of the Order wear it on the left breast of their coats, when they are not habited in their Mantles.

In addition to the foregoing Insignia, another Badge is sometimes worn. This is a George, within an inscribed Garter, suspended from a dark-blue ribbon, which passes over the wearer's left shoulder, bend-sinisterwise.[1]

HENRY the FIFTH appointed, as OFFICERS for the service of the Order, a PRELATE, REGISTRAR, and USHER, called the USHER OF THE BLACK ROD : with these were subsequently associated a CHANCELLOR and Special HERALD. The PRELATE is the BISHOP of WINCHESTER, and his successors in the See. In virtue of his office, he wears the George, surmounted by a Mitre, pendent from a blue ribbon, in addition to his episcopal vestments. Until 1836, the BISHOP of SALISBURY fulfilled the duties of CHANCELLOR, when the dignity was attached to the See of OXFORD. The DEAN of WINDSOR is the REGISTRAR.

It is commonly asserted that previous to the reign of HENRY the EIGHTH, the duties of the Herald of the Order were performed by 'WINDSOR HERALD'; and that, by an edict passed during the reign of that monarch, a KING-OF-ARMS was appointed, called 'GARTER,' who was invested with sovereign power over the College of Heralds, and whose special function it was to attend Installations, and other business connected with the Noble Order from which he derived his title.[2] This, Beltz points out in his *Memorials*

---

[1] Knights only wear the Collars of the various Orders when they are fully robed. These occasions are very rare, being only on grand State ceremonies, such as Coronations, &c., and usually at Levées, once in the season, known as *Collar-days*. The Jewels are commonly suspended from a ribbon.

[2] Her Majesty has recently dispensed with the statutes and regulations formerly observed in regard to installation into this Most Noble Order. The Dukes of Richmond, Beaufort, and Rutland, for example, were created Knights Companions by letters patent, under the Royal sign manual, and the Great Seal of the Order. The ceremonial, however, is still continued in the creation of foreign Knights of the Order.

of the Order of the Garter (p. lviii.) is incorrect, for WILLIAM BRUGES was appointed Garter King-of-Arms as early as the year 1417. See also the will of William Bruges, transcribed in the *Testamenta Vetusta* of Sir Henry Nicolas.

Some Heralds and Antiquaries—particularly those of Scotland—attribute to the MOST NOBLE AND ANCIENT ORDER OF THE THISTLE an earlier origin than to the Garter. That it was at least coeval with it appears from some of the coins of ROBERT the SECOND of SCOTLAND (A.D. 1370–1390), which bear on the reverse the figure of St. Andrew, supporting his Saltire, which, with the Motto, constitutes the Badge of the Order. Anterior to this there is no authentic record, although tradition assigns its institution to a period far more remote. During the Sixteenth Century, this Order was permitted to fall into disuse, but was revived by King JAMES the SECOND of ENGLAND. By a statute passed in the reign of Queen ANNE, the fashion and manner of wearing the Insignia were definitely determined ; and by a further edict of WILLIAM the FOURTH, it was decreed that the number of Knights should be sixteen, exclusive of the Sovereign.

The INSIGNIA worn by Knights of the Thistle are the STAR, COLLAR, and JEWEL.

The STAR is of chased silver, and is formed by a Saltire, or Cross of St. Andrew, conjoined with a Lozenge : in the centre is a Thistle proper, on an irradiated gold field, placed within a circle of green enamel, upon which is inscribed in gold letters the Motto of the Order : *Nemo me impune lacessit.*

The COLLAR is composed of sixteen Thistles—in allusion to the number of Knights—each between two of its leaves, alternating with four sprigs of Rue interlaced. From the Collar depends an eight-pointed star of silver, charged with a figure of St. Andrew—the Patron Saint of Scotland—

In 1881, GARTER, and the other officials, invested the King of Spain, in Madrid, in due and ancient form ; and the King of Saxony in 1882.

habited in a purple surcoat and green mantle, supporting a Saltire.

The JEWEL is worn in the same manner as the lesser George of the Knights of the Garter, dependent from a dark-green ribbon. It consists of a figure of St. Andrew, surrounded by an oval band of green enamel, edged with gold, bearing in letters of the same the Motto of the Order.

The OFFICERS attached to this Noble Order are : the

Fig. 368.—Star of the Order of the Thistle.

DEAN ; LORD LYON, KING-OF-ARMS ; and the USHER OF THE GREEN ROD : each distinguished by the peculiar Badge of his office.

THE MOST ILLUSTRIOUS ORDER OF ST. PATRICK was instituted by GEORGE the THIRD, as a decoration for Irish Nobles analogous to the Orders of St. George and St. Andrew. Twenty-two Knights, besides the Lord Lieutenant of Ireland, who is *ex-officio* GRAND MASTER, and the Sovereign, constitute the Order. The INSIGNIA of the Knights of St. Patrick are :

The MANTLE : which is of light blue, lined with white silk.

The COLLAR : composed of red and white Roses, within a Bordure charged with Trefoils, alternating with Harps and Knots of gold. In the centre is an Imperial Crown, from which depend a Harp of gold and the BADGE ; which is of oval form, and consists of the Saltire of St. Patrick, surmounted by a Trefoil, slipped : charged on each cusp with an Imperial Crown, all proper ; surrounded by a band of blue enamel, on which is inscribed the MOTTO, *Quis separabit?* and the date of the institution of the Order, MDCCLXXXIII. ; the whole within a Bordure gold, charged with Trefoils vert. The Badge is sometimes worn without the Collar ; in which case it is suspended from a light-blue ribbon, passing over the right shoulder.

The STAR is of chased silver, similar in form to that worn by Knights of the Garter. The Badge of St. Patrick, borne in the centre, is round, and the Bordure of Trefoils is wanting.

The OFFICERS are : the PRELATE, the CHANCELLOR, the REGISTRAR, and the GENEALOGIST ; assisted by ULSTER KING-OF-ARMS, two HERALDS, and four PURSUIVANTS.

THE MOST HONOURABLE ORDER OF THE BATH was founded in the year 1399. It was subsequently allowed to fall into disuse, but was reorganised by GEORGE the FIRST in 1725. Bathing was formerly one of the principal ceremonies observed at the installation of all Knights ; but the custom has long since been discontinued, and serves now but to give a title to one of the most distinguished of the Orders of Knighthood :—

> ' Accingitur gladio super femur miles,
> Absit dissolutio, absint actus viles.
> Corpus novi militis solet balneari,
> · Ut a factis vetitis discat emundari.'

(*The Battle of Lewes: Harl. MS.* 978, *fol.* 128 *et seq., ll.* 167–170.)

Prior to the year 1815 there existed no difference in point of rank amongst the Companions ; but at the termination of the War, when so many claimants appeared for honourable distinction, it was decided to divide the Order of the Bath into three Grades, entitled, KNIGHTS GRAND CROSS (G.C.B.), KNIGHTS COMMANDERS (K.C.B.), and KNIGHTS COMPANIONS (C.B.).

The COLLAR is composed of nine Imperial Crowns and eight groups of Roses, Shamrocks, and Thistles, with a Sceptre in pale, in the centre of each group ; linked together with seventeen knots, all of gold, enamelled proper ; the knots being white.

The Knights of this Order have two distinct Badges— one for the Military Knights, and another for the Civil and Diplomatic.

The BADGE of the MILITARY and NAVAL KNIGHTS is a gold star of eight points, enamelled white, having on each point a small ball, and in each of the four angles a Lion of England. In the centre, on a field enamelled white, are the Rose, Shamrock, and Thistle, surmounted by a Sceptre in pale, between three Imperial Crowns, one and two, all proper. Surrounding these is a red circular fillet, bearing the MOTTO, *Tria juncta in uno*, in letters of gold. The whole is encircled with a double wreath of laurel proper, edged gold, on which the Lions stand. On the bottom limb of the Cross is a Scroll of blue enamel, charged with the words, *Ich Dien*, in golden letters.

When the Collar is not worn, the Badge depends from a ribbon of crimson ducape, which, for Knights of the First Class (G.C.B.), passes bendwise across their right shoulders: the Second Class (K.C.B.) wear the Badge around their necks, pendent from a narrower ribbon ; and the Third Class (C.B.), from the button-hole of the coat, by a still narrower ribbon.

The STAR of the GRAND CROSS is in the form of a Lozenge, composed of rays of silver. In the centre is the Badge ; the balls at the points of the Cross, and the Lions, being omitted.

The STAR of the KNIGHTS COMMANDERS is similar to the preceding, except that the rays do not extend beyond the

Fig. 369.— Star of the Order of the Bath.

Cross, but arise from the angles, which in the Badge are occupied by the Lions. These Stars are worn on the left breast, in addition to the Collar, or Ribbon, and Badge. COMPANIONS of the Order (C.B.) are not entitled to wear any Insignia beyond their Badge, pendent from a ribbon, as before described.

The BADGE of the three Classes of the DIPLOMATIC and CIVIL KNIGHTS, is the Rose, Shamrock, Thistle, Sceptre, and Crowns, encircled by the Motto, as borne by the Military and Naval Knights, without other addition. It is oval, however, instead of round.

The STAR of the CIVIL G.C.B. is the same as the Military, except that the Crowns only appear in the centre (fig. 369). The wreath of laurel, and the Motto, *Ich Dien*, are omitted from the Star of the K.C.B.

THE MOST DISTINGUISHED ORDER OF ST. MICHAEL AND ST. GEORGE was instituted in the year 1818 by GEORGE the FOURTH, whilst Prince Regent, for the purpose of affording a special decoration to the natives of Malta and the Ionian Isles, shortly after the cession of those islands to England. This Order, like that of the Bath, is divided into three Classes—KNIGHTS GRAND CROSS, KNIGHTS COMMANDERS, and COMPANIONS.

The COLLAR, which is only worn by Knights Grand Cross and Commanders, is composed of Lions of England, Maltese Crosses, and the Monograms S.M. and S.G.—in commemoration of the Patron Saints of the Order—recurring alternately, and linked together with small chains. The several parts are formed entirely of gold, the crosses being enamelled white. From the centre, between two Lions, and immediately beneath as many sheaves of seven arrows, surmounted by an Imperial Crown, depends the BADGE, which is a Cross of fourteen points enamelled white, with a narrow fimbriation of burnished gold, below an Imperial Crown. In the centre of the Cross is, on one side of the Badge, a representation of St. Michael, and on the reverse, St. George, both enclosed within a circular blue fillet inscribed with the MOTTO, *Auspicium melioris Ævi*. In the place of the Collar, the Badge may depend from a dark-blue ribbon with a scarlet stripe down the centre, the three Degrees of the Order being distinguished by the width of the ribbon.

The STAR of KNIGHTS GRAND CROSS is septagonal, and is formed of alternate rays of gold and silver, richly chased. Over all is the red Cross of St. George, fimbriated gold, charged in the centre with a figure of St. Michael, within a band bearing the Motto of the Order. The STAR of KNIGHTS COMMANDERS is a Cross of eight points set saltirewise, the angles being filled with rays of silver, surmounted by the Cross of St. George, &c., as in the Star of the superior Degree, but somewhat plainer.

THE MOST EXALTED ORDER OF THE STAR OF INDIA.—

This Order, as originally instituted by her Majesty on the 23rd of February, 1862, consisted of a SOVEREIGN, who is the King or Queen of Great Britain regnant ; a GRAND MASTER, who is the Viceroy or Governor-General of India for the time being ; and twenty-five KNIGHTS, with such HONORARY KNIGHTS as the Sovereign may please to appoint; but on the 24th of May, 1866, her Majesty increased the number of Knights from twenty-five to a hundred and seventy-five, dividing them into three Classes, as follows :

First Class, consisting of twenty-five members, styled KNIGHTS GRAND COMMANDERS ; *Second Class*, consisting of fifty members, styled KNIGHTS COMMANDERS ; *Third Class*, consisting of one hundred members, styled COMPANIONS.

The INSIGNIA of KNIGHTS GRAND COMMANDERS are : the COLLAR, which is composed of a Lotus-flower of four cusps ; two Palm-branches, set saltirewise, and tied with a ribbon ; and an Heraldic Rose, alternately—all of gold enamelled proper, and connected by a double chain, also of gold. In the centre, between two Lotus-flowers, is placed an Imperial Crown, enamelled proper, from which, by a small ring, depends the BADGE.

The BADGE is a chamfered mullet, set with brilliants, below which is an oval medallion of onyx cameo, having a profile bust of her Majesty, the whole encircled by a band enamelled azure, fimbriated with brilliants, bearing the MOTTO of the Order—*Heaven's Light our Guide.*

The STAR is a mullet of brilliants set upon a field of gold, and surrounded by a Garter of light-blue enamel, tied in a knot at base, and inscribed with the Motto ; the whole being set upon a wavy star of gold.

In the SECOND CLASS, the mullet from which the Jewel depends is of silver, and the latter is surrounded by a plain gold border. It is suspended round the neck by a white ribbon, with blue edges. The Star is set upon rays of silver.

COMPANIONS of the THIRD CLASS wear no Star ; neither is there any mullet above the Jewel.

In the regulations respecting this Order, issued on the 24th of May, 1866, it is enacted that ' it shall be competent for the Sovereign of the said Order to confer the dignity of a Knight Grand Commander of the same upon such Native Princes and Chiefs of India as shall have entitled themselves to the Royal favour, and upon such British subjects as have, by important and loyal services rendered by them to the Indian Empire, merited such Royal favour ; and that, as regards the Second and Third Classes of the Order, no persons shall be nominated thereto who shall not, by their conduct or services in the Indian Empire, have merited such Royal favour.'

The Royal Order of Victoria and Albert.—This illustrious Order differs essentially from any of the preceding, inasmuch as it is conferred solely upon Ladies, similar to the *Order of Isabel,* of Spain, and of the *Lady of the Jewelled Cross,* of Austria. It was instituted by her Majesty, on the 10th of February, 1862, in commemoration of her marriage with the late Prince Consort ; ' to be enjoyed,' as stated in the Preamble, ' by our most dear children, the Princesses of our Royal House, and by such other Princesses upon whom we, from time to time, shall think fit to confer the same.'

By the rules originally established, it was ordained that her Majesty—and, after her death, the Kings and Queens regnant of Great Britain—should be the Sovereign of the new Order ; that the 10th of February of every year should be deemed the Anniversary of the Institution ; that it should be competent for her Majesty and her successors to confer the decoration of the Order upon the female descendants and wives of the male descendants of the late Prince Consort and her Majesty, as well as upon Queens and Princesses of Foreign Houses connected by blood or amity.

The Decoration of the Order consists of an onyx cameo, bearing a profile likeness of the late Prince Consort, surmounted by that of her Majesty, within an oval frame set with brilliants, dependent from an Imperial Crown of precious stones, attached to a white moiré ribbon an inch and a half in width, tied in a bow, and worn upon the left shoulder.

Since the institution of the foregoing Order, her Majesty has been pleased to extend the DECORATION to other Ladies besides those for whom it was originally intended. The SECOND CLASS is bestowed upon the Mistress of the Robes, Lady of the Bedchamber, or other Ladies holding office in the Royal Household. The DECORATION is similar to that of the Family Order, except that it is smaller, and is set with but four brilliants and twenty pearls, instead of seventy brilliants, as in the First Class. The Imperial Crown from which the Jewel depends is enamelled proper.

The THIRD CLASS is conferred upon such Ladies as hold, or have held, the office of Bedchamber-women, or other similar position, inferior to those Ladies of the Second Class. The DECORATION consists of a Monogram, composed of the letters V., P., and A., in gold, pierced, and ornamented with pearls and brilliants, suspended from an Imperial Crown enamelled proper, and enriched with brilliants.

The DECORATION of both the Second and Third Classes is attached to a bow of white moiré ribbon an inch in width, and worn in the same manner as that of the First Class.

The student who seeks for further knowledge on the subject of the Orders of Knighthood, is referred to John Hunter's *Description of the Insignia of the Orders of British Knighthood . . . shewing the manner of wearing them, and proper mode of using them in Heraldry . . .* (London, fol. 1844) ; and Burke's *Orders of Knighthood.*

The custom of wearing Collars and Neck-chains as badges of office dates probably from about the Fourteenth Century, and survived until comparatively modern times ; for Goodman, Bishop of Gloucester, in his *Court of King James the First,* writes that, at the Feasts of St. George, he

R

had 'seen very near ten thousand chains of gold stirring.' 'Go, sir ! rub your chain with crumbs,' says Sir Toby Belch to Malvolio ; thus showing that, in Shakespeare's day, even House-stewards wore such Badges.   ' Every attempt,' writes Beltz, 'has failed to carry the practice of conferring Collars in this country before the fourteenth year of Richard the Second, when, on the twelfth of October 1390, magnificent jousts were held in Smithfield, and the king distributed his cognisance of the white Hart pendent from a collar of Crosses de genet—or Broom-cods—of gold.' Of Collars worn as Decorations of honour, or Badges indicative of political partisanship, the most worthy of note are— the Lancastrian Collar of S.S., or *Esses*, as it was sometimes written ; and the Yorkist Collar of Suns and Roses. These constituted Decorations in themselves, and were totally distinct from the Collars of Knighthood previously described.

The COLLAR of S.S. was instituted by HENRY the FOURTH, during the reign of his immediate predecessor, but the signification of the device has not been clearly ascertained ; it is, however, generally supposed to be the repeated Initial of *Soverayne*, HENRY's favourite Motto. By a statute passed in the second year of that Monarch's reign, permission was granted to all Sons of the King, and to Dukes, Earls, Barons, and Lesser Barons (*Barones minores*), 'to use the livery of our Lord the King of his Collar, as well in his absence as in his presence,' and to Knights and Esquires in his presence only. It seems also to have been frequently conferred upon, or adopted by, Ladies. In NORTHLEIGH Church, OXFORDSHIRE, the monumental effigies of WILLIAM WILCOTES and his wife (A.D. 1407–11) are both decorated with a Collar of S.S., as are also the DUKE and DUCHESS of SOMERSET, in WIMBORNE MINSTER, DORSET (A.D. 1444) ; and SIR ROBERT and LADY WHITTINGHAM (*temp*. Hen. VI.), in ALDBURY Church, HERTFORDSHIRE (fig. 370). In DIGSWELL Church, also in HERTFORDSHIRE, is a brass to JOHN PERIENT

(A.D. 1442) and his wife. The Lady has a Collar of S.S. She also bears on the left lapel of her mantle the Lancastrian Badge of the Swan, ducally gorged and chained, of the De Bohuns. By a decree of Henry the Eighth, its use was forbidden to Esquires and Ladies.

Fig. 370.

The King-of-Arms, and Heralds ; the Lord Mayor of London ; the two Chief-Justices ; the Chief-Baron ; the Sergeants-at-Arms, and certain officers of the Royal Household, still wear a Collar of S.S. as a mark of their official dignity.

Considerable difference exists in the form and pattern of this decoration. Sometimes the letters were simply linked together by rings, as in the illustration at page 190, which is taken from the effigy of William Phelip, Lord Bardolph, K.G., in Dennington Church. More frequently they were fastened upon a band or ribbon, as in the instances of Sir John Cheney, in Salisbury Cathedral, which has for a pendant[1] the Portcullis of Henry the Seventh, surmounted by a Rose ; of Thomas, Duke of Clarence, second son of Henry the Fourth, who was killed in the year

---

[1] The ring, which turns on a swivel, as seen pendent from the collar, is called a *Toret*. The word — corrupted into *Terret* — is still used by harness-makers, and signifies the rings through which the bridle-reins pass.

R 2

1420 (1 ?), and whose effigy is in the chapel of ST. MICHAEL,
at CANTERBURY ; and of JOHN GOWER, the poet, in ST.
SAVIOUR'S Church, SOUTHWARK, to which is attached a Swan,
which was the Badge of the De Bohuns, and which Gower,
as Poet-Laureate, and adherent of Henry Bolingbroke,
probably wore as a portion of the King's Livery. Again,
we find them alternating with other devices, as in the Collar
worn by the Lord Mayor of London, which consists of S.S.,
Tudor Roses, and Lacs-d'amour, linked together so that each
S. is between a Rose and a Knot. In the centre is a Portcullis, from which depends the Jewel, which is the City
Arms cut in onyx, within an oval garter of blue enamel, inscribed with the civic Motto, *Domine, dirige nos*—the whole
surrounded by the Emblems of the United Kingdom in
brilliants. This Collar was presented to the Corporation by
Sir John Allyn, and was first worn by Sir William Laxton
in the year 1544.

In the Issue Roll of the Exchequer, Michaelmas, 8
Henry IV., occurs the following entry :—' Paid 3 November
to Christopher Tildesley, Citizen and Goldsmith of London,
for a collar of gold worked with the Motto Soveignez, and
the letter S. and ten annulets garnished with nine pearls,
twelve diamonds, eight rubies, eight sapphires, and a large
clasp in shape of a triangle with a large ruby set in it, and
garnished with four pearls £385 6s. 8d. ; ' and in the King's
Book of Payments, for August 1519, now preserved in the
Record Office, this entry is made :—' To Sir Richard Wingfield for a Collar of Esses, 53¾ oz. at 40 shillings the ounce,
and £6 for fashion.'

HENRY the EIGHTH seems to have been the last monarch
who wore the Collar of S.S. ; and his will, as well as that of
his father, is sealed with a signet on which are the Royal
Arms surrounded by the Collar, having a Rose between two
Portcullises for a pendant.

A very excellent paper on the subject of the King's
Livery in connection with the Collar of S.S. will be found

in the *Retrospective Review*, Second Series, vol. ii. p. 500, *et seq.*

The COLLAR of the YORKIST faction was formed by alternate Suns and White Roses. The Badge of the House of MARCH, a *Lion sejant argent*, usually depends from the Collar, though occasionally we find its place occupied by a White Rose. RICHARD the THIRD, and his adherents, adopted a White Boar ; and HENRY the SEVENTH, who was at all times anxious to exhibit his connection with both the rival houses, added to his Collar of S.S. the Portcullis of the BEAUFORTS. Occasionally he substituted for the Portcullis a Tudor Rose.

The sculptured effigy of SIR JOHN CROSBY, in the Church of GREAT ST. HELEN'S, in the City of LONDON (A.D. 1475), affords a fine example of a Yorkist Collar, from which the annexed illustration is copied.

Fig. 371.

In the original, the Suns and Roses near the pendant are somewhat mutilated. I have therefore substituted perfect examples as they appear on other portions of the Collar.

In BRANCEPETH Church, DURHAM, is an effigy of RALPH, second EARL of WESTMORELAND (A.D. 1484), decorated with a Yorkist Collar of Roses-en-soleil ; to which is attached the Boar of RICHARD the THIRD. On the effigy of his Countess is a Collar composed of alternate Suns and Roses, from which depends a plain lozenge-shaped Jewel.

SIR JOHN SAY, who died in 1473, and whose Brass in BROXBOURNE Church, HERTFORDSHIRE, was executed during his lifetime, is proved by the Collar of Suns and Roses which encircles his neck to have been an adherent of the Yorkist faction. The pendant is concealed by the upraised hands.

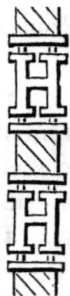

Somewhat analogous to the Collar of S.S. was the decoration instituted by HENRY the EIGHTH formed by the letter H, alternating with a link of gold, but which seems to have been worn only by the King himself. At LEE PRIORY, KENT, is a portrait of that monarch, by Holbein, decorated with a chain of gold, as in the accompanying cut.

Fig. 372.   At the Society of Antiquaries is a portrait of HENRY the SEVENTH in which appears a Collar composed of Roses-en-soleil, alternating with knots, as here reproduced.

Fig. 373.

At Windsor Castle is a portrait of PRINCE HENRY, afterwards HENRY the EIGHTH, in which the Collar is composed of red and white Roses alternately, with a knot, similar to that shown above, between each Rose.

CHAPTER XIX

SEALS AND MONUMENTS

I HAVE already adverted to the valuable assistance which Seals afford in the study of early Heraldry. Before we proceed to consider this subject in an Armorial point of view, it may not be uninteresting to notice briefly the manner in which Seals were employed in the pre-heraldic period, and the causes which, in after-ages, led to their general adoption for legal and other purposes.

The primary object for which Seals were devised was, without doubt, to furnish a mark of attestation to important documents in cases where the contracting parties were unable to subscribe their names ; and the practice of sealing was subsequently continued when the original purpose for which it was instituted had ceased. The custom of using Seals as a token of authenticity dates from an extremely remote period. Tribal distinctions seem to have been used in the form of Signets and Seals, even in the time of the patriarch Jacob. The Signet of Judah is the earliest mentioned instance in the Bible of a Seal as being the property of the wearer, known by an appropriate inscription. This was about the year 1730 B.C., so that writing and engraving Signets have certainly been in existence three thousand six hundred years—about two hundred and fifty years before Moses wrote the Book of Genesis. The Hebrew word rendered Signet (Gen. xxxviii. 18) denotes a Ring-Seal, with which impressions were made to ascertain property ; and

from Jeremiah xxii. 24 it seems that they were worn on
the hand, though they might also have been suspended from
the neck by a ribbon, as they are still worn by the Arabs.
Again, we read of Jezebel sealing letters with the King's
Seal ; of Darius sealing a decree with his own Signet, and
with those of his lords ; and in several other places in the
Old Testament reference is made to the practice.

In the British Museum, many impressions of ancient
Egyptian Seals are preserved. They are for the most part
square, and formed of fine clay, being affixed to the documents by strips of papyrus or cord. They seldom bear the
names of individuals, unless the contracting parties were of
regal dignity ; most of them are impressed with the sacred
names of the deities.

Amongst all classes of the Romans, Seals were commonly
in use. By an edict of Nero it was ordered that every
testator should affix his Seal to his will, and that it should
be further attested by the Seals of seven witnesses. No particular device seems to have been adopted by the Roman
Emperors upon their *sigilla* ; thus we find that of Julius
Cæsar bearing a representation of Venus ; Augustus, a
Sphinx, and sometimes the head of Alexander the Great.

In our own country, the earliest certain record we possess
of a Seal being attached to an important document dates
from the era of EDWARD the CONFESSOR. Anterior to this
period, however, documents are extant to which are appended
such a sentence as the following, which appears on a charter
of EDWY, brother of EDGAR (A.D. 956) : '*Ego Edwinus* . . .
meum donum proprio sigillo confirmavi ;' but it is extremely
doubtful whether the term *sigillum* does not rather refer to
the *Mark* of EDWY—the *Signum*, or Sign of the Cross.
Indeed, his brother EDGAR, in a charter to Crowland Abbey
(A.D. 966), expressly mentions this, in the following words :
'*Ego Edgardus* . . . *istud chirographium cum signo Sanctæ
Crucis confirmavi.*' The Sign of the Cross, attached to a
deed, seems to have been commonly employed as a sacred

pledge to render a compact binding, even in cases where the contracting parties were able to affix their signatures. In the charter of the foundation of the Abbey of St. Martin, by WILLIAM the FIRST,[1] a small Cross is placed in the centre of the signatures of the King and the fourteen nobles who attested it. The accompanying illustration is a facsimile of

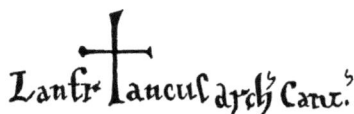

Lanfr Lancuſ aych Cant.

Fig. 374.

the signature of LANFRANCUS, ARCHBISHOP of CANTERBURY, one of the witnesses. Sir H. Spelman writes : ' So superstitiously did those Times think of the Crosse, that they held all things sanctified that bare the signe of it ; and therefore used it religiously in their Charters ; ' and from this circumstance may be deduced the custom which still obtains amongst persons unable to write of affixing their Cross or Mark. The earliest regal autograph known to exist is that of King RICHARD the SECOND. In the St. Martin's charter, it is probable that William affixed the Cross ; but the signature itself is evidently written by a clerk.

I have said that the earliest English Seal of which we possess an impression is that of the CONFESSOR : there exist, however, two others which, if authentic, are still older. One is a brass matrix of ÆLFRIC, EARL of MERCIA, found near WINCHESTER in the year 1832; and the other is an impression of the Seal of ETHELWALD, BISHOP of DUNWICH, found near the Monastery of Eye in 1821, and now preserved in the British Museum. These nobles were contemporaries, and lived about fifty years before the Accession of the CONFESSOR. It was not until after the Norman Conquest that wax impressions of Seals were regarded as necessary addenda to legal documents ; for although the CONFESSOR attached his

[1] *Bib. Harl. Chart. Antiq.*, 83a, xii.

Great Seal to certain Deeds and Charters, yet many bore no other mark of attestation than the *Signum Crucis* : but from the end of the Eleventh Century very few documents of importance exist which do not bear an impressed stamp on wax.   Originally, no one below the rank of a Baron was entitled to a seal ; but 'as land became more and more sub-infeudated, and wealth generally more distributed, the use of Seals was diffused among all classes legally competent to acquire or aliene property.'—*Archæological Journal*, vol. v.

The earliest manner in which Seals were attached to documents was *en placard*—that is, simply impressed on the margin of the parchment ; but shortly after other methods were devised. They were sometimes affixed by a parchment label to the bottom of the document, or suspended by silk cords ; at other times a strip was cut from the bottom, to the end of which the Seal was appended.   The object of these latter methods was, to enable the wax to receive an impression on each side.   The Great Seals of England are thus pendent, and bear a double device.   On the Obverse, which is sometimes itself called the Seal, appears an equestrian figure of the King ; and on the Reverse, or Counterseal, he is represented enthroned.

As the production of a new matrix was attended with a considerable expense, we find many of the early English Kings, by a slight alteration, utilising the Seals of their predecessors ; but from the time of Henry the Seventh a new Seal was engraved for every successive sovereign. That adopted by the Commonwealth deserves notice as much for the delicacy of its execution as for the curious devices upon it.   On the Obverse, usually occupied by an equestrian figure of the Reigning Monarch, was engraved, *A Map of England and Ireland ; in the Channel, a Fleet ; in chief, a Shield of St. George ; and in base, a Shield of Ireland.* Legend : *The Great Seale of England*, 1651. Reverse : *The House of Commons in Session.* Legend : *In the third Yeare of Freedome by God's Blessing restored*, 1651.

An interesting paper on the subject of the Great Seals of England between the years 1648 and 1660, written by W. D. Cooper, F.S.A., will be found in the *Archæologia*, vol. xxxviii.

Other objects than wax impressions were occasionally used as *Signa*, and appended to documents ; for we read of one monarch making his knife take the place of a Seal ; and it is recorded that ' King John, while he was Earle of Moriton, to his grant of yᵉ Church of Hope in Derbyshire made unto yᵉ canons of Litchfield, affixed his gold ring wᵗʰ a Turkye stone in it, to yᵉ silke string whereunto yᵉ seale was putt wᵗʰ this expression—Non solum sigilli mei Impressione, sed proprii annuli appositione roboravi.'—*Harl. MS. No.* 4630.

No relics of more importance to the Armorist exist, and on which greater reliance can be placed, than Seals ; for the devices thereon represented must always be those actually borne by their possessors at the time of their employment. On many ancient Deeds and Charters no dates are inserted, and Seals frequently afford the only evidence by which they can be determined.

The date of Seals can, in the majority of instances, be approximately ascertained by attention to the following general distinctions. Prior to the Thirteenth Century they were for the most part oval, and pointed ; those of secular Nobles bearing a representation of their possessors on horseback, without any Heraldic device. Until the Twelfth Century Roman capitals were generally used ; but about that era Gothic letters were adopted for the legends, which usually commenced with the form SI., SIG., or SIGILL. At the close of that century they were highly embellished, and Armorial Bearings began to appear, depicted on a shield. During the Fourteenth Century the paternal Arms were usually represented in the centre, dimidiated, and subsequently impaled, with those of the wife of him to whom the Seal belonged, ensigned with Helmet, Crest, and Mantling, and surrounded by small escutcheons, on which appeared the Arms of those Families with whom he claimed connection. During this era the legend was usually preceded by a Cross ; and later, by a Rose or Star. Towards the end of this century we find Seals protected by *Fenders*, which were formed of plaited twigs, rushes, straw, or paper, twisted around the impressions to protect them from injury. In the succeeding century the highest excellence of art was attained, and Seals were generally larger than at any other period. Quarterings were now exhibited, and the entire Seal was richly embellished with all the external ornaments of the shield, marks of Cadency being strictly attended to. From this period Seals began to lose their distinctive character ; but they almost invariably bore upon them the date of their adoption. The Seals of Ecclesiastics are nearly always of a pointed oval form, and the official Seals of Bishops are of that shape at the present day. The earliest ecclesiastical Seals bear a half-length impression of their possessors, who, shortly after the Conquest, are represented holding a pastoral staff in the left hand, the right being raised in the act of Benediction. During the Twelfth Century they appear at full length, either seated or standing ; and in the two succeeding centuries they are represented as seated, in full Episcopal vestments, usually under a canopy of more or less elaborate workmanship. The Papal leaden *Bullæ* were first instituted after the fall of the Western Empire ; the oldest known being that of Deusdedit (A.D. 615), which bears the figure of a Man standing between a Lion and a Lamb, and the Greek letters A and Ω. During the Thirteenth Century the Bullæ were somewhat larger than before, and bore a Cross between the heads of St. Peter and St. Paul, with the name of the Pope inscribed at full length, which hitherto had been signified only by a monogram. The Seals of Bullæ relating to matters of Justice were attached by a hempen cord ; but to those of Grace, by strands of silk.

The use of Seals on the Continent dates from an earlier

period than in England, although it is doubtful whether they really possess the high antiquity commonly asserted. CHARLEMAGNE, who was contemporary with the first of our Saxon Kings, is *said* to have added to the Royal Seal of France the words ' DEI GRATIA.' Subsequent to the time of HUGH CAPET (A.D. 987) the French Monarchs appeared holding a sceptre in the right hand. All Seals in France were impressed upon the parchment, *en placard*, until the reign of PHILIP the SECOND (A.D. 1180), from which period they were appended.

Much valuable information on the subject of Seals will be found in *Harl. MS. No.* 6079, written by Henry Lilly, Rouge-Rose Herald (*temp.* Elizab.), from which the following extract is made, the orthography of which I have taken the liberty of modernising : ' At first the king only, and a few other of the nobility beside him, used the seal. Afterwards, noblemen for the most part, and some others, as a man may see in the *History of Battle Abbey*, when Richard Lucye, Chief-Justice of England in the time of King Henry II., is reported to have blamed a mean subject for that he used a private seal, whereas that pertaineth (as he said) to the king and nobility only. At this time also (as John Ross noteth) they used to engrave in their seals their own pictures and counterfeits, covered with a long coat over their armour. After this, the gentlemen of the better sort took up the fashion ; and because they were not all warriors, they made seals engraved with their several coats, a shield of Arms, for difference' sake, as the same author reporteth. At length, about the time of King Edward III., sealing became very common ; so that not only such as bore Arms used the seal, but other men fashioned to themselves signets of their own device,— some taking the letters of their own name, some flowers, some knots and flourishes, some birds or beasts, or some other things, as now beheld daily in use.' See also Dugdale's *History of Warwickshire*, vol. ii. page 921. Also, if the reader be fortunate enough to find it, *A Dissertation on Seals,* by G. Lewis, 174 . . . The treatise is frequently referred to by writers on the subject ; but I have never been able to see a copy, though I once narrowly missed it in a second-hand bookseller's catalogue under the heading of Phocæ.

The device on the Sigillum Secretum, or Privy Seal, often differed as much from the Armorial Bearings as the Impress did from the Badge or Crest. I may quote as an example the Seal of John de Cusance, who, in the year 1342, attested a deed by affixing a Seal bearing a profile head, with the motto, *Je suis jolis e guay* ; his proper Arms being *an Eagle displayed* (*Mus. Brit. Add. Chart. No.* 1532).

In 1437, Sir John Fray, Chief-Baron of the Exchequer, attested a deed with the seal here engraved. It will be seen

Fig. 375.—Seal of Sir John Fray.

that the legend reads ' Thenk fayr Thenk ' (Þ = th) [1], or ' Thenk ay Thenk ' ; and that the word ' Fayr,' is simply an anagram of ' Fray.'

The colour of the wax affords but little evidence of the date of the impression : it may, however, be stated that, in general, wax of its natural colour—I refer, of course, to beeswax—bespeaks an earlier period than when tinted. Wafers were not introduced until the close of the Sixteenth Century, and sealing-wax—as now in ordinary use—until the Seventeenth.

The evidence afforded by Monumental Effigies,

---

[1] From the resemblance of the old character Þ to y, the word ' the,' originally written þe, afterwards became ' ye,' usually written yᵉ, to distinguish it from the personal pronoun.

BRASSES, and INSCRIPTIONS, cannot in all cases be so implicitly relied on by the student of Heraldry as that of Seals ; those records excepted which were executed shortly after the decease of the persons whose memory they were intended to perpetuate : in which cases it is impossible to overrate the value of such contemporaneous witnesses, whether as records of the existing fashion of Armour, Weapons, Vestments, or Heraldic Bearings. Reference has been made in another place to the palpable incorrectness of the blazoning of some of the early Shields of Arms represented on the tomb of QUEEN ELIZABETH ; and many similar instances might be adduced. Speaking of the errors sometimes found in monumental inscriptions, Mr. Grimaldi says : ' Many instances are on record of the incorrectness of inscriptions, which arises from various causes : executors are not always well informed on the subject; frequently all transactions relating to funerals and monuments (of eminent men especially) are under the direction of an undertaker, a man seldom very careful or very learned ; he, again, hands over half of his orders to the stonemason, a man probably of less learning ; and, if we often see the most absurd orthography in Epitaphs, there is less reason to impute infallibility to the chisel when carving dates. The monuments of Sterne and Goldsmith may be referred to as notorious proofs : in the latter, there is an error of no less than three years. . . . It therefore becomes especially the duty of genealogists to be careful against placing implicit dependence, in important cases, upon monumental inscriptions. Perhaps the proper light in which to regard them, should be rather as guides and helps to more accurate information, than as containing in themselves authentic evidence.' An error on a Seal, whether proceeding from carelessness or ignorance, could not fail of immediate detection ; and if such error were of any importance, it would be rectified at once. It would be impossible in such a Manual as this, treating of Heraldry generally, to devote sufficient space to a full consideration of this interesting and important branch of the subject. Stothard's *Monuments* ; Boutell's *Brasses*, and *Christian Monuments* ; Cutts's *Manual for the Study of Sepulchral Slabs and Crosses* ; and the Journals of the Archæological and other kindred Societies, will be found replete with interest to the student of Monumental Heraldry.

When Armorial Bearings are depicted both on the kirtle and the mantle of a female figure, it is usual to place the Arms of her family on the inner garment ; and on the outer, those of her husband, typifying that the husband is the outer shield and protection of his wife. A fine example of thus depicting hereditary and acquired Arms occurs in the East window of the Lady Chapel, in the Collegiate Church of WARWICK, wherein is represented ELEANOR, daughter and co-heir of RICHARD BEAUCHAMP, EARL of WARWICK, and wife of the DUKE of SOMERSET. When, however, the Mantle only is embroidered with Arms, those Arms are usually the family Arms of the lady, as for example at BROXBOURNE, where ELIZABETH, Lady SAY, is covered with a Mantle emblazoned with her paternal Arms of CHENEY, while the impaled Arms of her husband and herself are on a shield above her.

Fig 376.—Seal of Thomas Charleton (A.D. 1420).

CHAPTER XX

FLAGS

THE custom of depicting Heraldic Devices upon FLAGS has been practised from the remotest period of antiquity ; indeed, as I have before remarked, Flags were probably charged with certain distinctive figures Ages before such devices were borne upon Shields. In the Bayeux Tapestry, some of the Normans appear bearing lances, to which are attached small Flags, charged with a Cross, as in the margin. This can scarcely be considered as a Norman Heraldic Charge, for the Cross was universally adopted as a Symbol by all Christian nations, and was impressed on Saxon coins long anterior to the Conquest.

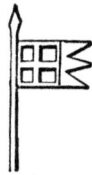

Fig. 377.

Several varieties of Flags were formerly employed, indicating by their form and size the rank of the bearer. The use of many of these, however, has now become obsolete ; but, as frequent allusion is made to them in History and in ancient Ballads, it is necessary that the modern Herald should be acquainted with the names and significations of the Flags of former times. In the following passage from *Marmion*, several Flags, now disused, are particularised :

> ' Nor marked they less, where in the air
> A thousand streamers flaunted fair :
> Various in shape, device, and hue—
> Green, sanguine, purple, red, and blue,
> Broad, narrow, swallow-tailed, and square,
> Scroll, pennon, pensil, bandrol, there
> O'er the pavilions flew.

s

Highest and midmost was descried
The Royal banner, floating wide ;
    The staff, a pine-tree strong and straight,
Pitched deeply in a massive stone,
Which still in memory is shown.
    Yet beneath the Standard's weight,
Whene'er the western wind unrolled,
With toil, the huge and cumbrous fold,
    And gave to view the dazzling field,
    Where, in proud Scotland's Royal shield,
The ruddy Lion ramped in gold.'

The same rules are to be observed in blazoning a Flag as in blazoning a Shield ; observing that the former is always supposed to be transparent : if, therefore, the material of which it is composed be so thick as to be opaque, the Charges on the other side must be drawn in reverse, so that the several devices exactly cover each other ; in other words, all Charges (except those intended to be contourné) should appear as though advancing towards the Staff.

The length of a Flag, from the Staff to the end, is called the *Fly ;* and the depth, the *Dip.*

The BANNER (fig. 378) was a small Flag, nearly square, or a *Pennon* (fig. 380) with the points torn off.   It was formerly the custom for a Sovereign on the field of battle to reward a Knight who was the leader of fifty Men-at-arms, besides Archers, for any particular act of gallantry by tearing the points off his Pennon ; thus converting it into a Banner.   Thenceforward the Knight was entitled to emblazon his Arms upon a square Shield, and was styled a Knight Banneret.   Barnes, in his *Wars of Edward the Third*, writes that, before the Battle of Nagera, LORD JOHN CHANDOS brought his Pennon to EDWARD the BLACK PRINCE, requesting permission to hoist it as a Banner.   The Prince took the Flag, and, having torn off the tail, returned it, saying : 'Sir John, behold, here is your Banner ; God send you much joy and honour with it.'

The Banner (on which were emblazoned all the quarterings of him to whom it belonged) was attached to a staff or lance, or, more frequently, depended from a trumpet—which custom is still retained by the Trumpeters of the Household Brigade. We read in Shakespeare :—

'I will a Banner from a Trumpet take, and use it for my haste ;'

and again, in Chaucer :—

'On every trump hanging a brode bannere
Of fine tartarium[1] full richly bete ;
Every trumpet his lordis armes bere.'

A good example of a Banner attached to an upright staff is to be found in the Chapel of St. Paul, in WESTMINSTER Abbey. At each corner of the tomb of LEWIS ROBSART, K.G., Standard-bearer to King HENRY the FIFTH, is a Banner of his Arms carved in stone, in bold relief. Two of these Banners are as represented in the margin, supported by a Lion ; and in the other two, supported by a Falcon, the third

Fig. 378.

quarter is occupied by three Buckles, and the fourth by a Chaplet.

The Flags carried by Cavalry regi-ments, though usually called *Standards*, should properly be styled *Banners*. The term *Colours* is applied to the Flags of Foot regiments.

On the *Royal Banner*, commonly called the *Standard*, are displayed the quartered Arms of the United Kingdom ; and on the *Ensign*, or *Union Jack*,[2] the Crosses of England, Scotland, and Ireland,

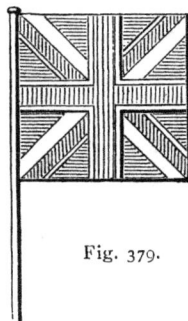

Fig. 379.

---

[1] 'A fine cloth manufactured in Tartary.'—*Du Cange.*
  '*His cote armure was of cloth of Tars.*'—*Knight's Tale.*
[2] The term *Jack* is probably a corruption of *Jacques*, or James,

S 2

blazoned as follows : *Azure ; the Saltires of St. Patrick and St. Andrew, quarterly per saltire, counterchanged, argent and gules ; the latter fimbriated of the second ; surmounted by the Cross of St. George of the third, fimbriated as the last.*

The first Union Jack, devised in the year 1606, consisted of the Saltire of St. Andrew, surmounted by the Cross of St. George, the latter fimbriated. The present Ensign (fig. 379) has served to typify the United Kingdom since the year 1801.

It is a curious fact that, on the existing bronze currency, the shield on which Britannia is represented as seated is incorrectly blazoned. The national Ensign is made to appear as a single Saltire, surmounted by a Cross, both fimbriated ; and the same device is sculptured on the marble Monument to General Howe, in St. Paul's Cathedral. On the medals of the Exhibition of 1862 the inaccuracy is, if possible, still more flagrant. The Union of the three kingdoms is there represented by a plain Saltire, surmounted by a fimbriated Cross—in fact, the Ensign of the Seventeenth and Eighteenth Centuries.

However little a man may know of Heraldry in general, an Englishman should at least know his own *Union Jack ;* but how few do ! The following letter, which appeared in a Country newspaper, though flippantly written, should be carefully read. Not being signed by me, I may be permitted to speak of it in high terms of commendation :—

PITY POOR JACK.

SIR,—I am not a grumbler, though I am treated very badly. How, sir, may I ask, would you like to be hung up by your heels? or how would any of your readers like to stand on their heads for a week together ? And yet I, who am (with the exception of my cousin, the Standard) the most noble bit of bunting in the world, am, even in the

during whose reign, as every reader of history is aware, the Union between England and Scotland was effected.

loyal county of Hertford, constantly displayed upside down, and am thus turned from a symbol of rejoicing into a signal of distress, and all because the descendants of those who marched and sailed under me to victory will not take the trouble to find out how I ought to be hoisted.

But, sir, I should probably have gone on and suffered in silence if I had not come across the following paragraph in your paper of November 16th :—' Mr. —— had two Union Jacks—the *red* and the *white*.'—How, sir, could you, being a *blue*, mistake my children, the ensigns, for me ? I will, therefore, give a short sketch of my history.

Long before I was known to the world as Jack, I was the Banner of Saint George. I was a white flag, with a red Cross ; thus I flew at Agincourt ; thus I appear at coronations, and a few other State occasions ; and thus I denote the presence of an English Admiral.

In 1606 the Banner of Saint Andrew—Azure ; a Saltire argent (blue with white diagonal cross) —was united to that of Saint George by virtue of a royal ordinance given on April 12th, 4 Jac. I. Heralds thus described me then : —' The Cross of Saint Andrew, surmounted by that of Saint George, the latter fimbriated argent ' (*i.e.* bordered white).

I continued in this state until the 1st January, 1801, when upon the Union with Ireland it became necessary to incorporate the Cross of Saint Patrick—Argent ; a Saltire gules (white, a red diagonal Cross) ; and I am thus described in a royal Proclamation of that date :— ' Azure ; the Crosses saltire of Saint Andrew and Saint Patrick, quarterly per saltire, counterchanged argent and gules ; the latter fimbriated, and the second surmounted by the Cross of Saint George, of the third, fimbriated as the saltire.'

In 1606 the Heralds departed from their own rules in forming me. Instead of quartering my two Crosses they endeavoured to make them into one. The Heralds of 1801 followed their example ; and the result is that I am now a heraldic absurdity, though, having flown over so many glorious fights, probably no attempt to alter me would succeed. Sir Harris Nicolas tried to get me slightly altered in 1832 : he wanted me to appear as I do on the bronze coinage, where I am represented wrongly, though perhaps sensibly, thus :—The Cross of Saint Andrew, surmounted by that of Saint Patrick, over all the Cross of Saint George, fimbriated argent. But I have not been re-arranged yet, and I don't suppose I ever shall be, so I will try to describe myself in plain English. I am a blue flag, divided into four quarters by a red Cross, with a narrow white border. Each quarter is divided by a red diagonal bar, with white border from corner to centre ; but the borders are not of equal width, *those nearest the staff being broad above and narrow below, those in my fly,* i.e. *in my second and fourth quarters, being narrow above and broad below.* Therefore, sir, if any of your loyal

readers have occasion to hoist me, I hope they will see that the broad
white border of the diagonal Cross is uppermost—next the staff.

One word more and I have done, ' Hoist me right up ' ; don't have
me flying four or five inches from the staff-head.   I have to fly half-
mast sometimes, and it is hard to be made to do so on occasions of
rejoicing.—I am, Sir, your obedient servant,

UNION JACK.

February 12, 1873.

The BANNER-ROLL, or BANDROL, and GUYDHOMME, or
GUIDON, were small Banners, edged with fringe, or twisted
silk, and rounded at the *Fly*, charged with the separate
quarterings of a Noble, and were usually displayed at
funeral processions.

The PENNON was a small narrow Flag indented at the
Fly, resembling the modern BURGEE.   It was usually affixed

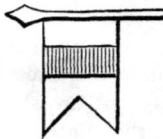

Fig. 380.

to the end of a lance, from which, when in
actual use, it depended ; and the Charges
thereon were so emblazoned as to appear
correctly when the lance was held in a horizontal position.   Thus, fig. 380 would represent *Argent ; a Fess gules*.   If the lance were
carried in an erect position, the *Fess gules* would become
a *Pale azure*.

In his *Canterbury Tales*, Chaucer puts the following
words into the mouth of the Knight :—

> ' And by hys bannere borne is hys pennon
> Of gold full riche.'

Sir Walter Scott thus alludes to this Flag in *Marmion* :—

> ' The trustiest of the four
> On high his forky pennon bore ;
> Like swallow's tail in shape and hue,
> Fluttered the streamer glossy blue,
> Where, blazoned sable, as before,
> The towering falcon seemed to soar.'

PENONCELS, or PENSILS, were small narrow Pennons,
usually borne to ensign the Helmet, or to form part of the
caparisons of the Knight's Charger, though they were some-

times affixed to lances, as appears from a line of the *Lyfe of Alesaunder*, a metrical Romance of the Fourteenth Century :

> ' Many a fair pencel on spere.'

The ANCIENT was a small Banner or Pennon. The bearer of it was called by the same name, and held a position in the Army somewhat analogous to the Ensign of modern days. This circumstance explains that passage in *Othello* where Cassio, in speaking to Iago, says :—

> ' The Lieutenant is to be saved before the Ancient.'

The PAVON was a peculiarly-shaped Flag, somewhat like a Gyron attached to a spear. The accompanying cut is taken from an illuminated Psalter executed for Sir Geoffrey Loutterell about the year 1340. The original is charged with the Arms of Sir Geoffrey : *Azure ; a Bend between six Martlets argent.*

Fig. 381.

The GONFANNON was a Banner, or Guidon, bordered with fringe or twisted silk, and usually supported as shown in the annexed illustration. In the *Lyfe of Alesaunder*, before alluded to, we read :—

> ' Ther gonfanons and their penselles
> Wer well wrought off grene sendels.' [1]

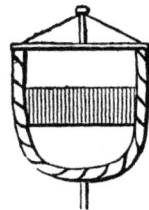

Fig. 382.

The STANDARD was a Flag somewhat resembling an elongated Pennon. It did not, like the Banner, indicate a distinctive mark of honour, but might be borne by any noble commander, irrespective of his rank ; the only restriction observed being that of its length : a King's Standard was eight to nine yards long : a Duke's, seven ; a Marquess's, six and a half ; an Earl's, six ; a Viscount's, five and a half ; a Baron's, five ; a Banneret's, four and a half ;

[1] ' Sendale was a thynne stuffe lyke sarcenett, and of a raw kynde of sylke or sarcenett, but coarser and narrower than the sarcenett now ys.'—*Animadversions on Speight's Chaucer*, by Thynne, A.D. 1598.

and a Knight's, four. The Banner, it has been already mentioned, was always charged with the *Arms* of its owner ; but on the Standard the *Crest* or *Badge*, and *Motto*, only were exhibited ; the Field being composed of the Livery Colours. When the Livery of a Family consisted of more than one colour—as the Tudor Sovereigns, for example, who bore argent and vert—the Standard was always parted per fess of such Colours. Towards the staff was emblazoned the Cross of St. George ; then followed the Badge or Badges, repeated an indefinite number of times ; surmounted by narrow Bends, on which was inscribed the Motto, or *Cri-de-guerre ;* the whole being usually surrounded by a roll of silk, company of the Livery Colours. The Charges were so depicted upon the Standard as to appear correct when it was *developed* by the wind in a horizontal position. On account of its size, it was not generally carried in the hand, like a Banner, but the staff to which it was attached was fixed in the ground—hence its name.

The following interesting List of Royal Standards is taken from a MS. in the College of Heralds, A.D. 1590, marked I. 2. As it would be almost impossible, on account of the number and peculiar position of the Charges, to describe a Standard in the same manner as a Shield of Arms, I have adopted a method which will, by reference to the example given below—the standard of EDWARD the FOURTH—be sufficiently intelligible.

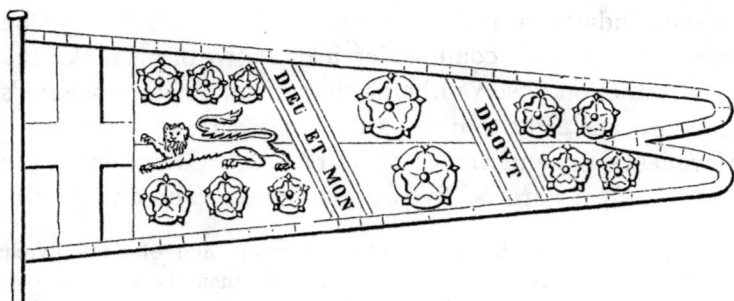

Fig. 383.

The Cross of St. George—Per fess, azure and gules—A Lion of England imperially crowned, between three roses gules in chief, and as many argent in base, barbed, seeded, and irradiated or—DIEU ET MON—*In chief a rose gules, and in base another argent*—DROYT—*In chief two roses gules, and in base as many argent.*

EDWARD III. *The Cross of St. George—Per fess azure and gules—A Lion of England imperially crowned ; in chief a coronet of crosses paté and fleurs-de-lys, between two clouds irradiated proper ; and in base a cloud between two coronets*—DIEU ET MON—*In chief a coronet, and in base an irradiated cloud*—DROYT—*Quarterly : 1 and 4. An irradiated cloud ; 2 and 3. A coronet.*

RICHARD II. *The Cross of St. George—Argent and vert—A Hart lodged argent, attired, unguled, ducally gorged and chained or, between four suns in splendour*—DIEU ET MON—*Two suns in splendour*—DROYT—*Four suns in splendour.*

HENRY V. *The Cross of St. George—Argent and azure—A Swan with wings displayed argent, beaked gules, membered sable, ducally gorged and chained or, between three stumps of trees, one in dexter chief, and two in base of the last*—DIEU ET MON—*Two stumps of trees in pale or*—DROYT—*Five stumps of trees, three in chief, and two in base.*

Another of HENRY V. *The Cross of St. George—Argent and azure—A heraldic Antelope at gaze argent, maned, tufted, ducally gorged and chained or, chain reflexed over the back, between four roses gules*—DIEU ET MON—*Two roses in pale gules*—DROYT—*Five roses in saltire gules.*

HENRY VII. *The Cross of St. George—Argent and vert—A Dragon gules, between two roses of the last in chief, and three in base, argent*—DIEU ET MON—*A rose gules in chief, and another argent in base*—DROIT—*In chief three roses gules, and in base two argent.*

On another Standard of HENRY VII. appears *a Grey-*

hound courant argent, collared gules ; the whole being semé of Tudor roses, Portcullises, and Fleurs-de-lys or.

The Standards displayed at the Funeral of the Protector afford a curious example of Republican Armory. That for England was as follows : *The Cross of St. George—gules throughout—a Lion of England imperially crowned statant on a crown—*PAX QUÆRITUR*—*BELLO*—the field promiscuously strewed with the letters O.P. or.*

Much valuable information on the subject of Flags will be found in the *Art Journal* for the years 1859-60-61.

During the Thirteenth Century, the custom originated in England of surmounting the pinnacles and towers of Castles with VANES, bearing the Arms of the lord. These were probably in the first instance but Banners or *Fanions*— hence *Fane,* and, more recently, *Vane—*which were displayed on the most conspicuous part of a Castle as a mark of supremacy, in the manner we still see them ; which custom might have taken its origin from the practice of victorious generals erecting their Standards, or Banners, on the most elevated spot of the battle-field, or newly-acquired territory, as the first act of possession.

Marchangy, in his *Gaule poétique,* writes : ' Le droit de placer des girouettes sur un château, n'appartint, dans l'origine, qu'à ceux qui les premiers étaient montés à l'assaut, et qui avaient arboré leur bannière sur le rempart ennemi. Aussi donnait-on à ces girouettes la figure d'un drapeau, et l'on y peignait les armoiries du maître du lieu.' In *Mémoires sur l'ancienne Chevalerie,* by La Curne de Sainte Palaye, we read : ' Les gentilshommes seuls avaient le privilège de parer de girouettes le faîte de leurs maisons. Ces girouettes étaient en pointe comme les pennons pour les simples chevaliers, et carrées comme les bannières pour les chevaliers bannerets.'

The following extract is translated from the same curious and interesting work : ' In the enterprise of Saintré, himself and his companions bore on their helmets two Banners, between which was a diamond, destined to be the reward of those who should prove their victors. Saintré proposed a *pas d'armes* to the English, between Gravelines and Calais, which was accepted by the Count of Bonquincan and his companions. On the Sunday, the first day of the month, in the morning, after saying Mass, the said Lord and Count of Bonquincan arrived, and a brave company with him, who had placed on the highest wing of his house his banner, which he had brought from England, bordered with silver,' &c. Bonquincan thus, though the challenged party, flew his *Fanion* in defiance, in attestation of his right.

Unfortunately, the action of the weather has destroyed the most interesting examples of Vanes, those only of a comparatively recent date remaining to us.

Fig. 384.

Vane above the Library of Lambeth Palace.

CHAPTER XXI

GENEALOGIES AND FAMILY HISTORIES

' Family tradition and genealogical history are the very reverse of amber, which, itself a valuable substance, usually includes flies, straws, and other trifles ; whereas these studies, being themselves very insignificant and trifling, do, nevertheless, serve to perpetuate a great deal of what is rare and valuable in ancient manners, and to record many curious and minute facts, which could have been preserved and conveyed through no other medium.'—SIR WALTER SCOTT.

ARRANGING Genealogies in a tabular form, so as to exhibit clearly and concisely the lineal descent of a Family, with its collateral branches, forms one of the most important vocations of the Herald. In the acquisition of this art, the Science of Heraldry may justly be deemed to culminate ; for he who would profess to be a Genealogist must not only possess a perfect knowledge of the Charges used in Armory, but must also be intimately acquainted with the laws of Blazoning and Marshalling. I do not mean to say that, without this knowledge, it is impossible to draw up a Pedigree in a tabular form, for that is merely mechanical employment, which anyone who can read and write can easily learn to accomplish in a few hours ; but to deduce from such Genealogy the Armorial Bearings to which each member in the scheme would be entitled, and the manner of bearing them, requires the science of a Herald.

It is essential, in Ancestral Charts, to append a short account of the principal events in the lives of the chief members of the Family ; such as the time and place of Birth, Baptism, Marriage, Death, and place of Interment ;

together with their Profession, or the offices they may have held, and any circumstances worthy of note with which they may have been connected. A copious record of this description is commonly called a GENEALOGY; but when the names only are inserted, with the dates of Birth and Death and the Matrimonial connections, it is usually styled a PEDIGREE. Both words, however, are frequently used in the same signification. Assuming that this difference exists between a Genealogy and a Pedigree, the latter is utterly worthless, unless it be designed merely as a chart to indicate family connections. It is the easiest thing in the world to assert, John, born 1760; married, 1785, Mary, and had issue John, William, and Henry, and died 1820; but quite a different thing to prove it. The entry respecting this apocryphal John should run: 'John, eldest son; born 3 June and baptised 14 June, 1760, at St. Mary's, Chester; M.A. St. John's Coll. Camb. 1801; Instituted to Rectory of St. Peter, Ely, 13 May, 1803; married at St. Ann's, Ipswich, 3 July, 1785, Mary, daughter and co-heir of Henry Brown, of Ipswich, Esq., and Susan, his wife; died at Plymouth 14 August, 1820, and buried in St. Charles's Church there. Will dated 13 May, 1810; proved in London, 30 October, 1810, by Mary, his widow, and John, his eldest son.' Here we have a complete history of the individual, with such definite references to the essential points, that if correct they can be established, and if 'fudged,' they can be easily disproved.

In a tabulated pedigree all those persons of one generation should be arranged *in the same horizontal line.* If the names be too numerous to permit their insertion on one line, and the record be made in a book, so that it is impossible to enlarge the sheet, the horizontal line may be continued on the following leaf; and when a Pedigree extends to the bottom of a page, Letters of the Alphabet, or Numbers, should be placed under the name of every individual which appears on the last line; and the same Letters, or Numbers, must be carried to the top of the next page, so as clearly to indicate the continuation of the chart.

It frequently happens when Pedigrees are printed, that space forbids such an arrangement, and that *drop-lines* are obliged to be used. I here give, as examples, a skeleton pedigree (omitting details), as it should be drawn up, and the same as it would appear in a book of less width than this :—

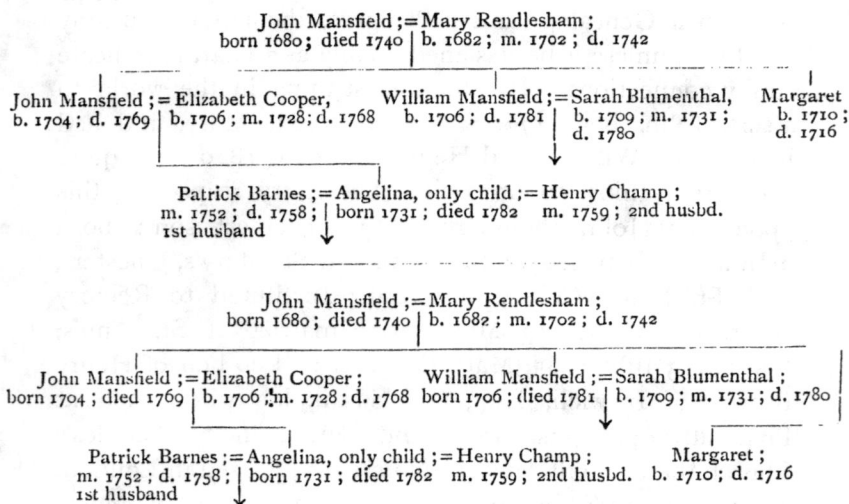

John Mansfield ;=Mary Rendlesham ;
born 1680; died 1740 | b. 1682 ; m. 1702 ; d. 1742

| John Mansfield ;=Elizabeth Cooper,
b. 1704 ; d. 1769 \| b. 1706 ; m. 1728; d. 1768 | William Mansfield ;=Sarah Blumenthal,
b. 1706 ; d. 1781 \| b. 1709 ; m. 1731 ;
d. 1780 | Margaret
b. 1710 ;
d. 1716 |

Patrick Barnes ;=Angelina, only child ;=Henry Champ ;
m. 1752 ; d. 1758 ; | born 1731 ; died 1782   m. 1759 ; 2nd husbd.
1st husband

John Mansfield ;=Mary Rendlesham ;
born 1680; died 1740 | b. 1682 ; m. 1702 ; d. 1742

| John Mansfield ;=Elizabeth Cooper ;
born 1704 ; died 1769 \| b. 1706 ; m. 1728 ; d. 1768 | William Mansfield ;=Sarah Blumenthal ;
born 1706 ; died 1781 \| b. 1709 ; m. 1731 ; d. 1780 | |

Patrick Barnes ;=Angelina, only child ;=Henry Champ ;   Margaret ;
m. 1752 ; d. 1758 ; | born 1731 ; died 1782   m. 1759 ; 2nd husbd.   b. 1710 ; d. 1716
1st husband

It will be noticed that in the second scheme, Margaret, who belongs to the second generation, is brought down to the same level as her niece Angelina. The drop-line, however, shows that Margaret is sister to John and William. Drop-lines should never be used unless it is absolutely necessary. In charts in which there is ample space there is no excuse for them.

In enumerating Issue, it is better to commence on the dexter side with the eldest child, and so continue towards the sinister ; by which means seniority is plainly indicated, when the dates of Birth are not appended. Some Genealogists, however, depart from this practice, and arrange the sons and daughters in two groups : others keep the main line of descent in a vertical column ; but this is sometimes attended with some difficulty. I usually put the eldest son's wife on his right, that is, on the left on the chart. This I do to shorten the extension line. Others insist that the husband should always be on the dexter side of his wife. These, however, are but minor details, to which no great importance attaches ; the primary consideration to be borne in mind is, as I have before stated, to keep the generations separate.

The following are the most frequent Abbreviations and Marks to be met with in Genealogies :

Born	*na.* . . .	Natus, or nata.
Son and Heir	*fil. et hær.* ,	Filius et hæres.
Daughter and Heir. . .	,, ,, .	Filia et hæres.
Married	*m. d.* . . .	{ Matrimonio duxit (for a son).
,, ...	*nup.* . . .	Nupsit (for a daughter).
Died	*ob.* . . .	Obiit.
,, an infant	*ob. inf.* . .	Obiit infans.
,, in youth	*ob. juv.* . .	Obiit juvenis.
,, a minor.	*ob. inf. æt.* .	Obiit infra ætatem.
,, a bachelor	*ob. cœl.* . .	Obiit cœlebs.
,, a spinster	*ob. inn.* . .	Obiit innupta.
,, without issue . . .	*ob. s. p.* . .	Obiit sine prole.
,, ,, lawful issue .	*ob. s. p. leg.*	Obiit sine prole legitimatâ.
,, ,, male issue. .	*ob. s. p. mas.*	Obiit sine prole masculâ.
,, ,, surviving issue	*ob. s. p. s.* .	Obiit sine prole superstite.
,, in the lifetime of his or her father . .	*ob. v. p.* .	Obiit vitâ patris.
Age, of his or her . . .	*æt.* . . .	Ætatis.
Buried	*sepult.* . .	Sepultus, or sepulta.
In the county of	*com.* . .	Comitatu.
Was living, or lived (in the time of)	*viv.,* or *vix.*	Vivans, or vixit.

= signifies that the two persons between whose names such mark appears were husband and wife.

↓, when placed under a person's name, signifies that he or she had children whom it is unnecessary to specify.

× signifies extinction of that branch of the Family.

n.f.—ne fallor—implies a doubt ; sometimes represented by a note of interrogation.

The following Abbreviations are generally employed in modern Genealogies:—

Born . . . . b.
Married . . . . mar.
Died . . . . d.
Buried . . . . bu.
Son and heir . . . . s. & h.
Daughter and heir, or Co-heir . . . dau. & h., or coh.
Mon. Ins., or M. I., signifies that there is a Monumental Inscription in the church where the person referred to is buried.

In the example on the next page, it will be seen that Henry Holland—whose arms were, *Per Fess az. and gu., three Fleurs-de-lys arg.*—married Alice, the daughter and co-heir of Henry Mailmaing. Their daughter Jane married Thomas Goldwell, whose son William, in right of his mother, quartered the Arms of Goldwell, Holland, and Mailmaing. Alice Haute, William Goldwell's wife, was heir to four Coats—Haute, Surrenden, Gatton, and Dene : hence their daughter Joan, who married Thomas Toke, of Bere, brought in Goldwell, Holland, Mailmaing, Haute, Surrenden, Gatton, and Dene, to the Escutcheon of the Tokes,—from whom are descended the existing families of the Tookes, Tukes, and Tucks.

The task of tracing the Pedigree of a family is frequently one of considerable difficulty, more especially if the name of such family be of common occurrence. For the assistance of those who may be desirous of discovering their own or others' ancestry, I subjoin a few directions, attention to which will generally bring such investigations to a suc-cessful issue. It would be advisable, in the first place, to ascertain at the College of Heralds what records, if any, are there to be found of the Family whose descent is required. Pedigrees are, in most instances, deposited with the Heralds, on receiving a Grant or Confirmation of Arms ; and with Peers of the Realm this is compulsory. These Pedigrees are frequently continued by the grantee's descendants. The re-cords in the Family Bible, or other documents of a similar

Figs. 385 to 391

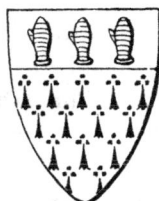

HENRY HOLLAND, of Fetton, *ob.* 10 Ric. II.=ALICE, d. and coh. of HENRY MAIL-
MAING.

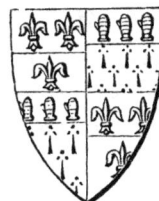

THOMAS GOLDWELL, of Godington, =JANE, d. and coh. of HENRY HOLLAND.
Co. Kent, *ob.* 5 H. V.

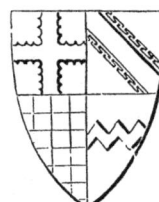

WILLIAM GOLDWELL, of Godington, = ALICE, d. and coh. of JOHN HAUTE.
viv. 5 H. VI.

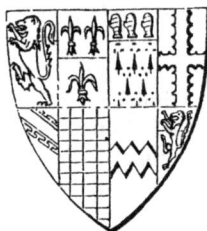

The bottom Shield represents the Arms brought in by JOAN GOLDWELL.

T

nature, will usually give two or three generations : beyond
these (should the College of Heralds afford no assistance),
reference must be made to Parochial and other local Registers,
and Wills.   The latter frequently supply a valuable clue
to collateral branches of the Family.[1]   Old numbers of
The Annual Register and *The Gentleman's Magazine*, Army
Lists, and College Registers, will also, in many instances, be
found of great service.   If the Pedigree can be traced up to
the middle of the Seventeenth Century, and the Family were
at that time entitled to Armorial Bearings, the *Visitations
of the Heralds* may carry it three generations higher, or
more.   The real labour now commences ; and unless the
Family were during the Sixteenth Century either Noble, or
were landed proprietors, further research is almost useless.
County Histories, Documents in the Public Record Office
(particularly Subsidy Rolls, for in them will be found the
names of *every* householder assessed), and, in some cases,
Municipal Archives and Monastic Chartularies, must now be
carefully and patiently examined ; [2] the genealogist bearing

---

[1] The transcripts of Wills of all persons who resided in or around
London are to be found at Somerset House, as are also those of many
persons in the Country who devised property of any considerable
amount ; but sometimes, particularly when only small properties were
bequeathed, the Executors would prove the Wills in the Court of the
Bishop within whose Diocese they were situated.   Some Dioceses contained an exempt jurisdiction, called a Peculiar, in which many Wills
were proved.   Individuals are sometimes supposed to have died intestate,
when their Wills are really deposited in some insignificant Peculiar, or
perhaps at Peterborough, York, or Durham.   The records of the Cir-
cumcision of Jewish infants are carefully preserved in the Synagogues.
Full details of their parentage are given, long before they were required by the Registration Act of 1837.   The Society of Friends, commonly called Quakers, are admirable genealogists.   Unfortunately, many
of their early records are lost ; but those that exist are absolutely
perfect in every essential particular.

[2] Mr. W. J. Hardy, F.S.A., and Mr. W. Page, F.S.A., whose
valuable labours are justly appreciated by every worker in the Antiquarian field, have recently (1893) issued a Calendar of the *Feet of
Fines* for London and Middlesex from the reign of Richard I. to the

in mind that no reliance can be placed on the orthography of proper names, either of persons or places. Except in a few rare instances, it is utterly impossible to trace a Pedigree beyond the time of Richard the Second ; and those persons who assert that their Ancestors 'came over with the Conqueror' derive their authority chiefly, if not wholly, from Tradition, or their own imagination. For the same reason that it is difficult for such persons to prove their assertion, it is equally difficult to refute it.

Nothing is more common than for a person bearing a certain name to imagine that he is necessarily connected with another family of the same name. Samuel Johnson, the retired tradesman, anxious to trace his pedigree, may be of the same family as the Lexicographer, but the chances are that he is not. In the London newspapers of the 14th September, 1870, appeared an account of an Inquest on an infant who was found in Tolmers Square. The child was taken to the Workhouse, where it subsequently died. At the Inquest it was described as ' Joseph Smith, parents unknown.' The Coroner asked how, if the parents were unknown, it was called Joseph Smith. The reply was that when a deserted child was brought into the Workhouse, it was given the name of one of the Guardians, and Mr. Joseph Smith happening to be the Chairman for that week, the child was named after him.

Thousands of children have received their names at the hands of the Parish Beadle. ' Dr. Lankester held an Inquest at Marylebone Workhouse, on the body of a female child which had been christened Elizabeth Wimpole, from the circumstance that it had been found in an area in Wimpole Street. . . .' (*Standard*, Nov. 15, 1872). I knew a

year 1834. The *Pedes Finium*, preserved in the Public Record Office, are of the utmost service to the genealogist, for, dealing as they do mostly with the conveyance of land, persons from every part of the country, and in every station of life, are mentioned. These records have hitherto been unindexed, and, therefore, to a great extent, unavailable to the searcher.

T 2

person called Mornington, who was brought up in the Foundling Hospital, and received her name from the fact of having been found, when an infant, in Mornington Crescent.

Many of the descendants of such children, now perhaps in good circumstances, but ignorant of their origin, fondly imagine that they are allied to the noble families whose names they bear.

Further, it must be borne in mind that it was not until the Fifteenth Century that Surnames among the lower classes became general. Before that period (although serfdom no longer existed), it was much the same in England as it was in the United States thirty years ago : that is, two slaves, neither with any further name than John, would for distinction sake be called by their master's name, and those names they and their descendants retained after their emancipation.

Again, private soldiers, sailors, and actors, seldom give their real names when they commence their career ; and in the majority of cases the name so assumed is that by which they and their descendants are known.

At the same time, it must be borne in mind that the pronunciation of proper names has done much to baffle the genealogist. The Moons, Boons, and Bones of to-day un-doubtedly derive their patronymics (whether directly or indirectly I cannot pretend to say) from the de Mohuns and the de Bohuns. Puddefat and Puddephatt are to-day common family names in the western part of Hertfordshire. By various records I have traced the name through Pudifer and Pedifer to Pied-de-fer, in which form it appears in an *Inquisitio post mortem* in the time of Edward III.

The *Visitations of the Heralds* are invaluable to the Genealogist. These Visitations were made for the purpose of examining the right by which the persons within the respective Heraldic Provinces bore Arms, or were styled Esquires or Gentlemen. The results of these official in-quiries were carefully collected, and subsequently recorded in the College of Heralds. The earliest Visitation which

PARADIGM of ALPHABETS

Set Chancery		Common Chancery		Court Hand		Secretary Stuart Period
A	a	A	a	A	o	A a
B	b	C	b	A	B	B b
C	c	C	t	C	o	tt t
D	d	D	d	D	d	D d
E	e	E	e	E	o	E v
ff	f	ff	f	ff	f	ff f
G	g	G	g	D	g	C g
h	h	h	h	h	h	G l
I	i	J	i	I	1	z i
k	k	k	k	k	k	k k
l	l	l	l	l	l	l l
M	m	M	m	M	III	M m
N	n	N	n	N	II	N n
O	o	O	o	O	o	O o
P	p	P	p	P	p	U k
Q	q	Q	q	Q	q	R q
R	rz	R	zl	R	zl	R v
S	sz	S	s	O	s	G s s
T	t	T	t	T	b	C t
U	uv	S	v	U	u	U u
W	w	W	ww	W	ww	H w
X	x	X	x	X	x	V x
Y	y	Y	y	Y	y	Y y
Z	3	Z	z	Z	z	Z z

we possess took place in 1528-9, by order of a Commission granted and executed by Thomas Benoilt, *Clarencieux ;* although informal Visitations were made in the reigns of HENRY the FOURTH, EDWARD the FOURTH, and HENRY the SEVENTH, of which only fragments remain. Until 1687, when the last Visitation was made, they were regularly conducted every twenty or thirty years. Unfortunately for the Genealogist, dates are, for the most part, omitted in these recorded Pedigrees ; but, by collating them with the Visitations of other Counties and periods, the dates can generally be approximated with tolerable precision. It is much to be regretted that these MSS. are now dispersed in various places : some are to be found in the Libraries of Queen's College, Oxford ; Caius College, Cambridge ; and in those of other provincial towns ; while some are in private collections : but by far the greatest number are preserved in the British Museum and the College of Heralds.

Some of the Visitations and earlier documents have been legibly copied and published ; but as these constitute but a small part of the entire collection, it is absolutely necessary that the student should be able to decipher the originals. In Astle's *Origin and Progress of Writing* (4to, 1803), and Wright's *Court Hand Restored* (sq. 8vo, 1773), ample directions will be found for the acquirement of a knowledge of the various styles of caligraphy practised in England, down to the reign of ELIZABETH ; but as the Visitations commenced from about the period where these authors conclude, I have deemed it advisable to furnish a few examples of later styles, taken from Manuscripts preserved in the British Museum.

The accompanying tabular Alphabet shows the principal alterations and modifications which have at various times been effected in the formation of letters. It must not, however, be regarded as a complete Paradigm ; for even contemporary scribes frequently differed widely from each other in their caligraphy.

Caley, in a Parliamentary Return on the Public Records

This ys the petigre of Sr Henry Boynton knyght of Sadbere

Xpofer (*Christopher*) Boynton of Sadbere maried Elisabeth daught of Strangwys of Ketton and by her he had yssue Xpofer son & heyre

They The saide Massies became lords of Grafton, and to quarter the seconde Coate aforeshewed ; And hee the said William Massye Maryed, Anne Massye doughter to John Massye of Coddington

Harl. MS. No. 1499.   *Anno* 1530.

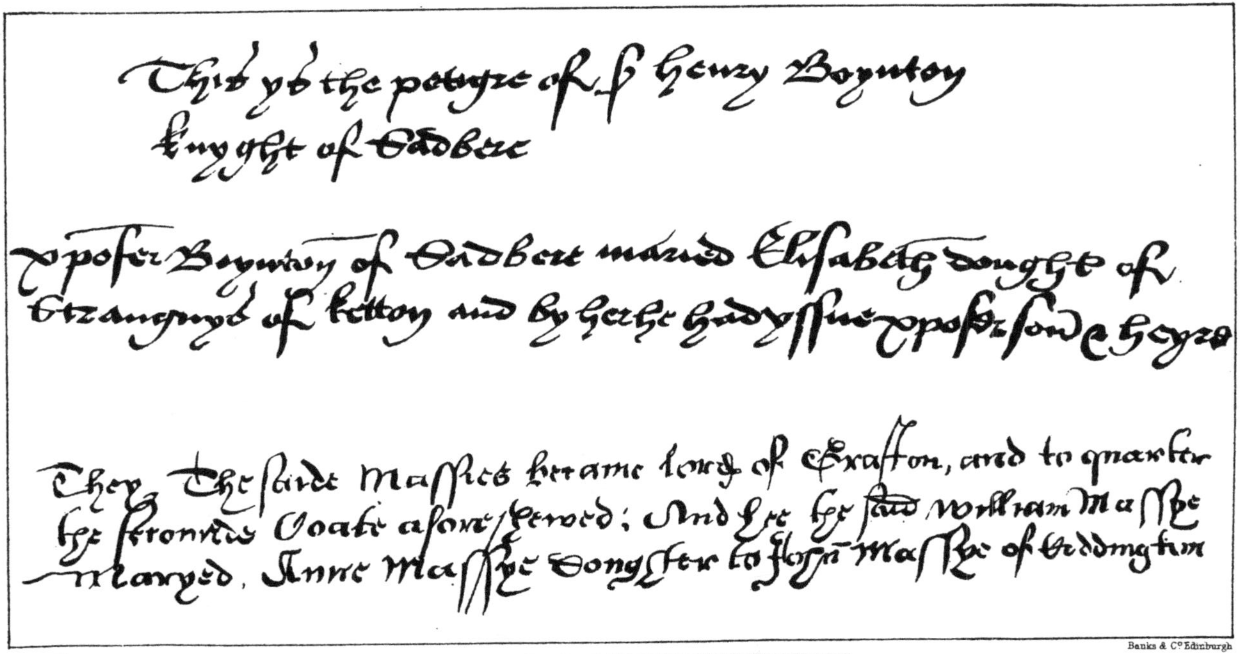

Pl. 3.

FAC-SIMILE OF HERALDS' VISITATIONS

Banks & Cᵒ Edinburgh

of the Kingdom ordered in 1803, writes : 'From the Norman Conquest until the reign of Henry the Third, the Character or Hand-Writing of Ancient Records is in general plain and perspicuous ; of this latter reign, however, there are many Records which cannot be read with facility, on account of the intricacy of the character, and the number of abbreviations.

'The same observations may be applied to Records from this reign until that of Edward the Third inclusive.

'From this period downwards, I have experimentally found that less difficulty occurs in reading and translating Records, and that the Hands used from the reign of Richard the Second to that of Philip and Mary are such as may be read without much trouble.

'Hitherto, each reign appears to have had a set or uniform character ; but in the reign of Elizabeth and her successors, the Clerical Mode seems to have been in a great measure abandoned, and each transcriber to have written according to his own fancy ; and it is observable that the English Records of the Sixteenth and Seventeenth Centuries are in general more difficult to be read than the Latin Records of preceding Ages.'

A more general uniformity of Character was preserved in early legal documents, from the circumstance that they were all prepared by the Clergy, who throughout Europe formed one body ; but as the art of writing became more general amongst the Laity, other styles were introduced.

In order to familiarise the student with the style of writing usually found in the Visitations, I have annexed facsimiles of portions of Heraldic Manuscripts preserved amongst the Harleian Collection.

The greater part of the Visitations are written in the manner of the examples in Plate 4. These are by far the most difficult of any to decipher ; but a few hours of careful application will enable the student to read them with tolerable ease. When names of places occur—such as Villages or Country-seats—with which the reader is unac-

Ric. (*Richard*) Hunt sun = Ann d. & heire   = Tho : Soame of
& heire   of Tho : Knighton | Botteler in Norff
2 husband

John Hunt
of Hunts
Hall in Essex

Willm
ob. s. p.

Alice ux
John Day
of London

Tho : Soame = Elisebeth
sonn & heire   d. of Robert
Alington sun
& heire of Sr
Giles

Stephen
Soame
of London
maior

Willm

John South Cote Judge of
the Comon pleas mared
Elizebeth eldest daughter
& heire of Wdlm Robins
of london Alderman he died
the 18 of Aprill 1585.

These be the Right Armes
of Whightbred of Whight
Notley in Com Essex as doth appere
by the Regester & Records of
my office the same wh in myne
office—&c.

Harl. MS. No. 1541. *Anno* 1634.

FAC-SIMILE OF HERALDS' VISITATIONS

Banks & Cᵒ Edinburgh

quainted, he should always refer to a Gazetteer of the County to obtain the correct orthography.

An experienced reader of Manuscripts possesses one great advantage, inasmuch as he can generally see at the first glance the nature of a document ; and, being familiar with the form in which such instruments are couched, can arrive at its contents without having to decipher one-fourth of it. The most common description of Charters, and those of the greatest value to the Genealogist, are deeds ostensibly of gift, but really of sale ; and these are almost universally worded as follows : *Sciant presentes et futuri quod ego Petrus de Bartone filius Johannis de Bartone dedi concessi et hac presenti carta mea confirmavi Rogero et Henrico filiis meis et heredibus ac assignatis eorum unam acram terræ arabilis cum pertinentiis suis in parochia de Witford vocatam Langcroft et jacentem inter pratum Roberti Warner et messuagium meum quod Radulphus le Hunt pater Aliciæ uxoris meæ mihi dedit. Habendum et tenendum totam predictam acram terræ arabilis cum pertinentiis suis predictis Rogero et Henrico heredibus ac assignatis eorum de capitale domino feodi per servicia inde debita et de jure consueta. Et ego predictus Petrus et heredes mei predictam acram terræ arabilis cum pertinentiis predictis Rogero et Henrico heredibus ac assignatis eorum contra omnes gentes warantizabimus imperpetuum. In cujus rei testimonium huic presentæ cartæ sigillum meum apposui. Hiis testibus . . . Data apud Excestre die dominica proxima post festum sancti Pauli apostoli anno regni regis Edwardi tertii post conquestum nono.*

Supposing that the student has a knowledge of Latin, with a *Ducange* or *Spelman*[1] to resolve the barbarous monastic words, and has mastered the Alphabet, he has still to become acquainted with the various abbreviations generally used. It would be impossible in this place to give all the

[1] In old editions of *Ainsworth's* Dictionary there is a good Glossary of Mediæval Latin words, quite sufficient for ordinary use.

contractions to be found in old MSS. ; I therefore content myself with giving the most frequent :—

ꝰ⟩=er, at the end or middle of a word ; never at the beginning.   Example :   Integ̃=Integer ;   Eñ⟩vis= Enervis ; ꝑminus=Terminus ; Inꝑea = Interea ; Magist̃ = Magister.   It may also serve as ar, ir, or, or ur.

ꝰ=us final.   Ex. : Exꝑnꝰ=Externus ; Domꝰ=Domus.

ʒ=rum, genitive plural.   Ex. : Horʒ=Horum.

b₃=bus final.   Ex. : Omnib₃=Omnibus.

p=per.   Ex. : pfecit=Perfecit.

ꝓ=pro.   Ex. : ꝓfectꝰ=Profectus.

p and ꝓ are also used in the middle and at the end of words, as Sup=Super ; and Imꝓbe=Improbe.

p̃=pre or præ.   Ex. : p̃dictꝰ=Predictus.

A line through a long letter, as h, or over a short one, as m, indicates that there is an omission of one or more letters.   Thus, Joħes = Johannes ; Ric̃us = Ricardus ; Acrā = Acram ; Dominū = Dominum ; łre nr̃e=Litteræ nostræ ; Miłłimo = Millesimo ; ħeas = Habeas ; ꝑtūū= Perpetuum.

The *Inquisitiones post Mortem,* in the Record Office, are of the utmost value.   Their tenor is 'Inquisition taken at (time and place) before A. B. the King's escheator ; C. D. &c. being jury, who say upon their oath that E. F. on the day he died was possessed of (particulars of estates at length, how acquired, and how held).   And that the said E. F. died on the . . . and that G. H. is his son and next heir, and of the age of . . . years.'

If the student will carefully apply himself to the study of a Fourteenth Century deed in good condition, he will be surprised at his own cleverness in being able to decipher that which a few hours before appeared as unintelligible as an Egyptian papyrus.

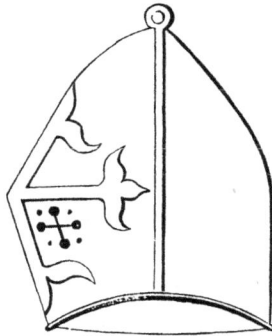

Fig. 392.—From the Effigy of SIR WILLIAM DE STAUNTON, in STAUNTON Church, NOTTS (A.D. 1326).

CHAPTER XXII

HATCHMENTS

HATCHMENTS [1] are lozenge-shaped frames charged with a Shield of Arms, and usually affixed to the front of a house on the death of one of its principal inmates. In delineating a Hatchment, certain rules are observed, by which it is clearly indicated whether the deceased person were single, or married ; a widower, or widow ; and also the rank to which he or she was entitled.

If the deceased person were a Bachelor, the whole of the field on which his Shield is placed should be black, and all the accessories—such as Coronet, Crest, Supporters, &c.— which usually ensigned his Shield should appear in the composition. In the place of his family Motto, some legend of a religious tendency is commonly inscribed on the Motto-scroll (Fig. 393).

[1] The Initial letter is taken from a small window in the North Aisle of King Henry the Seventh's Chapel, Westminster Abbey.

The Arms of an unmarried Lady are charged upon a
Lozenge ; a knot of ribbons takes the place of a Crest, and
the Motto is omitted.   In other respects her Hatchment is
similar to that of a Bachelor.

As in every case Armorial Insignia on Hatchments are
marshalled in accordance with the regulations already speci‐
fied, the Arms of a Widower appear impaled with those of
his late wife ; or, if she were an Heiress, they would be
charged upon an Inescutcheon of Pretence, ensigned with
the usual extra-scutal accessories.

The accompanying diagram (Fig. 394) exemplifies the

Fig. 393.   Fig. 394.

manner in which a Widow would exhibit her bereavement
to the world.

It will be observed that that portion of the frame on which
the Arms of the wife rest is white, showing that she survives ;
while the dexter side, on which the Arms of her late husband
are placed, is black.   If the wife were dead, and the husband
were still living, this arrangement would be reversed — the
Arms, as before, appearing upon a Shield.   On the death of
a Widow, the Arms of her late husband and herself would
be impaled upon a Lozenge, without Crest or Motto.   Im-

paled Arms on a Shield, on a Hatchment all black, bespeaks the death of a Widower.

On the decease of a Bishop,—who impales his Paternal Arms with those of his See,—the sinister side, on which his own Arms appear, is black ; that portion of the field over which his Official Arms are placed being white. Above the Shield is his Mitre, behind which two Pastoral Staves are usually placed in saltire. Bishops never use Supporters. In the case of the wife of a Bishop dying during the lifetime of her husband, two Shields, placed side by side on the same Hatchment, would be employed. On the dexter Shield, resting on a white field, would appear the Arms of the Bishop, and those of his See, impaled ; and, on the sinister Shield, his Paternal Arms, and his late wife's also impaled— the latter upon a black field.

In like manner, two separate Shields are employed if the husband were decorated with the Order of the Garter, Bath, &c. ; that on the dexter containing the Knight's Paternal Coat of Arms, surrounded by the Motto of the Order ; and that on the sinister being charged with the two coats impaled in the usual manner. In all the fore-going instances, such persons as are entitled to Supporters and Coronets have them duly set forth.

The Hatchment of a Bachelor may readily be distin-guished from that of a Widower, by observing that the Arms of the former are either single or quartered ; whilst the latter are impaled. The same distinction obtains between the Hatchments of a Spinster and Widower.

CHAPTER XXIII

DRAWING AND EMBLAZONING

MBLAZONING[1] may be regarded as the Art of which Armory is the Science; and, indeed, the two are so intimately connected that the student who can lay claim to no other acquirement than a knowledge of the technical terms employed by Heralds, and is unable from a written Blazon to delineate a Coat of Arms correctly and artistically, cannot consider his heraldic education complete. In the few plain directions which are subjoined for the guidance of those who wish to learn something of the Art of Emblazoning, only the mechanical processes to be adopted can be pointed out : manipulative skill must be acquired by practice ; but no amount of instruction can impart true artistic feeling. It is a generally received opinion that Heraldry affords but little scope for artistic talent : this, however, is far from being the case ; in proof of which, it is but necessary to

[1] The initial letter is taken from the Grant to Edward the Black Prince, by Edward the Third, of the Duchy of Aquitaine. (*Mus. Brit.*, *Cot. Lib.*, *Nero D.* VII.)

compare some of the beautiful specimens of the Mediæval Ages with others of the Seventeenth and Eighteenth Centuries.

It does not follow that because a person is a good ' artist ' in the common acceptation of the term, he would therefore be a good emblazoner.   The Armorist is sometimes permitted, and even necessitated, to employ a certain amount of conventionalism, both of form and colour, in the execution of his designs, which is not allowed to the 'artist.'   In Sir John Ferne's *Blazon of Gentrie* two characters are introduced who hold a disquisition on this subject.   One objects to an Eagle being represented as *chequé*, affirming that he never saw a bird of that tincture ; to whom the other replies : ' Do you finde fault with it because the Eagle is not borne to her nature ?   Avoyd that phantasie as speedily as you can.   Although things borne according to their nature and colour be very commendable, yet is there as good misteries and honourable intendements in Coats wherein be borne fishes, beastes, fowles, &c., different from their nature.'

When drawing a Charge, one should endeavour to make it fill the space at command as fully as possible ; though by so doing it may appear somewhat disproportioned : thus, the cross *humetté* on page 61 might sometimes appear as at fig. 395, and at others as at fig. 396, according to the shape of the space to be filled.

Fig. 395.

In delineating Animals, the modern emblazoner should neither be too anxious to represent them with such scrupulous exactness as though they were intended to illustrate a work on Natural History, nor should he servilely imitate the examples of the early practitioners of the art, who, through want of knowledge, violated the laws of drawing and of Nature.   In repre-

Fig. 396.

senting purely conventional or conventionalised beings, such as Griffins or Dolphins, of course the Armorist of the present

day must strictly adhere to those forms originally ascribed
to them in Heraldry ; but there is no reason why, in
delineating natural Charges, he should perpetuate the mis-
conceptions of the early Emblazoners.   In an Illumination
I examined lately, a Heron and an Eagle were represented
as *volant*, with their legs hanging straight down.   Now,
this is manifestly wrong ; for wading birds extend their
legs horizontally to their entire length while flying, and
short-legged birds draw theirs close to their bodies, so that
they press against the thighs, leaving little more than the
claws visible.

There is no greater field for the display of artistic talent
in Armory than in the arrangement of the various accessories of the Shield.   It scarcely falls within the limits of a
work treating of the whole science in general to furnish
many examples of this particular branch of the subject, but
the accompanying outline may be advantageously adopted
for the Achievement of an Esquire or Gentleman.

Fig. 397.

The Achievement on the Brass to Sir John Say, in
Broxbourne Church, Hertfordshire (A.D. 1473), is particularly graceful and effective.   (See Title-page.)

The method of representing the Tinctures of Coats of
Arms by lines drawn in certain directions has been described

at page 52. Another mode is sometimes made use of, when a simple sketch or memorandum of the Charges and Tinctures is required, known as TRICKING. Nearly all the Coats of Arms contained in the Visitations of the Heralds are represented in this manner, effected by making a rough drawing of the Coat, and indicating the Tinctures by Initial letters, as follows :—

Or	O., or Or.
Argent	A.
Gules	G.
Azure	B., for Blue
Vert	V.
Sable	S.
Purpure	P.
Proper	Ppr.
Ermine	E., or Er.

These Abbreviations are also sometimes used in the Visitations in blazoning Arms.

The example in the margin is a facsimile of the Arms of the family of BALDINGTON, of OXFORD, taken from the Visitation of that County (*Harl. MS. No.* 1541) ; which would be blazoned : *Argent ; on a Chevron sable, between three Pellets, as many Roses of the field.*

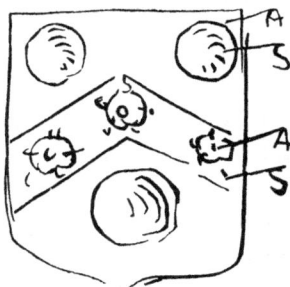

Fig. 398.

When a Charge is repeated upon a Shield, the number is sometimes, for the sake of brevity, indicated by figures placed on the spots which such repeated Charges would occupy, as in the accompanying illustration, which represents the Arms of GILLY, of SUFFOLK and ESSEX : *Or ; a Pale between four Fleurs-de-lys gules.*

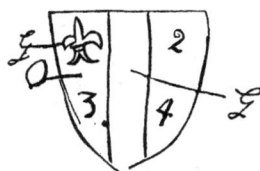

Fig. 399.

Much difficulty is frequently experienced in accurately
determining the Fess-point in a Heater, or Kite-shaped
Shield, in consequence of its narrow Base ; for if the Fess-
point be taken as the exact centre, and the Shield be divided
horizontally by a line drawn through that point, the upper
portion will be found greatly to preponde-
rate over the lower.   In a Shield of this
form, it is advisable to cut off from the
Base about one-ninth of its entire length,
and to place the Fess-point midway between
such dividing-line and the top of the Shield.
The same allowance should be granted when
the Escutcheon is to be divided into three
parts, so as to determine the depth of a charged Chief.   It
is of the utmost importance to fix the Fess-point correctly ;
for, unless that be done, it is impossible to draw any of the
Honourable Ordinaries so that they shall occupy their
proper positions.

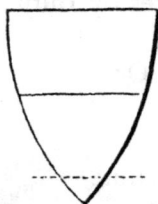

Fig. 400.

The Tinctures of the Field, Charges, and Crest, being
specified in the Blazon, and those of the Wreath and Helmet
implied, it is only in the Mantling and Motto-scroll that the
emblazoner has an opportunity of exhibiting his artistic
combination of colour.   In an Achievement of Arms, con-
trast is frequently more effective than harmony.   If, therefore, the dominant Tincture of the Escutcheon or its Charges
be Blue, the Mantling may be Orange ; if Red, Green ; if
Yellow, Purple ; and *vice versâ*.[1]   It is the general custom
to depict the Mantling Green, irrespective of the other colours
in the composition ; which practice cannot be too strenuously

---

[1] Some authorities assert that the Mantling should derive its Tincture from the field of the Escutcheon ; but I see no adequate reason
why this rule should be adopted, especially as Heralds themselves
persistently disregard it.   If any system be followed, the Mantling
should be of the same Tincture as the *Livery Colours ;* but as so few
Families, out of the thousands which are entitled to Armorial distinctions, possess Livery Colours, it is almost useless to lay down such a
law on the subject.

deprecated. It has been remarked that the liberal use of green in decorative art has ever marked its decadence ; and by this one feature alone we can, with tolerable accuracy, determine whether an Illumination be prior or subsequent to the Sixteenth Century, from about which time the decline of artistic feeling in Emblazoning and Illuminating may be reckoned.[1]

I shall now proceed to mention briefly the various mechanical appliances to be used, and the progressive steps to be taken, in emblazoning a Coat of Arms. Nearly all the important Armorial records which remain to us are executed upon Vellum ; and this material is still chiefly employed by modern Armorists. I would advise the student, however, to make his first essays on drawing-paper, or 'London board'—being less expensive, and easier to work upon. To prepare the vellum, it should be slightly but thoroughly damped on the outside, which can be distinguished from the face by a slight roughness : it should then, while soft, be stretched evenly on a board with drawing-pins, or the edges may be fastened with glue ; but the former method is preferable. When the skin is perfectly dry, it should be dusted over with a little powdered chalk, contained in a roll of flannel, and afterwards wiped with a clean cloth. This removes all grease that may be upon its surface. If, subsequently, colours refuse to lay evenly, a little prepared ox-gall, mixed with them, will overcome the difficulty. I do not recommend—I merely say that it is equally efficacious, if the refractory surface be licked once or twice with the tongue, or saliva applied with a brush.

Vellum does not permit the erasure of pencil-marks as readily as paper ; for which reason, unless the emblazoner be tolerably proficient, it is advisable to draw the outline of

---

[1] 'The term "illuminated," used for those drawings executed in gold and body-colour, in ancient manuscripts, is derived from the name applied to the artists who produced them. They were termed *Illuminators* (Lat. *illuminatores*, Fr. *enlumineurs*); whence the name given to the paintings executed by them.'—*Fairholt.*

the intended subject on paper, and transfer it to the vellum, or cardboard, in the following manner : Place over the face of the vellum a piece of black transfer-paper, and over this the original draft, being careful to pin the latter to the board in several places, so as to prevent any change in its position.   Then, with a hard pencil, trace the outline, using an even and gentle pressure.   By removing one or two of the pins, and carefully lifting the draft and black paper, it can be readily seen whether any part of the outline has been omitted : if so, refasten the paper, and supply the deficiency. This method can only be employed when the draft is made on thin paper : if it be on cardboard, it will be necessary to make a copy of it on tracing-paper, by pinning the latter over the draft, and carefully following the outline with a pencil. The emblazoner should not be too anxious to secure small details in the transfer : these can be better supplied afterwards ; it is quite sufficient to trace the general outline. A piece of stale bread is preferable to india-rubber for clean- ing the vellum and erasing pencil-lines.   Tracing-paper, as sold in the shops, is frequently greasy, and when used, espe- cially on vellum, causes the colours subsequently employed to flow irregularly.   It is easily prepared, by rubbing one side of a sheet of foreign post, or 'whited brown' paper, with a broad-pointed Cumberland B.B.B. pencil, or with a block of stove blacklead.   The powdered grate-lead will answer very well, if a pad of wadding be used to rub it over the surface.   Red transfers can be produced by preparing the thin paper with powdered red chalk.   By using paper blackened on one side only, the back of the draft is preserved clean. It is obvious that, if two objects are to be represented in the same attitude, but reversed—such as wings conjoined, two Lions combattant, or the two sides of a Mantling—it is only necessary to turn the tracing.

While on the subject of tracings, it may not be out of place to tell the *young* student how to *rub* monumental Brasses.   Carefully dust the brass, so as to remove any dirt that may be on it. Then lay on it a strip of white paper. The best is *thin* 'lining paper,' which costs at the paper-hanger's about $2\frac{1}{2}d$. the piece—i.e. twelve yards. *Good* paper is *bad* : it is too thick. Then put weights on the paper, to keep it in position—hassocks or cushions do admirably—and with the hand press heavily on the most delicate parts of the brass work, so as to squeeze the paper into the details of the engraved surface beneath. Then, with a piece of shoemaker's heel-ball (it is made in three qualities ; get the softest), rub the surface of the paper, being careful not to touch the stone slab outside the brass. For a delicate rubbing (a much worn coin for example), tissue-paper should be used, and well pressed on the object for a minute or two with the thumb. Should the original be very slightly in relief, heel-ball will not render all the details. In that case a thick unguent should be made with lamp-black and lard, applied with a pad or dabber. This pad is simply a small bunch of rags tied up in a cloth. The pad should be thoroughly blackened, but still as sparingly as possible. Then, with the blackened pad, *lightly* rub the surface of the paper, and if the operation be carefully performed, details will appear on the paper scarcely visible on the original.

Rubbings of Inscriptions on Church Bells are frequently very difficult to make, as the letters stand in too high relief, and the surface is not plane. The best way is to take a strip of thin cartridge paper, paste it one side, above and below the Inscription, and stick it on the bell. While yet damp, press it firmly with the hand, on, and *into*, the Inscription. When quite dry, get a piece of ' uppers ' leather, damp it, and rub the lettering.

After this digression let us return to our vellum drawing.

When the pencil outline is complete, it should be carefully inked over with a fine steel pen. For this process it is important that the best Indian Ink should be employed ; for if an inferior description, or Lamp-black, be used, when the colours are applied the outline will ' run,' and ruin the work. It would be well to test the permanency of the Indian

Ink before using it upon the vellum. Every straight line, however short, should be ruled ; nothing mars the general appearance of a Coat of Arms more than an irregular, jagged outline. When the whole has been inked-in, all pencil-marks should be removed with a piece of bread ; for they become indelibly fixed if washed over with colour.

In this state the drawing is ready to receive the Tinctures. The first to be applied are the Metals. There are three methods of gilding, viz. with gold-leaf, shell-gold, and gold-paper. When the first is employed, the surface intended to be gilded must be painted with gilding-size, and, when nearly dry, the leaf laid over it, and gently pressed with a pad of wadding. The superfluous gold from the edges can be removed with a dry brush. It is advisable to dilute the size with water, and to give the vellum two coats, allowing the first to dry ; and, at the moment of applying the leaf, to breathe upon the size. Amateurs usually experience great difficulty in using the 'tip'—the wide, flat brush with which the gold is applied. Simple as the operation seems when performed by an adroit gilder, it requires considerable dex-terity and practice to lift a sheet of the metal from the book with the tip, and lay it flat on the 'cushion,' previous to its being cut with a blunt knife or spatula into the required size. A much easier plan is to take a piece of thin paper, a trifle larger than the sheet, rub it well with beeswax, and insert it in the book of gold leaf. With a slight pressure, the gold adheres to the paper ; yet not so firmly but that it readily leaves it when placed on the sized surface, and gently rubbed on the back. One great advantage of this method is, that no more gold is used than is absolutely required ; there are, consequently, no 'skewings,' as gilders term the waste metal—which, by the way, are, by custom, the workman's perquisite.

Great care, and some little skill, are required to produce an even surface with shell-gold ; nevertheless, it is the best adapted for general use. The most frequent mistake made by beginners in the use of this material is, that they do not fill the brush sufficiently full ; the consequence is irregular patches, some but half gilded. Green shell-gold, which is a modern preparation, is very useful in adding brilliancy to certain Charges, such as Dragons, &c., when tinctured *vert* ; but its use should be but sparingly adopted. Another method of gilding is by cutting out the intended figure in gold-paper, previously gummed at the back and permitted to dry. This material should only be employed in cases where a large surface is to be covered. For Church Decorations, or similar purposes, it does well enough, but gold-paper should never be used when any pretence is made to ' finish.'

When leaf or shell gold is used, after it is quite dry a piece of writing-paper must be placed over the gilded surface and rubbed quickly and firmly with an agate burnisher, to brighten the gold beneath. With gold-paper this is unnecessary.

Gold Charges may be represented in relief by coating the surface intended to be gilded with a preparation called Raising Composition, the vellum having been previously roughened with a knife to make the composition adhere. As many coats of this composition should be applied as may be found requisite, allowing each coat to dry before another is laid on. It must then be sized, and gilded with leaf, in the manner previously described. In burnishing raised gold, the agate should come in direct contact with the metal.

After the flat Gold Charge is laid down, its details must be picked out with yellows and browns, according to the intensity required.

Or may be represented with Gamboge, Cadmium Yellow, or Indian Yellow, shaded with Yellow Ochre, Burnt Sienna, or Carmine. Chrome must be particularly guarded against, as it rapidly becomes discoloured. The brilliant and opaque variety of Cadmium Yellow recently introduced by Messrs. Winsor and Newton, under the name of Aurora Yellow, is a perfect substitute for Chrome, and promises to be of the greatest value to Illuminators. Of all the Yellows for representing *or*, Aurora Yellow, Aureolin, and Primrose Aureolin are most to be recommended.

For *Argent*, silver shell or leaf may be employed, if the drawing is to be placed under glass, and kept airtight. On account of the liability of silver to oxidise and turn black when exposed to the air, Platinum or Aluminium are preferable, although they are not so brilliant. Chinese White answers for *Argent*, when Colours are used in the place of Metals.

For the remaining Heraldic Tinctures the following Colours should be employed :

Gules : Vermilion ; shaded with Carmine, Crimson Lake, or the newly-introduced Alizarin Crimson ; the last-named having the advantage in respect of permanence.

Azure : Ultramarine or Cobalt ; shaded with Prussian Blue or Indigo. A beginner should not attempt to cover a large surface, particularly if it be irregular in outline, with Cobalt, as this Colour exhibits a most perverse tendency to dry in patches. French Blue is almost as brilliant as Ultramarine, and is, moreover, much less in price. Both of these Colours work very smoothly. New Blue, a pale variety of French Blue, also answers admirably.

Sable : Lamp-black. When dry, the shadow-side may be deepened with gum-water.

Vert : Prussian Blue and Gamboge mixed ; shaded with Moss Green or Carmine. Emerald Green is occasionally useful in Mantlings, when tinctured *vert ;* but it does not work well, and is easily displaced if another Colour be laid over it. Viridian, more or less modified with Aureolin makes a very bright and permanent green.

Purpure : Indian Purple, or a mixture of Carmine and Cobalt ; shaded with gum or Burnt Carmine. Alizarin Crimson, mixed with the new colour known as Permanent Violet, forms an excellent Purpure.

Tenné : Carmine, Gamboge or Indian Yellow, and Burnt Sienna ; shaded with Umber or Vandyke Brown.

Sanguine : Dragon's Blood ; shaded with Burnt Carmine.

It frequently happens that the beauty of an Illumination is marred by a want of uniformity of tone in those tinctures which are composed of others, such as Vert, Purpure, &c. : to obviate this difficulty, Messrs. Winsor and Newton have recently introduced a box of Heraldic Colours containing all the Tinctures, simple and compound, employed in the art, whereby the operations of the emblazoner are much facilitated. From the experience which I have had both in heraldic and other illumination, I consider the Colours of the above-named makers to stand unrivalled, not only for brilliancy and permanence, but for the ease with which they may be applied.

DIAPERING, as a method of relieving the monotony of a large plain surface by means of a kind of pattern composed of small devices constantly repeated, has been already noticed at pp. 78–81.

In conclusion, I must impress upon the student the absolute necessity of cleanliness in all his manipulations, if he wish to produce a brilliant result. The palette, or saucer, should be scrupulously clean, and free from dust ; the brushes should always be carefully washed before they are laid aside ; and the water with which the Colours are mixed should be frequently changed, if the brushes are rinsed in it. When a Compound Colour has to be prepared, such as Green, one cake of Colour must never be rubbed in a saucer containing another Colour ; but a separate saucer must be used for each, and the colours afterwards mixed with a brush. The Yellows are particularly liable to have their brilliancy impaired if they come in contact with the least trace of any other Colour. If, however, prepared Heraldic Colours be used, the Illuminator will be spared the trouble and uncertainty of mixing compound tinctures.

CHAPTER XXIV

FRENCH HERALDRY

I T was probably amongst the Germans that the system of Armory which now obtains in England derived its origin. To the French, however, must be accorded the credit of reducing it to a Science—as would appear from the terms which are employed in it ; if, indeed, we had not learned the fact from History. It might be supposed, as English Armorists originally received their instruction directly from the French, that the systems adopted in both countries would be identical. Such, however, is not the case. In course of years, modifications of details, and, in many instances, considerable differences in the significations of terms, have arisen, which have at length caused a wide separation between the Armory of France and that of England.

Many of the terms used in Blazoning bear the same meaning in both languages ; but there are some important differences, both in the principal Charges and the method of employing them, which render a study of French Heraldry highly necessary. The *Bar*, for example, is unknown to French Armorists ; with them, the *Fess* has no diminutive ; that which they designate a *Barre* is with us a *Bend-sinister*. The *Mullet*, in France, is always represented of six points, and pierced ; while the *Étoile* has but five points, which are straight, and not, as in England, wavy. The *Chevron* is drawn very much higher, and, when there is no Charge in the centre Chief, it extends almost to the top of the Es-cutcheon ; the *Bordure,* also, occupies considerably more space than with us. Dragons are always drawn as Wy-verns ; and the Cockatrice is never seen on Shields of French Arms.

The Tincture *Vert* is invariably rendered in French, *Sinople ; Vert* is found only in very ancient documents. It will be seen also, by reference to the List of Terms at pp. 314–316, that *Party per bend, Bend-sinister, Fess,* and *Pale,* are each expressed by certain distinctive terms. In blazon-ing a Field or Charge which is *gutté,* the French always specify the particular guttæ by the Tincture : for example, they would not blazon fig. 147 as *Gutté de larmes,* but *Gutté d'azur,* which is more simple than the English system, and ought to be generally adopted.

Colour is frequently imposed upon Colour, and, when so done, is expressed by the term *Cousu,* as in the Blazon of the Arms of *Le Camus,* which is, *De gueules ; un Pélican d'argent, ensanglanté de gueules, dans son aire ; au Chef cousu d'azur, chargé d'un Fleur-de-lys or ;* which would be blazoned in English, *Gules ; a Pelican in her piety argent, vulning herself proper ; on a Chief azure, a Fleur-de-lys or.* In German,[1] Italian, and Spanish Armory, also, Colour frequently appears upon Colour ; the Arms of the Spanish Inquisition were : *Sable ; a Cross vert.*

Another important point in which the English and French Heralds differ is in Marshalling. The latter do not impale the Arms of Husband and Wife, but place them *accolé,* on two separate Shields. The Issue impale their Parents' Arms when, under similar circumstances, in Eng-land they would be entitled to quarter them.. I have before mentioned, in the chapter on Cadency, that the Bordure Compony was formerly employed as a Brisure to indicate

---

[1] A peculiarity of German Heraldry is, that the Charges are placed indifferently, either moving towards the Dexter or Sinister, and some-times *affronté.*

illegitimate descent ; but, in France, the Bordure serves as
a Mark of Difference for the younger lawful children.
There, a natural son bears, or ought to bear, his Paternal
Arms upon one of the principal Ordinaries.

The Heralds of Spain make use of Marks of Difference
in the same manner as in England, but carried to a greater
extent.   Instead of nine Marks, they have thirty-six—that
is, a distinctive device as a Brisure for each of twelve sons
for three generations—*pater, avus*, and *proavus*.

The following selection of Arms will exemplify some of
the technicalities of French Blazonry :

*D'azur ; à la bande d'or chargée de trois écrevisses de
gueules, et accompagnée de trois molettes d'éperon d'or, posées
deux et une ;* borne by PELLETIER.   In English : *Azure ; on
a Bend between three Mullets of six points, two and one or,
as many Lobsters gules.*

*Écartelé : aux 1 et 4, de sable, à l'aigle d'argent au vol
éployé, semée de Croissants du champ, et chargée sur l'estomac
d'une Croix du même : aux 2 et 3, d'or, au laurier de sinople,
et un chef de gueules ;* DE VALORY : In English : *Quarterly
of four : 1 and 4. Sable ; an Eagle displayed argent, semé of
Crescents, and charged on the breast with a Cross of the first :
2 and 3.   Or ; a Laurel-tree vert, and a Chief gules.*

The Arms of His Grace the DUKE of DEVONSHIRE would
thus be described by a French Herald : *Écartelé : aux 1 et 4,
d'argent, à trois recontres de Cerf de sable, posés deux
et un : au 2, tranché bastillé d'argent et de gueules :
au 3, échiqueté d'argent et d'azur, et une fasce de gueules
brochante.*

Some of the Charges in Continental Armory—particularly
that of Spain—appear most grotesque to English Heralds.
Animals, for instance, are represented as talking to each
other ; and many Shields of Arms seem as if they were
designed to illustrate the Fables of Æsop.   Napoleon is
said to have remarked, on seeing for the first time the
various Quarterings to which his wife was entitled, in which

were comprised a goodly assortment of zoological curiosities :
' Parbleu ! il y a beaucoup d'*animaux* dans cette famille-là ! '

But little attention is paid by French Heralds either to
Crests or Mottoes (*devises*); but all the *Noblesse*, that is,
those entitled to bear Arms, ensign their Shields with a
Coronet ; and the Coat, when thus ensigned, is said to be
Timbré.

The Arms of most of the great Officers of State were,
under the *Ancien Régime* of France, supported by devices
emblematic of their office. Thus, the Admiral of France
had two Anchors ; the Vice-Admiral, one. The Grand
Louvetier (wolf-hunter) had wolves' heads ; and the Grand
Butler, two Bottles.

The French make a distinction between *Supporters* and
Tenans ; and both may sometimes be seen ensigning a Shield,
as in the Arms of ALBRET. In this instance, the lower part
of the Escutcheon is *supported* on either side by a Lion, the
head covered by a helmet ; on each Lion stands an Eagle,
which, with one foot, *holds* the upper portion.

In 1789, amongst the general annihilation of all aristocratic distinctions, the office of *Juge d'armes* was abrogated :
it was restored under the *régime* of Buonaparte, to be again
extinguished in 1848. A law was passed in 1856 forbidding
the unlawful assumption of Surnames ; but in this regulation no mention was made of Armorial Bearings ; hence it
follows that in France, at the present time, anyone is at
liberty to devise and bear whatever Arms his inclination
may dictate—and the Republican Inclination *does* dictate,
frequently in the most startling manner.

French and German Nobility has become cheap for the
reason that all the descendants of a Baron; for example, are
Barons. A. B. is made a Baron : he has ten sons—they are all
Barons : each has ten sons—they also are Barons. Thus
there are, or may be, a hundred and eleven Barons A. B.
living at the same time, each styling himself as Baron A. B.

For the assistance of those who may wish to extend their

researches to the Heraldry of France, I subjoin a list of the
principal terms, with their English significations. I have
not considered it necessary to insert those which are the
same, or nearly so, in both languages.

Abouti	Conjoined.
Accolé	Collared : also used to express two Swords, &c., placed behind a Shield ; and two Shields side by side.
Accompagné . . .	Between.
Accroupi . . .	Lodged.
Acorné	Attired.
Aislé	Winged.
Ajouré	Voided : generally applied to open windows of Castles.
Armoyé	Usually applied to a Mantling or Lambrequin, when charged with Arms.
Arraché	Erased ; eradicated.
Assemblé . . .	Dovetailed.
Assis	Sejant.
Bande	Bend.
Barre	Bend-sinister.
Bouse	Water-Bouget.
Brochant . . .	Debruised.
Caudé	Coward : applied to Lions.
Chausé	Party per chevron.
Chaussé trappe . .	Caltrap.
Clariné	Gorged with small bells.
Contre-bretessé . .	Embattled.
Contre-écartelé . .	Quarterly-quartered.
Contre-fascé . . .	Barry-paly.
Contre-hermine . .	Ermines.
Coquille de St. Jacques .	Escallop.
Coquille de St Michel .	Escallop without ears.

Cotise	Bendlet.
Cotoyé	Cotised.
Coupé	Party per fess.
Crenellé	Embattled.
Croissant . . .	Crescent.
Danché	Indented.
Dechaussé . . .	Without claws.
Demi-vol . . .	A wing.
Ecaillé	Scaled.
Écartelé . . .	Quarterly.
Écartelé en sautoir .	Party per saltire.
Échiqueté . . .	Checky.
Environné . . .	In Orle.
Éployé	Displayed.
Étoile	Mullet.
Fasce	Fess.
Fascé	Barry.
Fusé	Fusil.
Gerbe	Garb.
Hermine . . .	Ermine.
Jumelles	Bars gemel.
Lampassé . . .	Langued.
Mantelé	{ Party per chevron, extending to the top of the Escutcheon.
Martinet	Martlet.
Molette	Étoile.
Morné	Disarmed.
Ombré	Adumbrated.
Onglé	Taloned : applied to birds.
Pannes	Furs.
Parti	Party per pale.
Parti de l'un à l'autre .	Counterchanged (see fig. 159).
Parti de l'un en l'autre .	Counterchanged (see fig. 160).
Peri	{ Reduced in size : generally equivalent to couped.
Pointe	Base.

Posé	{ Placed : as, Posé en bande bendwise.
Quintefeuille . . .	Cinquefoil.
Rencontré . . .	{ Affronté : applied to Animals' heads.
Sautoir	Saltire.
Sinople	Vert.
Sur le tout . . .	Over all.
Sur le tout du tout . .	A second Inescutcheon.
Taillé	Party per bend-sinister.
Tavalures . . .	Ermine spots.
Tranché	Party per bend.
Treffle	Trefoil.
Vergette	Pallet.
Vire	Annulet.
Viudé	Voided.
Vivré	{ Dancetté : when applied to Serpents, gliding.

Fig. 401.

Arms of DE CUSANCE, of Burgundy.

CHAPTER XXV

AMERICAN HERALDRY

MANY people imagine—and none are more loud in the assertion than Americans themselves—that in the great Western Republic the species of gentilitial registration denominated Heraldry is uncared for. This, however, is far from being the fact. Even amongst the partisans of political equality there is a large majority anxious to exhibit their individual superiority. In proof of which, I may mention that a gentleman connected with the College of Heralds recently informed me that the fees received from America constitute one of the most important sources of the revenue of that Institution.

The 'Aristocracy of America derives its origin principally from three sources : from the *Knickerbocker* Families of New York—the VAN BURENS, the STUYVESANTS, the VAN CAMPENS, the RENSELLAERS, the VAN DAMS ; from the Cavaliers who founded the Colony of Virginia—the BEVERLEYS, the FAIRFAXES, the HARRISONS, the SEDDONS, the BERKELEYS ; and from the Puritans of New England—the APPLETONS, the WINTHROPS, the RICHMONDS, the LATHROPS, the CHAUNCYS, the WADES, the FOSTERS, &c. It is no matter of surprise that Americans, particularly those of the Eastern States, with all their veneration for Republican principles, should be desirous of tracing their origin to the early settlers, and of proving their descent from those single-hearted, God

x

fearing men who sought in a foreign land that religious liberty which was denied them at home. True, that when they landed in America they shot down the natives, and took forcible possession of their land, without remorse. That, however, was simply a matter of detail, and is still the inevitable consequence whenever strength and civilisation are opposed to weakness and barbarism. Æsop's *Wolf and the Lamb* is a Parable, not a Fable.

It should be remembered, moreover, that the early Colonists of New England were, with but few exceptions, men of family ; for, in those days, a large sum of money was required to equip a vessel for a long voyage, and provide the means of subsistence when they were arrived at their destination.

At the same time, it must not be forgotten that during the Sixteenth and Seventeenth Centuries many persons were 'deported' to the Colonies on political grounds, nominally as labourers, but really as slaves. Many of these, however, may have been of good families, though reduced in circumstances by their adherence to the losing cause, whether of politics or religion. It is a matter of much difficulty to trace the connection of such emigrants with their English paternal stem.

It is curious to note, amidst the simplicity of the Puritans' lives—a simplicity which has passed into a proverb—the tenacity with which they clung to certain Old-World customs. Their Seals, probably brought from England, and much of their Plate, were engraved with their Arms ; and the same, with the addition of the title *Armiger*, are inscribed on many of their tombstones.[1]

---

[1] The following are a few examples in confirmation of the above :

In Dorchester Churchyard, Massachusetts.—WILLIAM POOLE, died 1674 : *Azure ; a Lion rampant argent, within eight Fleurs-de-lys in orle or.*

Salem Churchyard, Massachusetts.—PICKMAN : *Gules ; two Battle-axes in saltire or, cantoned by four Martlets argent.*

Not the least commendable characteristic of the Pilgrim Fathers was the scrupulous accuracy with which they recorded the births and marriages of their children.[1] These documents were carried down to the period of the Revolution, when, for about twenty years, their continuity was somewhat broken. But when the Republic was firmly established, and order once more obtained, the records were continued, though under different auspices. Thus it follows that, if a descendant of the early settlers can trace his ancestry as far back as the middle of the Eighteenth Century, there is seldom much difficulty in clearly determining to what English Family he is allied.

Unfortunately, there is not in the United States of America any Institution analogous to our College of Heralds ; the consequence is, there are probably more *Assumptive Arms* borne in that country than anywhere else. Nor are the bearers of such Arms to be so much blamed as the unscrupulous self-styled Heralds who supply them. The advertising London tradesmen who profess to find Arms are for the most part less anxious to give themselves the trouble of examining the requisite documents—even if they possess the necessary ability to do so, which many certainly do not—than they are of securing the fee. If, therefore, they cannot readily *find* in the printed pages of Burke, they do not hesitate to draw from the depths of their imagination. Many American gentlemen consequently engrave their plate, and adorn the panels of their carriages,

---

King's Chapel-yard, Boston.—WINSLOW : *Argent ; on a Bend gules, eight Lozenges conjoined or ;* and in the same place, on a tomb of the SAVAGE Family : *Argent ; six Lioncels sable.*

Copp's Yard, Boston.—MOUNTFORT : *Bendy of eight, or and azure.*

Charlestown, Massachusetts.—LEMON : *Azure ; a Fess between three Dolphins, two and one, embowed or.*

Granary Yard, Boston.—TOTHILL : *Azure ; on a Bend argent, cotised or, a Lion passant sable.*

[1] See Nathaniel Hawthorne's *Scarlet Letter.*

with heraldic insignia to which they have no right whatever :
and this, too, though they may have an hereditary claim to
Arms as ancient and honourable as those of a Talbot or a
Hastings. Nor have native professors of the science been
behindhand in distributing their worthless favours. The
names of Thomas Johnson, John Coles, and Nathaniel Hurd,
are notorious in New England as those of manufacturers of
fictitious Arms and Pedigrees ; and in New York at the
present day are many self-styled Heralds who, having failed
in honest trades, have fallen to Pedigree-making, as they
might have to Fortune-telling, to make a living.

So, too, with regard to their Corporate Heraldry : it is
much to be regretted that no competent authority should
have taken cognisance of the Arms borne by the individual
States. The National Arms are at once dignified and elo-
quent : *An Eagle with wings displayed, holding in its dexter
claw a sheaf of Arrows, and in its sinister a Thunderbolt,
all proper ; on the breast a Shield argent, charged with six
Pallets gules* (constituting the thirteen original States, i.e.
seven white and six red) ; *on a Chief azure, forty-four
Stars of the first* (the present number). Motto : *E pluribus
unum.*[1] The Flag is equally well conceived : in this, the
Pallets are Barrulets, and for the Chief is substituted a
Canton, on which are as many Stars as there are States.[2]

[1] Originally there were but thirteen Stars on the chief. The others
have been added as Territories have become States, by reason of the
increase of inhabitants in those Territories. The five remaining Territories, viz. Utah, Arizona, New Mexico, Alaska, and the Indian
Territory, will in process of time become States, and as each comes
into the Union another Star will be added to the National Arms. It
is probable that one of the present large States will be divided, so that
the grand and *final* total of Stars will be fifty. It may be noted by the
way that the American *Stars* are not Stars at all. They are *Mullets*
five points, unpierced, as officially decreed on the 4th July, 1818.
Previous to that time, that is from the 14th June, 1777, the so-called
Stars were eight pointed.

[2] Previous to the Civil War a curious difference was observed
in blazoning the National Flag. In the Northern States it was : *Argent ;*

But what shall be said of the Devices assumed by the separate States? Old Guillim himself would have been sorely puzzled had he seen the following blazon of the Arms of KANSAS : *Two Ox-teams and Wagons, between a Man ploughing in sinister foreground, and Indians hunting Buffaloes in dexter middle-distance ; on sinister, a River and double-funnelled, hurricane-decked Steamer: behind Mountains in distance, the Sun rising ; on sky, in half-circle, thirty-seven Stars, all proper.* Motto : *Ad Astra per aspera.*

I confess myself utterly unable to do justice to a verbal blazon of the Arms of OREGON. Perhaps the following will give some idea of this heraldic curiosity : *On a Fess, the words,* THE UNION ; *in Chief a Landscape, an Ox-wagon, a Deer, Trees, Mountains, and Prairie ; in distance, the Sea, thereon a sailing Ship and a Steamer ; in base, a Plough, Rake, Scythe, Garbs,* &c.—which I may venture to blazon as, *All any how.*

The Devices of the thirteen original States approach much nearer to the standard of true Heraldry ; several, indeed, are unexceptionable. As these have already become in some degree historical, it may be interesting to mention them. All the Tinctures are supposed to be *proper.*

NEW YORK : *From behind a Mountain, the rising Sun.* Crest : *An Eagle with wings addorsed, holding in its dexter claw a Ball.* Supporters : Dexter : *Justice holding in her dexter hand a Fasces, and in her sinister hand a Rod ;* Sinister : *Liberty holding in her sinister hand a Staff, on the top of which a Cap of Liberty.* Motto : *Excelsior.*

CONNECTICUT : *Three Apple-trees, two and one.* Motto : *Qui transtulit, sustinet.*

six Barrulets gules ; on a Canton azure, thirty-four Stars of the first. In the Southern States it was : *Gules ; six Barrulets argent, &c.* In the former case the Canton rested on a white stripe ; and in the latter, on a red. This difference was never officially recognised.

MASSACHUSETTS : *An Indian holding in his dexter hand a Bow, and in his sinister hand an Arrow : in dexter chief an Étoile.* Crest : *A Cubit Arm grasping in the hand a Sword.* Motto : *Ense petit pacem, sub libertate quietem.*

RHODE ISLAND: *Flotant erect on waves of the Sea, a Shield charged with an Anchor, flukes in base, from the ring a Cable pendent.* Motto : *Hope.*

NEW HAMPSHIRE : *A Ship on the Stocks ; on the horizon, at sinister side, the Sun in splendour.*

NEW JERSEY : *Three Ploughs in pale.* Crest : *A Nag's head couped.* Supporters : Dexter : *Liberty, holding in her dexter hand a Wand, on the top thereof a Phrygian Cap ;* Sinister : *Plenty, holding in her sinister hand a Cornucopia.*

PENNSYLVANIA : *Per fess azure and vert ; on a Fess or, between a Ship in full sail on Waves, proper, in chief, and three Garbs of the third in base, a Plough of the fourth.* Crest : *An Eagle rising.* Supporters : *Two Horses caparisoned for draught, sable.* Motto : *Virtue, Liberty, Independence.*

DELAWARE : *Arg. ; a Fess gules, between a Garb and ear of Maize in chief, proper ; and a Bull passant in base of the last.* Supporters : Dexter : *A Labourer holding in his dexter hand a Rake, and in his sinister, as a* Crest, *a Ship.* Sinister : *A Hunter habited in fur, holding in his dexter hand a Fowling-piece.* Motto : *Liberty and Independence.*

MARYLAND : *Quarterly: 1 and 4. Two Pallets, surmounted by a Bend ; 2 and 3. A Cross pommé.* Crest : *An Eagle with wings displayed.* Supporters : Dexter : *A Husbandman holding in his dexter hand a Spade ;* Sinister: *A Fisherman holding in his sinister hand a Fish.* Motto : *Crescite et multiplicamini.*

VIRGINIA : *A female Figure in Roman armour holding in her dexter hand a Sword, point in base, and in her sinister hand a Spear, treading on a Dead Man armed ; lying on the ground, broken fetters.* Motto : *Sic semper Tyrannis.*

NORTH CAROLINA : *On dexter side, Liberty seated ; and on sinister, Plenty erect, reclining her dexter arm on a Cornucopia, and holding in her sinister hand an ear of Maize.*

SOUTH CAROLINA : *Pendent from the branches of a Palm-tree, two Shields ; in base, as many sheaves of Arrows in saltire.*

GEORGIA : *Three Caryatides, inscribed on bases, Moderation, Justice, and Wisdom, supporting the front of a Grecian Temple ; Tympanum irradiated ; above, the word* 'CONSTI-TUTION' *: in front, standing by sea-shore, a Revolutionary Soldier armed.*

The foregoing Blazons, though somewhat imperfect, are the best I can give. Great want of uniformity occurs both in colouring and drawing the various Arms. I have only given Heraldic Tinctures where the same are well established.

Already an attempt has been made in America to restrain in some measure the indiscriminate bearing of Arms. The question has been raised in Congress whether it would not be advisable to compel all those who use Arms to register them in the United States Court, and to pay an annual tax for the same, as in England. It is also proposed to inscribe at the bottom of the Shield the date when such Arms were first granted or assumed ; any infraction of the law to be punished by a fine. Wholesome as this regulation would be in restraining the too general use of Arms, it falls short of what it should be ; for, according to the proposed law, any one will be at liberty to adopt whatever Arms he may please, provided he pay his ten or twenty dollars a year. No provision is made for new grants, or for examining the authenticity of alleged claims ; it is simply a device to increase the revenue of the country. Nevertheless, it is calculated to be productive of much good, and is probably but the precursor of a legally-established College of Heralds.

The following incident—which I believe actually occurred

some years ago—aptly illustrates the light in which Armorial
Bearings are regarded by many wealthy Americans. During
the residence of our Ambassador, Mr. Crampton, in Wash-
ington, a carriage which he brought from England was sent
to a carriage-builder's to be repaired. Sometime afterwards,
on Mr. Crampton going to the factory, he was surprised to
see several *buggies*, *sulkies*, and *wagons*, each bearing his
Arms. In astonishment, he turned to the attendant, and
directing his notice to the carriages in question, inquired if,
they were built for him. ' I reckon not, sir,' was the reply ;
' you see, when your carriage was here, some of our citizens
admired the pattern of your Arms, and concluded to have
them painted on their carriages too !'

During a recent visit to the United States I noticed
many carriages with Arms painted on their panels. Some
of the Arms I knew to be incorrect : at the same time, many
other carriages, which bore a simple Monogram, might with
propriety have been emblazoned with Arms. Americans are
an eminently practical people ; and inasmuch as there is no
competent authority to regulate the bearing of Arms, many
who are entitled to the distinction refuse to avail themselves
of their prerogative.

The United States has many earnest and capable
genealogists, but, as far as I know—and I have taken pains
to inform myself—there is absolutely no professional worthy
of the title. The *New England Historic Genealogical
Society*, and the *Historical Society of Pennsylvania*, have
done good and worthy service. Of W. H. WHITMORE, and
especially of JOHN WARD DEAN, both of Boston, America
may well be proud. In the same State of Massachusetts
are Henry Fitz-Gilbert Waters, W. S. Appleton, Hon.
R. C. Winthrop, J. R. Rollins, Edward Russell, E. B.
Crane, and others : nor should the name of the late John
Savage be omitted from the honourable list. The State of
New York can boast of Hon. Levi Parsons, James Gibson,
George Burnaby, and R. Woodward : in Connecticut are

Ashbel Woodward, and Charles A. White : and little Rhode Island has two worthy representatives in Ira B. Peck, and John Osborne Austin. These, and others whom I could mention, are earnest and honest workers in the fields of historical research, but unfortunately they are not *professionals*. The number of privately-printed Genealogies which have been issued during the past few years conclusively shows that the commendable pride of Ancestry has a great hold on Americans—as, indeed, it has on anyone who values the reputation of his parents—and that it would be a national boon if some incorruptible authority, analogous to our College of Heralds, could be established among them.

I know J. W. Bouton, of 8 West 28th St., N. Y., Bookseller, to be a capable man to advise with, but he is not, nor does he profess to be, a Herald.

CHAPTER XXVI

LIVERIES

' . . . What though Arms and Crest unlike my own
Glare on its surface?   Who's to make it known?
No walking Guillim, Clarencieux, or Rouge Dragon
Infests our streets to put an envious gag on
My borrowed Arms and Crest.   That I'll rely on.
One care's at rest ; but now my liveries claim
My best attention, and my thought's best aim.
What shall the coats be?   Blue turned up with green,
And smalls contrived of darkest velveteen?
Or green with blue, and (pray don't, ladies, blush)
Continuations built of crimson plush !
'Tis passing hard for one unskilled like me
In dress, and such like vanity,
Such things to settle.'—*The Lay of the Sheriff.*—ANON.

THE custom of distributing clothes—or what in the
present day would be styled uniforms—amongst the
servants of the Crown, such as the Judges, Ministers,
Stewards, &c., dates from a period nearly coeval with the
Conquest (*Hist. Exch.* pp. 204–220).   This distribution was
termed a *Livrée ;* hence the more recent expression, *Livery.*[1]
About the beginning of the Fifteenth Century the practice
of giving Liveries to other than the civil servants of the
Crown became very general.   By the word *Livery* is not to
be understood simply clothes : it was frequently used to

---

[1] The distribution of provisions for the evening meal in the mansions of the nobility was also termed a *Livrée.*   Inhabitants of **Exeter**
need only to be reminded of Livery-dole, near Heavitree.

designate Collars, or other badges of partisanship. Nor were these distributed solely amongst the personal adherents of the king ; for we read that, in 1454, King HENRY the SIXTH directed six gold collars, forty silver-gilt, and sixty others of silver, 'of the order and livery of the king,' to be distributed amongst the principal inhabitants of Bâle, at the time when the General Council was assembled in that city. An allusion to the custom of sovereigns bestowing such collars upon their favourites, and upon those foreigners on whom it was intended to confer a mark of the royal consideration, occurs in the preface to the third volume of *Proceedings and Ordinances of the Privy Council of England*, by Sir Harris Nicolas (p. 68). It is also frequently mentioned in Rymer's *Fœdera*.

In like manner, the great feudal barons subsequently distributed Liveries amongst their dependents and retainers. It must not be considered that the wearing of Liveries was confined exclusively to the menial servants of the household, as at present, or was considered in any way more degrading than an officer of the Crown regards his distinctive uniform. The son of a duke would wear the Livery of the prince under whom he served ; and an earl's son might don the Livery of a duke without derogating from his dignity. Stowe gives an account of the EARL of OXFORD riding into the City to his house close by London Stone, preceded by eighty gentlemen attired in his Livery of Reading Tawny, with chains of gold around their necks, and followed by 100 tall yeomen in the same Livery, but without chains, and all having his cognisance of the *Blue Boar* embroidered on their left shoulders.

In the year 1454—the thirty-second of Henry the Sixth—the DUKE of YORK, with the view of increasing his influence, procured the authority of the Privy Council to bestow the king's Livery on eighty gentlemen whom he might select, all of whom were obliged to swear not to be retained by any person except with the especial license of the King.

In the days when the feudal Barons were as Kings in their own domains, and when Justice leaned to that side which could furnish the largest array of swords and spears, and strong right arms to wield them, it is not surprising that they should enlist mercenaries to serve under their banners—forming in themselves small standing armies—who were supplied with Liveries in the same manner as the lawful retainers.   To such an extent did this practice prevail in the Fourteenth Century, that RICHARD the SECOND, having a wholesome fear of the baronial power before his eyes, as exemplified in the history of his immediate predecessors, attempted to check it by the most severe enactments.   He ordered that 'no varlets called yeomen, nor none others of less estate than esquire, should use nor bear no badge or livery called livery of company of any lord within the realm, unless he be menial or familiar, or continual officer of the said lord.'   At the same time he ordered that all Purveyors for Lords and Nobles should display the Standards or Arms of their lords in the markets of the City of London, 'quod clarius sciri potuerit cui constant' (*Close Roll*, 21 *R. II. pars* 2 ; *m.* 24, *dorso*).

RICHARD the THIRD thus wrote on the 26th September, 1484, to the Mayor and Bailiffs of Bedford :—'Forasmoche as we understande that by reteindres geving of liveries clothinges signs and cognissances of tymes past within our said towne gret divisions and debates have growen and ensued amonges our subgiettes and inhabitaunts of the same not oonly to the gret perturbaunce and subversion of our peax and good rule to be had and continued there but also in manifest contempt of oure lawes in that behalve ordeigned . . . we woll and commaunde you to make open proclamacions in places convenient and accustumed there charging stractly on our behalve fromhensforth noon of thinhabitaunts within the same take or receive any reteyndors liveres clothinges or cognisaunce of any person or personnes of what estate degree or condicion soever. . . .' (*Harl. MS.* 433, *fol.* 188*b*).

By degrees the edicts regulating the distribution of Liveries were suffered to fall into abeyance ; and HENRY the SEVENTH found, on his Accession to the Throne, that the custom of maintaining mercenary soldiers was still greatly in vogue; a practice which the sagacious Monarch foresaw might be productive of prejudicial consequences towards himself : he therefore reiterated the order forbidding Nobles to distribute their Liveries amongst any other than their household servants without a license, on the pain of a heavy penalty. Little attention, however, was paid to this edict, as the following circumstance sufficiently proves. The King, being entertained at Castle Hedingham by JOHN DE VERE, EARL of OXFORD, the Earl, thinking to do his royal master honour, clad nearly a thousand hired retainers in his Livery, who formed an escort to conduct the King to the Castle. Henry complimented his entertainer on the magnificence of his reception, and hinted that it must cost the Earl a good round sum to maintain so many servants. 'They be none of mine household,' replied De Vere, 'but only some varlets I have hired to do your Grace reverence.' 'By my faith, my lord,' said the money-loving king, 'I thank you for your good cheer ; but I may not have my laws broken in my sight : my attorney must speak with you.' The result of the interview with the attorney was, that the Earl was mulcted in 15,000 marks. Queen MARY, during her short reign, granted thirty-nine licenses ; but ELIZABETH, during forty-five years, granted but fifteen. Her successor was even less liberal ; and by CHARLES the SECOND the custom was entirely abrogated. In *Quentin Durward*, Chap. XV., we read how the Countess HAMELINE of CROYES gave the Scottish hero of the Romance ' a richly embroidered kerchief of blue and silver, and pointing to the housing of her palfrey, and the plumes in her riding cap, desired him to observe that the colours were the same.'

SIR HENRY SIDNEY, in the year 1579, referring to the custom of nobles distributing Liveries amongst their hired retainers, writes : 'The use has no colour to be any longer maintained ; for, besides that it is detestable, it is dangerous to the State' (*Calend. Carew MSS., Lamb. Lib.*, 607, p. 136).

At the present time, at the first meeting for the year of the Court of Aldermen of the City of London, in December, Liveries, or Distributions of cloth, to certain officers are made. Thus, the Lord Chancellor, the Lord Chief Justice, the Master of the Rolls, the Lord Chamberlain, the Vice-Chamberlain, the Lord Steward, the Treasurer and Comptroller of the Household, the Home Secretary, the Foreign Secretary, the Attorney-General, the Solicitor-General, the Recorder, and the Common Serjeant, each receives four and a half yards of the best black cloth. The Town Clerk gets six yards of black cloth, and as many of green. His principal Clerk has four yards of each.

The primary purpose Liveries were intended to serve has long since been forgotten amongst us, and our coachmen and footmen alone remain as representatives of the splendour which once marked the households of the feudal nobility. Although much derogated from its ancient importance, the 'distribution of Liveries' is still a matter of some moment, demanding the attention of the Herald. At the present time, the too general custom is to rely on the taste of the tailor to prescribe that which is absolutely determined by the laws of Heraldry. A gentleman may wear garments of any colour his fancy may dictate, but he is not permitted such license with regard to the uniforms of his servants : the colours of these depend entirely on the Tinctures upon his Escutcheon. In both, the dominant colour should be the same ; the subsidiary colour of the Livery (or, as a tailor would call it, the trimmings—that is, the collar, cuffs, lining, and buttons) should be of the colour of the principal Charge. For example, a gentleman bears *Azure, a Fess or* : in this case, the coat of the servant should be blue, faced with yellow. But, supposing the Tinctures were reversed, and that the Field were *or* and the Fess *azure*, how then ?

—Would the coat be yellow, and the facing blue? No. Custom has decided that we must not dress our servants in golden and silver coats. Instead of yellow, we should employ drab; a lighter tint of the same colour doing duty for *argent*. But in the case of Dress-Liveries, which are only worn on special occasions, Coats should be of their proper colours—that is, absolute yellow or white, as the case may be. Custom also has forbidden us to dress our servants in scarlet coats. By prescription, red is the Royal Livery, and in lieu of that colour, Claret, or Chocolate, or Maroon should be used. M. de Saint-Epain, in his work entitled *L'Art de composer des Livrées au Milieu du XIXme Siècle*, carries out the principle before stated to an almost absurd degree, and gives minute directions for regulating the colour of every *visible* article of dress, whereby all dignity is entirely frittered away. At the risk of being myself condemned for trespassing on the grounds of the tailor, I subjoin a few examples in illustration of the proper method of composing Liveries:

Argent; a Lion rampant azure. Coat, light drab; Facings, blue.

Gules; an Eagle displayed or, within a Bordure argent. Coat, claret or chocolate; Facings, yellow; Buttons and Hatband, silver.

Or; a Fess chequé argent and azure, between a Mullet in chief gules, and a Crescent of the third in base. Coat, dark drab; Facings, blue; Buttons and Hatband, silver: and, to represent the Mullet, the edges of the coat might be bound with red, or have a red piping up the seams, or the rim of the hat looped up with red cord; though, according to the modern usage amongst tailors, which forbids the employment of more than two colours, the red would be entirely lost.

The Colours of HAMMERCLOTHS, as well as the pads on which the harness-saddle rests, on the backs of carriage-horses, are regulated by the same laws as Liveries, as are also the ribbons and bows on the horses' heads.

The uniform Livery of Widows is white (i.e. light drab), with black facings. Servants, when in mourning for the head of the family to which they are attached, should wear black clothes, unrelieved by any colour. Even the buttons should be of black cloth. The servant of a Military or Naval Officer should wear black clothes for twelve months after the death of his master. For any other member of the family he would wear his ordinary Livery with a black band around his left arm : but in either case his Cockade should be of black crape. The ridiculous custom of civilians, men and women, wearing a black band around their left arm, has recently come into vogue. By so doing they announce either that they are themselves Naval or Military Officers, or the Servants of Officers ; or, that having recently bought a light overcoat, they cannot afford to buy another.

The custom of thus deducing Livery-colours from the Tinctures on the Shield is, however, of comparatively recent date : there formerly existed no such regulation. The colours adopted by the different Royal Families of England sufficiently prove this ; for we find the PLANTAGENETS wearing White and Red ; the LANCASTRIANS, White and Blue ; the YORKISTS, Murrey and Blue ; the TUDORS, White and Green ; and the STUARTS, White. So, too, many of our oldest Families use their hereditary Liveries, which bear no relation whatever to the Tinctures of their Arms ; and it is these, and these only, which should justly be called LIVERY-COLOURS.

No man but one entrusted with the care of horses dare wear a canary and black waistcoat, which, as I have now come nearly to my journey's end, and the reader knows as much of Heraldry as I do, I may describe as *Barry or and sable, sleeves of the last.* The velveteen coat and leather leggings of the gamekeeper are also sacred.

There is as much attention paid at the present time to the *form* of servants' costumes, as to their *colours*. Each dependent of the family has assigned to him a particular dress, by which his office may be readily recognised. Thus, the overcoat of a footman is distinguished from that of a groom by its greater length, and by being made without outside pockets. A coachman is known by his three-cornered hat, curled wig, and the embroidered pockets of his coat—technically called the flap and frame. A curious circumstance respecting the coats of coachmen is, that by an inviolable sartorial custom pocket-flaps must always be made of the same width and depth, and placed at a prescribed distance from the buttons at the back, whatever may be the proportions of the wearer. Hence every coachman is obliged to adapt himself to the standard size, as though he were a guest of Procrustes.

Persons setting up a new establishment—and of necessity there must be many such—would do well (if they have no better adviser) to place themselves unreservedly in the hands of such practical men as Messrs. Wiseman, of Sackville Street, or Messrs. Hills, of Bond Street. There are, doubtless, other tradesmen, equally as good, who are familiar with the practical requirements of their customers as to Liveries or Naval, Military, or Civil Uniforms.

BUTTONS should always be of the dominant metal in the Arms, and charged with the master's Badge—not his Crest. The latter, as has been before stated (p. 133), belongs exclusively to the bearer of the Arms ; servants have no right whatever to them. Buttons should also be differenced with Marks of Cadency in the same manner as Arms and Crests : thus, the second son of the House of Pelham would bear a Crescent over a Buckle. Badges, like Crests and Mottoes, are quite arbitrary : if, therefore, a gentleman have not an hereditary Badge, he is at perfect liberty to devise one for himself, without any fear of incurring the censure of the College of Heralds. So little are the laws of Heraldry attended to with regard to Livery-buttons, that it is no uncommon occurrence to see the servants of *ladies* wearing

Y

them charged with a Crest, or with a Shield of Arms. A Livery-button maker recently told me, that a maiden lady applied to him to have some Buttons struck from her late father's die, on which were her paternal and maternal Arms impaled ; nor could any persuasion induce her to alter her determination. Flagrant as this is, it is perhaps surpassed by a statuary who, having been directed to carve a Coat of Arms upon a marble monument, took them from another, which was erected to the deceased's grandfather, in the same church : by which the ingenious stone-cutter made it appear that a young bachelor, aged ten, had married his own grandmother, who had been laid to rest nearly forty years before he was born.

A correspondent of the *Gentleman's Magazine* (May 1784) writes as follows : ' It has been a long time a matter of wonder to me that none of our genealogists have ever taken the least notice of the Liveries worn by the domestics in the several families whose pedigrees they describe. This I cannot help thinking a neglect, as we have thereby lost the colour of the Coat, as well as the facings, worn by the servants of our extinct nobility and gentry—except where the younger branches of certain houses have maintained a genteel rank, and thence been enabled to continue the use of such hereditary distinction. . . . We know that the Badge of the Earls of Warwick was the Bear and Ragged Staff ; that of the De Veres, Earls of Oxford, a Mullet : but no notice is taken of the colour of the Coat upon which such mark was borne, although, as an hereditary Cognisance, I think it of as much consequence to the world as their Crest, Motto, and, I had almost said, Coat-armour—the latter being a distinction borne by the chief himself—the former, that worn by his servants, and thereby rendered almost of equal importance ; and, indeed, since the disuse of shields and defensive armour, it is a more conspicuous distinction than the Arms themselves, as it is much oftener seen, and may be known at a greater distance. Wherefore, I would recommend it to the College of Arms, as a matter not unworthy of them, in all future entries of pedigrees, where the Livery is known, to note the Colours ; and the same of the ancient nobility and gentry, wherever it can be recovered. So, in all future editions of the Peerages and Baronetages, after the Crest and Motto, it would be well to add the Livery, giving the colour, facing, lace, or any peculiarity that may attend it : which practice, if introduced, would be a more certain means of making this sort of family distinction regular, and of conveying the same to posterity.'

COCKADES, affixed to the hats of servants, constitute an important part of Liveries ; their use, however, is not in any manner regulated by Heraldic laws. They were originally but the knots of the ribbon with which military men used to *cock* their broad-brimmed hats, and served the purpose of the button, or star, which ostensibly keeps up the flap of the modern cocked hat. The black Cockade, as now worn, is of German origin, and was not introduced into England before the time of George I. It was quickly adopted by the adherents of the Hanoverian party, and in the Rebellion constituted a conspicuous mark by which they were distinguished from the Stuart followers, who displayed a white Rose. Hence the expression 'to mount the cockade' was synonymous with becoming a soldier, and is frequently used in that sense in the party songs of the last century.

In 1782 the use of Cockades was prohibited in France to all but military men, who were compelled to wear one of white stuff ; but in the national enthusiasm a few years later the citizens assumed the tricoloured ribbon as the badge of patriotism, which was soon also given to the Army. At the Restoration, the white Cockade of the monarchy was restored, to be again succeeded by the tricolour in 1830.

Where no absolute law on the subject exists, it is, to many people, a matter of uncertainty to decide who are entitled to assume the distinction of Cockades. There should be no such uncertainty, for the privilege is confined to the servants of officers in her Majesty's service, or those who by courtesy may be regarded as such ; the theory being, that the servant is a private soldier, who, when not wearing his uniform, retains this badge as a mark of his profession. Doctors' servants, though frequently to be seen wearing Cockades, have no right to them whatever, unless their masters' names are to be found in the Army or Navy List. Cockade-wearing servants whose masters do not hold offices which represent the Crown have my authority to think their masters impostors. Any commissioned officer of the Crown, with an income of perhaps only 100*l.* a year, has an undoubted right to grace his footman's hat with a Cockade if he can afford it ; but a millionaire, not a commissioned officer, is denied the privilege. The Cockade worn by the servants of military officers is composed of black leather, arranged in the form of a corrugated cone, and surmounted by a cresting like a fan half-opened (fig. 402). The servants of naval officers, deputy-lieutenants, and gentlemen holding distinct offices under the Sovereign, bear a plain Cockade as at fig. 403. In both cases, the ribbon in the centre may be either black, or of the Livery-colours.

Fig. 402.   Fig. 403.

The servants of Foreign Ambassadors and Ministers abroad also wear Cockades, with the exception of America, I know, and Russia and France, I think. The German Cockade is black and white ; the Austrian, black and yellow ; the Portuguese, white and blue ; the Spanish, red ;

the Belgian, black, yellow, and red ; while that of the Netherlands is the National colour, orange.

EPAULETTES and AIGUILLETTES are generally worn by all those entitled to Cockades.

Under no circumstances are the servants of unmarried ladies allowed to wear Cockades or Epaulettes ; and it is extremely doubtful whether a widow can lay any more claim to them than to the Crest or Orders of her deceased husband.

During the reign of EDWARD the THIRD, the Companies of artificers and merchants who had previously been associated into Guilds—so called from their annually paying a *gild* or fine to the king—received Charters, and were enrolled into ‘ Mysteries ’ (Méstiers=Métier=Trade) or ‘ Crafts.’ At the same time, they adopted certain distinctive styles and colours of dress : thus we find the Grocers’ Company, on their first meeting in 1345, prescribed the Colours of their Livery. These Companies were originally intended as a means of mutual protection and assistance to members in the prosecution of their trades. EDWARD the THIRD fully appreciated the importance to the country of fostering the spirit of enterprise amongst its merchants : one of his first official acts, therefore, was to secure to them certain privileges and immunities, for the encouragement of the various arts at home. To this end he granted Charters, in the first year of his reign, to the Linen-armourers (subsequently styled Merchant Tailors), Gold-smiths, and Skinners, and himself became a member of the first-named Company, confirming their former gild licenses, and at the same time conferring upon them further privileges. His grandson RICHARD was also a Linen-armourer ; and nobles, both secular and ecclesiastical, quickly followed the Royal example.

The date of the assumption of Liveries by trading com-munities is uncertain : the earliest record I have been able to find occurs in Stowe’s *Survey*, where, in describing the marriage of EDWARD the FIRST with his second wife, MARGARET, at Canterbury, in 1329, he writes that the fraternities, to the number of six hundred, rode to meet the procession 'in one livery of red and white, with the cognisances of their mysteries embroidered on their arms.' The Liveries originally adopted by the various Companies have in no instance been continuously preserved ; many of them have undergone several modifications and changes.

There are, at the present time, seventy-seven Livery Companies in the City of London[1]: of these, the Mercers', Grocers', Drapers', Fishmongers', Goldsmiths', Skinners', Merchant Tailors', Haberdashers', Salters', Ironmongers', Vintners', and Clothworkers', are styled the twelve great Companies—the Arms of which, as constituting interesting examples of Corporate Heraldry, are subjoined :

1. The MERCERS : *Gules ; a Demi-Virgin, couped below the shoulders, with hair dishevelled, vested or, crowned with an Eastern Crown, within an Orle of Clouds, all proper.* Incorporated 17 Ed. III.

2. The GROCERS : *Argent ; a Chevron gules, between six Cloves in chief, and three in base sable.* Crest : *A loaded Camel trippant, proper.* Supporters : *Two Griffins per fess gules and or.* Motto : *God grant the grace.* Incorporated 27 Ed. III.

3. The DRAPERS : *Azure ; on three Clouds radiated, as many triple Crowns proper, the caps gules.* Crest : *A Ram lodged argent, horned and unguled or.* Supporters : *Two Lions or, pelleté.* Motto : *Unto God only be honour and glory.* Incorporated 38 Ed. III. ; Arms granted, 1439.

4. The FISHMONGERS : *Azure ; three Dolphins naiant in pale argent, between two pairs of Lucies saltirewise, proper, crowned or ; on a Chief gules, three pairs of Keys, endorsed in saltire, rings in base of the fourth.* Crest : *Two Arms embowed, supporting an Imperial Crown, proper.* Supporters : On the

---

[1] Thirty-one of these Companies have no Halls.

Dexter, *A Triton, body armed, head helmeted, holding in the dexter hand a Sword, all proper ;* on the Sinister, *A Mermaid.* Motto : *All worship to God only.* Incorporated 17 Ed III.

5. The GOLDSMITHS : *Quarterly of four :* 1 *and* 4. *Gules ; a Leopard's face or ;* 2 *and* 3. *Azure ; a Covered Cup, and in Chief two Buckles fesswise, tongues to the dexter, of the second.* Crest : *A Demi-Woman, holding in her dexter hand a pair of Scales, and in her sinister a Touchstone, proper.* Supporters : *Two Unicorns or.* Motto : *Justitia virtutum Regina.* Incorporated 1 Ed. III.

6. The SKINNERS : *Ermine ; on a Chief gules, three Prince's Coronets or, caps of the first.* Crest: *A Leopard passant, proper, gorged with a Garland of Leaves or.* Supporters : *An heraldic Tiger and a Wolf, both proper, and gorged with a Garland as the Crest.* Motto : *To God only be all glory.* Incorporated 1 Ed. III.

7. The MERCHANT TAILORS : *Argent ; a Tent between two Mantles gules, lined ermine ; on a Chief azure, a Lion passant-guardant or.* Crest : *A Paschal Lamb radiated, proper.* Supporters : *Two Camels or.* Motto : *Concordiâ parvæ res crescunt.* (See page 197.) Incorporated 1 Ed. III.

8. The HABERDASHERS : *Barry-nebulé of six, argent and azure ; on a Bend gules a Lion of England.* Crest : *Issuant from a Cloud argent, two Arms embowed, holding a Garland of laurel, proper.* Supporters : *Two Goats argent, attired and unguled or.* Motto : *Serve and obey.* Incorporated 26 Hen. VI. ; Arms granted, 21 Hen. VIII.

9. The SALTERS : *Per chevron azure and gules, three covered Cups argent.* Crest : *A Cubit Arm erect, issuing from Clouds,*

---

[1] The custom of wearing Badges is still continued by some of the Almspeople of this Company. Thirteen of them wear silver Badges bearing the Arms of Kneesworth ; six, a Badge with the Arms of Hunt, surmounted by a Dolphin ; two, a Badge with Edmond's Mark ; and one, a Badge with Hippesley's Arms ;— the persons whose names are mentioned having devised money towards the charity of the Company.

all proper, holding a Covered Cup (sprinkling salt), as in the Arms, argent. Motto : *Sal sapit omnia.* Incorporated 37 Ed. III.

10. The IRONMONGERS : *Argent ; on a Chevron gules, between three Gads of steel azure, as many pairs of Shackles or.* Crest : *Two Lizards erect, combattant, proper, chained and collared or.* Supporters : *None.* Motto : *God is our strength* Incorporated 3 Ed. IV.

11. The VINTNERS : *Sable ; a Chevron enarched, between three Tuns argent.* Crest : *A Bacchus.* Supporters : *None·* Motto : *None.* Incorporated 38 Ed. III.

12. The CLOTHWORKERS : *Sable ; a Chevron ermine, between two Habicks in Chief argent, and a Teazle slipped in base or.* Crest : *A Ram passant or.* Supporters : *Two Griffins or, pelleté.* Motto : *My trust is in God alone.* Incorporated 20 Ed. IV. ; Arms granted, 21 Hen. VIII.

Fig. 404.   Arms of the Barber-Surgeons

INDEX

PRINTED BY
SPOTTISWOODE AND CO., NEW-STREET SQUARE
LONDON